Postmarked: Bleeding Kansas

Letters from the Birthplace of The Civil War

Letters by Edward and Sarah Fitch
Foreword by Chad Lawhorn

Purple Duck Press

About this book

The Douglas County Historical Society first published the letters of Kansas pioneers Edward and Sarah Fitch in 1997. The title of that book was *Yours for Freedom in Kansas*. The society printed a limited number of copies, and the book went out of publication several years after its release. In the months just prior to the 150th anniversary of William Quantrill's raid on Lawrence, longtime Historical Society volunteer Carol Graham approached me about republishing *Yours for Freedom in Kansas*. About 20 letters that were included in *Yours for Freedom in Kansas* are not included in *Postmarked: Bleeding Kansas*. They primarily are letters written by Edward Fitch prior to his arrival in Kansas. *Yours for Freedom in Kansas* also had detailed footnotes that were the result of significant research by Historical Society officials John M. Peterson and others in the mid-1990s. Due to the short amount of time to produce this book prior to the 150th anniversary of Quantrill's raid, it was decided to not include the footnotes in this edition. For historians interested in seeing the entire cache of the Fitch letters and the footnotes, a copy of *Yours for Freedom in Kansas* is still available for review at the Douglas County Historical Society's Watkins Community Museum of History in downtown Lawrence.

The letters included in *Postmarked: Bleeding Kansas* are reprinted exactly as they appeared in *Yours for Freedom in Kansas*. Volunteers in the 1990s did painstaking work to format the handwritten letters of Edward and Sarah Fitch into book form. They were extremely diligent in copying the letters word for word. If a word was inserted for clarity's purposes, it is noted. Readers also will notice that occasionally the letters have a blank in the middle of a sentence. That is to denote that a word was included in the letter, but due to handwriting or condition issues, the volunteers were not able to determine the word.

Finally, there are a few people I would like to thank for bringing this book to market. Foremost are members of the Fitch family – in particular Roger Fitch, Edward's great-grandson — who took great care to save the letters from their ancestors so that they could be shared with the world. Closely behind those efforts are those of all the volunteers and officials at the Watkins Community Museum of History who spent their valuable time in the 1990s bringing these letters to life. They include, but likely are not limited to: Graham, Peterson, Steven Jansen and Dorothy Norris. I also would like to thank the current day leaders of the Douglas County Historical Society, particularly director Steve Nowak, who embraced the idea of bringing these letters to the public once again. But it is fair to say that this book would not have been possible if not for the efforts of one person: Carol Graham. It was Carol who had the vision to see that these letters – and the courageous lives of Edward and Sarah Fitch – deserved to again be remembered. Douglas County is such a rich place, in part, because we do not forget our history. But that does not happen by accident. It is because of caring, persistent people like Carol Graham who help ensure that Lawrence and Douglas County's important role in American history is not forgotten.

FOREWORD

I'm not a historian, and the title of this book proves it. The phrase "Birthplace of the Civil War" would make historians squirm and immediately begin searching for a place to attach a footnote. But since I'm not a historian, I don't squirm, and the most likely thing I am to do with a foot is to insert it in my own mouth. I'm a storyteller. I've been a professional journalist telling stories in Lawrence and Douglas County, Kansas for more than two decades. And when I first read the frontier letters of Edward and Sarah Fitch, I recognized them for what they are: A beginning.

The first letter with a Lawrence postmark from Edward Fitch is dated March 4, 1855. Indeed, that was very near the beginning. The first party of the New England Emigrant Aid Company arrived at the site that is now Lawrence on Aug. 1, 1854.

Edward's first letter was about tending school. He was a teacher at a school/boarding house that tended to about 10 to 15 men and boys. Edward told his parents how he would make breakfast each morning, spend six hours in the classroom, wash dishes after supper, haul water "seventy rods" in the evening, and find time to chop all the wood for the school's needs. Although he didn't ask in his first letter, the writings that soon would follow included multiple requests for his parents to send money. So, parents of modern day students of Kansas University can take comfort in knowing that cries for cash have been coming from Lawrence since nearly the beginning.

Edward – and eventually his wife, Sarah – would write much from Lawrence. Over the next eight years, the couple would write more than 150 letters to family members, mostly to Edward's parents back in Hopkinton, Mass.. Members of the Fitch family in the many decades to follow would save those letters. All who are interested in the beginnings of Lawrence, Kansas owe members of the Fitch family a debt of gratitude. The writings of Edward provide a look at the early life of Lawrence and the relentless routine of frontier living that often does not make it into the history books. That's because Edward Fitch is not the type of man history often shines a spotlight on. He was an ordinary man in many ways. He first was a teacher, later a farmer, and finally an employee at his father-in-law's book and stationery store. But in a sense, that's what makes these letters so interesting. Edward Fitch wrote the type of history many of us would have lived.

Well, that is, if we would have made the courageous decision to live in the very unordinary place of Lawrence. There was perhaps no other place in the country quite like Lawrence, Kansas in the mid-1850s. It has been said that while other cities were founded on commerce, Lawrence was founded on conviction. As the letters will attest, there certainly were many men looking to make their fortunes in Lawrence, but it also is true the conviction that slavery must be abolished permeated the community.

It permeated Edward. In some of the letters, you will read where Edward criticized both President Lincoln and his wife. While Lincoln was intent on maintaining the union of a country, Edward was intent on breaking the bonds of slavery. "Trying to fight a war without touching slavery is like trying to put out a fire without water," Edward wrote to his parents in 1862.

Edward knew about fire. You'll see several of Edward's letters back home included instructions for his parents to purchase a Navy Colt revolver and to send it to him, along with a thousand rounds of ammunition. He talked about the time period where he, nor any other sane man, ever left their homes without a Sharps rifle in their hands. And he wrote about death, first excitedly and eventually nonchalantly. From July, 23, 1856 – nearly a full five years before the battle of Ft. Sumter and the traditional history-book beginning of the war:

"We have had rather still times for this latitude.; true some two or three men have been shot at, and killed for going to Topeka to attend the meeting of the Free State Legislature, but such occurrences are so common here that they hardly cause a remark."

That paragraph says a lot about the condition of Lawrence and Douglas County in the mid-1850s. The history books may not say war had begun, but Douglas County certainly was suffering from perhaps the cruelest casualty of war – callousness toward death.

That's why I say with no hesitation that Edward and Sarah Fitch provided us dispatches from the birthplace of the Civil War. I'll leave it to some other book to argue whether Sumter or Bull Run or Douglas County's Battle of Black Jack was the true first battle of the Civil War. That's not what I mean when I say this area of Eastern Kansas and Western Missouri was the birthplace of the Civil War.

I'll concede this ground may not be where cannons were first precisely placed and men were ordered to march to secure a flank. Rather, this is the place where the idea for a Civil War was born. This is where beliefs turned to blood. Before every war, there first must be a line drawn. For the American Civil War, the line was drawn in Kansas. The men with the biggest sticks, who created that line in the sand, lived in Lawrence. Edward Fitch lived among them. His name will not show up in many history books with the likes of Lane or Robinson or Brown. His stick wasn't as big, but he carried something else into battle – a pen.

In the end, it may have been just as powerful. It tells an important story of an ordinary family making an extraordinary stand for a belief that would change a country. Along the way, there were the very human stories of failed crops, sick children, false hopes and lingering doubts.

Pieced together, Edward and Sarah's pen tells a story of warriors on a frontier, wondering if their country would follow them.

Perhaps the historians never will recognize those times as the beginning of the Civil War. That's all right. Edward and Sarah Fitch did, and that's good enough for me.

See for yourself.

Part I
Fitted for a Straight Jacket

August or September 1854

This letter was postmarked South Weymouth, Mass.. Edward had arrived there to stay with his uncle's family while he prepared to travel to Kansas.

Dear Mother

I arrived here this afternoon about 4 o'clock.   Doctor and Aunt Howe are well but the children have been sick with Dysentery and are not well yet.   Florinda says she has hardly been out of the house since you was here; she does not look very well.

I forgot one or two things that I ought to have told you before I left.

John must go to Barnards as soon as you get this and get the stock for three pair of boots that he said he would have ready Sat. and carry one pair of them to Baker and have him make them for me.   He has got the measure of my foot and said he would make them the early part of the week so John must get them there as soon as possible.   If Father has done anything about it since I was there very well; if not have this done without delay.

I want you to be ready to go to Worcester with me next Fri. if I should not get home Thursday night for I did not get half the things I wanted in Boston.   I got some Hd'k'f's and told Aunt Louisa to send them home by Father Sat. if she had a chance so that you could hem them before I get home.

The Teacher of the High School here boards with Doctor and he has four other men.   When I told him first that I was going to <u>Kansas</u> he said I ought to have <u>a straight Jacket On</u> (fine Anti-Slavery man that) and so I told him.

I find that the money that has been put into the bank here for me or given to the Doctor for that purpose amounts to between 11 & 12$ and there is interest on some of it since 1844 so there ought to be as much as 15,00 I should think, that will help me some.   I shall go from here tomorrow afternoon and I cannot tell exactly what time I shall be at home.   Tell John to keep things going as fast as possible.

Doctor and I are just going to the Bank.   I have seen Mrs. William Torrey and Capt. Torreys folks.   They all send much love to you as do Aunt Howe and Florinda.

I can't think of any more that I must write and so I will stop.
Your affectionate son,   E.P. Fitch

March 4, 1855

Postmarked Lawrence, Kansas

Dear Parents

Two weeks ago tomorrow the eastern mail arrived here that was delayed on the way by the storm.   It brought with it two letters from home, or one from Boston, written about the last of Jan.   They were the first I had rec'd of a later date than the 29 of Dec/ 54.   A day or two since I rec'd another from Father dated Feb 17th at the end of which he says 'write oftener'.   Now here I am away from home with half a dozen or more to write to me and I don't get but about one or two letters in a month and then ask me to write oftener.   I should like to receive one oftener at any rate and write them if I had time.   But I have covered any quantity of paper more than you have since I have been here.   Mother says she has written to me before since this year commenced but if she did not have arrived here.

I am so sleepy that I cannot write and I am going to leave your letters till I have more time and then I will answer them at length.

I have been keeping school for the past two weeks and we have had from 10 to 15 men to board.   I have to get up at about 5 o'clock in the morning, get breakfast for all the men then go into school and stay six hours and at night I have dishes to wash after supper and then I bring all the water seventy rods or more and I chop all the wood so you can guess how much time I have to write or anything else but I expect I shall soon have a better chance.

I have a bad cough.   _____ I'll write particulars soon.

Your aff. son   E.P. Fitch

I want to hear the news from town meeting tomorrow.   I have sent the Herald to you just as you said.

March 25, 1855

The notation of Em. A. Soc. refers to the New England Emigrant Aid Company, an abolitionist organization that was instrumental in the founding of Lawrence.

Dear Parents

My time has been very much occupied for a number of weeks and I have had not time to write letters at all.   I have not kept school any now for a little more than a week but I have had all I could do to take care of our boarders.   We have had sometimes 15 or 20 at once that had their meals here tho they did not all sleep here and now for three or four days I have had all the work to do alone as Mr. Stearns has done nothing 'at all' and I have had 13 or more regular boarders all the time besides lots of transient folks so you may guess that I have been somewhat busy.   I think now I shall sell out my share and if I get enough to make me square, that is just pay my living through the winter, I shall be pretty well satisfied tho I expected to make something when I commenced but Stearns has acted so about the Em. A. Soc. that he is not popular here and we suffer some for it -- you may have seen some of his letters in the papers, he writes for the Tribune (NY) and the Liberator also.   He is down on the E.A. Co. "like a thousand of brick".   I don't think so much of it as some do but I don't think quite so badly of it as he does for he says it has been a curse to the territory while I merely say it has not done as much good as I wish it had and as it ought to have done.   There are some things about it that I don't like at all.   You need not be surprised if the next news you hear from me is that I have decided to go to California.   There are a lot of young fellows going from here and I don't know but I shall go with them. We shall start about the 10th of May, and go by way of Salt Lake City. We can have 30, [$30] per month and found to drive [a] team out there; go in a train of about 100 wagons.

I want you, Father, to get the Boston Weekly Journal of Feb. 22nd if you have not seen it and read what Dr. Webb and Dr. Robinson write about Stearns and Willard.   And then get the Journal of April 6th or about that time and see the answers that they have just written.   Dr. Robinson has told some lies in that piece and no mistake -- but they have paid him off with truth mostly.   I shall if I can get and send along some papers with this letter that I want you to read the Editorials and see what they say about Em Aid Soc. to read and circulate.   There is a large mail at Westport now but we can't get it because the P.M. [postmaster] would not send to Lawrence until he received orders from the Department at Washington.

Our election will come on Friday and we shall have a hot time of it.   I expect almost that the pro slavery ticket will be elected but if it is there will be some Free State men on that.   I have not heard from you at home for some time; you ought to write oftener.   You can show this to any one that wants to see it.   The reason why I have not kept school has been that they have made my schoolroom into a boarding house, and many Emigrants are arriving and we can't accommodate them any other way.

Give my love to all.

Yours, E.P. Fitch

July 26, 1855

The lapse of four months between the date of the following letter and the previous one is accounted for by Edward's return, for reasons not known, to Massachusetts.   On his trip back to Kansas, he guided an Emigrant Aid Company party of twenty women and children which left Boston on July 24 and arrived in Kansas City on August 1.   (Herald of Freedom, Lawrence, August 11, 1855.)

Aboard a steamship referred to as Buckeye on Lake Erie

Dear Friends at Home ? _____ no, Hopkinton

We are here.   Our party which numbers just 20 including myself started in due time Tues P.M.

They are all women and children except two, who are a young gentleman and young lady.   The gentleman (?) being myself of course and the lady being a Miss Davis from Pawtucket who I suppose would not much care to be called one of the children though her mother and brothers & Sisters are with her, she being about sixteen (with the adjective before it)

The party are as follows.   Mrs. Davis with six children from Pawtucket going to Osawatomie (and I am going there too),   Mrs Baker with one child going to the same place,   Mrs Stone from Medford with five children going to Topeka & Mrs Banks with three children from Lynn going to Lawrence.   No interrogation mark.

We left Boston at half past one. I saw Olive at Worcester. Arrived at Albany about ten in the evening and left there by the N.Y. Central R.R.

about eleven.   Rode all night and at half past ten the next morning, twenty one hours from Boston, found us at Buffalo, 500 miles being 25 miles an hour leaving out the hour that was stopped at Albany and including other stops.   We took dinner and supper at the Rail Road Hotel, Buffalo and had a good parlor, and as many bedrooms as we wanted for $6.00 for the party.   I saw all our baggage safe on board the Buckeye State, the same steamer in which I crossed the lake ten months ago, day after tomorrow.   I procured three State rooms for the party and slept in the Cabin myself.   We had got nicely settled in a berth etc. last night when there came up a tremendous storm of wind thunder and rain, which gave us a start out of our sleep but it was soon over and this morning we are out of sight of land and all in good spirits.   None of us seasick yet.   There is quite a chop on the Lake as Albert says and the wind is quite fresh.

I have numbered this letter as the first home because I shall direct it to Father or Appleton but it is for all my Hopkinton friends to see that care enough about me to ask whether you have heard from me, and I want every one that hears or reads this letter and is going to write to me to number their letters all of them, so I shall know whether I receive all of them or not.   I shall try and remember to number all I write.

I remain with respects to all readers.

Edward P. Fitch

To my friends

We are just entering the Detroit River and shall be at the dock soon.   My family of children is so large that I shall have some trouble about keeping them together at Detroit.   I suppose especially as I have got to look close after the baggage.   Two of the trunks belonging to the party are now broken open, mine remaining whole yet.

Dear Parents

As I expected there were many things left undone or said that ought to have been attended to before I left home.   I meant to have had those boots that I wore home packed as there was room enough but I suppose they were not and I meant to have had some corn for seed and saved some ears of both kinds to shell for that purpose, but they are left not alone in their glory.   Uncle Fisher I am afraid wont want those potatoes nor McDermot either if they aren't sent pretty soon.   I meant to have attended to it but I forgot it.   Another thing I forgot I got that sugar oiled silk, pins, some court plaster and one or two other things charged to Father amounting to .62 cts at Bolles store.   He said he would take eggs 20 cts per doz in May.   I meant to have told about it but forgot it.   Elijah was there perhaps he knows about it.   Put your eggs in water so to be sure that you send no bad ones.

I told some of the milk folks that we should next time allow five or six per cent discount on all bills paid when they were first presented so Elijah ought to tell them the day before the bills are ready (or sooner) that you will allow them a discount and how much per cent and then the Disct ought to be marked on the bill so if Elijah collects he will know how much it is.   That will make a good many pay right up.   No discount on old bills of course unless perhaps this time.   Father thinks it will call in the old debts.

That box of candy that you got for me last fall I sent to you by Phipps.   I ought to have had it packed in to my box but I did not know that it was in Boston until I went in Tues.   Then I asked Mr. Pomeroy where I should find it out at Kansas.   He said he left it for Dr. Webb to send with a box of books.   I then asked Dr. Webb and he said it was round somewhere and just before we started he found it.   It was impossible for me to bring it unless I brought it in my hand all the way and so I sent it to you.   You had said better sell it if you can get anything for it.   It may be hurt for it doesn't keep good long.   I wanted to bring it with me but I could not at any rate.

I had some green corn for, or with my dinner in Buffalo yesterday; it rained all the time I was coming and was quite cool till yesterday afternoon when it cleared off quite warm but today it is cool and hazey.

We are close to Detroit have had a very pleasant passage across the Lake.   We shall start from Detroit at nine O clock this evening and probably arrive in Chicago tomorrow morning about 7 AM.

You will probably hear from me again at St. Louis.
Your affectionate Son
Edward P Fitch

Be sure and No. your letters to me so that I shall know whether I get all of them or not.   I am going to number mine and keep an account of them so that I can tell both when I write and when I receive a letter.
EPF

July 30, 1855

Aboard the Steamboat Martha Jewett on the Missouri River, 220 miles above St. Louis.

Dear Friends

      We arrived at Detroit on Thurs afternoon about 50 hours from Boston (pretty quick passage considering that we stopped about 10 hours in Buffalo). We staid in Detroit till nine O clock Thurs eve. when we took the cars for Chicago and, riding all night we arrived there about nine AM on Fri. We staid in Chicago till nine in the evening and started for St Louis. The road from Chicago to St Louis is very bad indeed some of the women were almost killed, they thought. The cars jumped up and down nearly a foot. We got to Alton about noon & into St Louis about 2 P.M. Sat. I found our Boat The Martha Jewett going to start right off for Kansas and engaged open passages, _____ Pierce to the contrary not withstanding, got our things on board immediately and we started about 5 O clock from St Louis. Went down to Jefferson Barracks and took on a company of soldiers going to Ft Leavenworth. The Martha Jewett is one of the tip top Boats (wine for Dinner every day) and has some good officers. Mr Silvia our clerk is quite a fine young man. Our Capt I have not got acquainted with. His name is Burton. If we have good luck now we shall be in Kansas City Wed. which will be a quick trip. I paid all our passages up [river] on the Boat and it amounted to $156.00. We have Mr & Mrs Fitch on board (Mrs. C. Baker). We have Col Sumner and family going to Leavenworth. They have been with us all the way from Buffalo. We have also some Southern folks who think they are some and have tried to insult me and my party in every possible way. They will set down and stop up one passage in the aft Deck and have told some of our folks that the <u>second class</u> did not belong on that side. Miss Davis is enough for them however and gives them as good as they sent. Two or three of the party are sick today but I have been very well all the time and am enjoying myself finely. We have been on sand bars two or three times a little while at a time. The longest time was about two hours. The Soldiers we have on board are all from Georgia.

      But the musquitos belong in Mo.

I want everybody that wants to should see this letter and if the looks dont suit them they must _____Yours externally internally eternally and
Fraternally

Edward P Fitch
Conducting Agt Kansas party

To All my friends

P R S V R Y P R F C T M N
V R K P T H S P R C P T S T N

      The above is a puzzle.   It only wants one letter to make it a perfect sentence.   Who'll tell me what it is and what the sentence is when it is supplied.
[Add an "E" Persevere Ye Perfect Men; Ever Keep The Precepts Ten]

July, 1855 (est.)

I have just been taking the rope off of my trunk and I am going to open it and get out a clean shirt if I can find one and if not I am going to buy one and then I am going up into town to take a bath & change my clothes, for I have not had a chance to wash before.   It will cost me twenty five cents but that is nothing to the pleasure of a bath and being clean here for it is as hot as it was in July at home.   We expect Mr Reeder, the Gov. of Kansas on board the Boat in a few minutes.   Write to me & tell Whittemore and Appleton to write direct to me at Kansas City Mo and I shall get it.   We had a lot of rain yesterday & this morning.

      Tell Fisher to stick to his party when he comes but he will not have to delay here as I have, for Mr St__ has just made arrangements with this Boat to take the next party from here the Mon. after they leave Boston instead of Sun. as they left yesterday.   I have taken some more brandy & sugar today and feel much better and shall not probably have to take any more.   I am afraid that I shall not be with the party when they organise as I meant to be.   I would not have the trouble that I have had since I left the party or they left one for 20$ and if they dont pay me ten I shall not be at all satisfied.   Be sure and write soon and write a long letter.   I am so dry that I dont know what to do and I dare not drink. Next time I come though I shall know what to do & I shall have less baggage if possible.

                  Yours, E.P. Fitch

Aug. 8, 1855

From Lawrence

Dear Parents

As I wrote before; we arrived in Kansas City the first inst. I left there the next afternoon just before night with Mr Stones folks, who were going to Topeka.   I drove a horse up for him and had my ride up and my things brought up to pay for it.   The fare from Kansas [City] to Lawrence on the mail coach is $2.50.   The river is still very low (though it has risen some within a day or two) and all three of the Boats that tried to Navigate the Kaw are stuck on sandbars-- two above and one below Lawrence.   I arrived here before noon on Sat. the 4th inst.   I found a great deal of alteration in the looks of things since I left here.   The Hotel is up almost three stories beside the basement and makes a fine appearance.   When done it will be a fine building.   There are many other good buildings now here.   One small one is painted white and lathed ready to plaster and there is one lathed & plastered, the only one in the place, that is one of the Cincinatti ready made houses and Mrs. Hall & Mrs. Hunt are going to keep boarders in it.   They will open in a few days.   Stearns & Campbell who were together when I went away have blowed up more than a month ago.   Stearns wife is here and he has got a lot on N.H. [New Hampshire] St. cor. of Henry St. and has a log cabin put up and a roof on it so that he and his wife sleep there.   She works during the day for Messrs. Hunt & Co. cooking for six men etc.   Stearns is out of funds to finish his house with and so nothing is being done on it now.

Campbell is still at the old place or he stays there nights and works out days.   The house is a perfect wreck almost.   There has been no care taken of it for a long time.   Stearns nor Campbell did not know me for some time.   I dont weigh so much now as I did when I started from home last Sept.   Then I weighed 131 1/2, now 130 and last winter I weighed 150 lbs.

I staid in the old house Sat night and Sun. morning.   We had quite a rainstorm which lasted some hours.   It rained in through all parts of the roof and wet everything but it cleared off before noon and was fair. I went to meeting in the afternoon and evening.   Wed. the day I landed in Kansas was a <u>very warm</u> day.   Thurs. was a <u>hot day</u>. Fri. <u>was hotter</u> & Sat/ was <u>the hottest</u> day I have seen.   The thermometer stood at 105 in the shade,that is <u>some</u>!   I believe they have not had any, or at least many, such days.   It was cooler Sun. after the shower.   Monday I spent looking around town and writing an article for the Herald which you will see I suppose in this weeks paper.

Tues. I went to see Mr Haskell and went to the Wakarusa to see Mr. Abbot's folks.   Walked a good ways and got very tired.
This morning about four Oclock it began to rain and rained right through the cloth roof onto me.   We got as wet as you please, so as soon as it was light enough I came into the schoolroom where I am now writing.   The school that they have now is not spoken very highly of by some.   We have a mail now three times a week.   It comes Tues. Thurs. & Sat nights & goes Mon. Wed. and Fri. mornings.   Closes at 7 Oclock.   It is almost seven and <u>I</u> shall have to close at any rate.

Your afft. Son Edward P. Fitch
Be sure & number all your letters. Notice Stearns letter in the Free State I sent you and the manifesto in the last Herald about the city site & settlement put there together.

Aug. 9, 1855

Marked private

Dear Parents and Brother Appleton- no one else

I wrote to you yesterday morning but have a good deal to write now.   I am sometimes sorry that I came out just at this time and sometimes not. I have got into a tight place and I expect in order to get through and come out square I shall <u>have to have</u> some more money. First with regard to my claim.   I think that perhaps I shall be able to hold it but I can't tell yet.   If I do I shall have to go on to it and do some things that will cost money and that I cant do without money.   I dont <u>write this because I want you to give me more money</u> or because I think you have not done enough for with <u>the exception of</u> What little more you will pay <u>me for the Buffalo & for what</u> work I did.   I did not mean to ask you for any more for you have done all you ought to be asked to, but nevertheless I am in a tight fix and shall have to have money to get out or else give up entirely the $225.00 that I have paid for claim & interest and begin new again.   By doing that I shall lose so much but may by industry make something with what Capital I now have.

On the other hand if I have a little more to put with this I may make the whole worth something to me sometime.   Experience keeps a

19

dear School but she has learnt me one thing at least and that is not to trust anybody but myself. I have learned that, perhaps by the loss of 300, & perhaps less. I find that Haskell took my frame off of the claim and sold it and at the same time offered to sell the claim with it to which he had no more shadow of a title than I have to the city of Boston. Next Wise got on to the claim but his house was torn down and he went off. Then Mr. Mott went on to it not knowing who it belonged to, as there was no frame on it and he had an acre of the grass turned and planted it with beans. His house was torn down, or before that Wood saw him and told him it was my claim and he told Wood that he would make it right with me if I came back. Then Wood told him to hold on to it. Soon after about the Fourth of July his house was torn down and the eighth of July a Mr. Moore from Illinois went on to it. Mr. Wise claimed it and tried to sell it to Moore first for $100, & finally they came within five dollars of trading, but he did not pay anything for it but went on to it. Pierce also, the man who bought my frame, claimed the claim but did not press his claim at all because he had another claim. Moore went on to it and put up a log cabin and is now living in it with his family. He put up his cabin the eighth of July. I went to see him Tuesday. He seemed to think he had a right there but when I told him the circumstances he was a little less sure but he said he did not know as I had any right. He only had my word for it and he had Wise's word that he owned it. He did not want to pay me for it nor would he say what he would take for what he had done. I have consulted Esqr. Emery and he thinks I shall be able to hold the claim. He is going to see the man himself and see what he can be made to do. Moore said that if Wood had told him that the claim was mine he should not have gone on to it but now he was on it he wanted to keep it.

I shall try hard to hold it but may not. I was at a meeting of the association last night and they are quarelling all the time. About my city property I must write another time. I was going to this time but Emery says keep easy. I shall in all probability publish a Notice forbiding any one to buy that note that that Wood holds and refuse to pay it. He did not look after my lot that I was to have for staying this winter and I have got none yet, but Emery says I should have one. More anon.

I may come to Mass again this fall but it is doubtful. I should if I had only worked it right coming out. Perhaps I shall have my school again. Good chance.

Your Edward P. Fitch

Aug. 12, 1855

Dear Parents

    I guess that you will begin to think that I don't do anything else but write letters home, well I have not done much of anything else yet since I got here that is any work and I am so much perplexed that I hardly know which side up I am half of the time.   It has rained almost if not quite everyday, since I arrived here a week ago, some part of the day. Last night about 6 O'clock it began to rain very hard and to thunder and lighten dreadfully.   It litterally poured down.   I never saw it rain harder and as to thunder and lightening all that I ever saw I heard was not a priming to what we had here.   The thunder was like the constant discharge of Artillery and the lightening kept the air all a blaze of light. Almost all the persons that I have heard speak of it say they never knew such a storm of thunder.   The lightening struck twice in the city.   The first time was just about sundown.   It struck the end of a house and went down both rafters to the ground.   And [at] one corner a door came up to the corner post and a man stood in the doorway.   There was an ax laid on the ground a few feet from him; he says the last he remembers was seeing a large ball of fire come right down and burst all to pieces close to him.   It stunned him and his wife who was in the house pretty bad.   They have now got over it.   The lightning tore the end off from the house some. The other time it struck it came down a post of a low house and tore the boards off pretty well.   Just inside of this post laying right along side of it was a bed and a woman in it.   Strange to say altho it split the post all up it did not hurt her but two children in the house were stunned considerable. Both were very narrow escapes.   We had one death in the city yesterday from Small pox, a child of Mr. Willis.   Today it has rained very hard a great part of the day.   Our rainy season which ought to come in June has just commenced.   I have no place to stay except the old house and when it rains outdoors it rains in there just as hard perhaps harder.

    Mr. Stearns hired a horse and wagon to go look for some butter Friday and took me with him to drive.   After we crossed the Wakaruse ten miles from here we had to go most of the time across the prairie where there is no road.   The grass on the high prairie is not more than a foot high but on the bottoms where we crossed it is as high as the middle of the horse and some of it some higher.   From Washington Creek which was some 12 miles from home we set out to come across to Blanton which is 5 miles from here.   We started through the grass where it was up to my waist saw a large copperhead snake come through where the grass was just as thick as it could grow and as high as my head.   The horse could but just draw us thro and we had to get out sometimes and look ahead for there were ravines that we might get into and break the wagon.   We finally got through this first bottom and were going up the hill when we heard   a rattlesnake but we kept on and luckily did not see him.   We finally got home about nine o'clock in the evening without having found any butter at all but we bought 12 doz ears of green corn for our market. Sat. we sold some 8 or 10 dollars worth of provisions in our market and made a pretty good profit in them.

Let everybody see this sheet that wants to and all that don't want to see it read it to. Remember me to all friends.   Tell Albert to write to me.

Edward P. Fitch

Sept. 8, 1855

Dear Parents

I believe it is not long since I wrote to you but important steps have been taken and of them you should be informed.   I don't know what I have written to you about my city affairs exactly but the facts are these: when I arrived here this summer I found that I could not have the lot for which I bargained on Mass. St. and I found that city property was almost valueless.   S. N. Wood had neglected my business and taking all things into consideration with the advice of another lawyer (fight dog with dog) I have concluded to protest Wood's note and in order to have anything to show for the two hundred dollars paid, I thought it best to improve the best lot in the interest deeded to me.   So last Tues. I made a bargain with a carpenter to build me a house on that lot and to go right to work on it and have it on before Allen, Woods agent, had a chance to jump the lot. Wed. & Thurs. Allen was gone to Big Spring, and Mr. Jones (the Carpenter) went to work and has begun to frame the building.   The house is to be 12 x 14 ft., ten feet posts, and will cost $175.00 I shall probably rent the lower part for about 1.50 per week and have the upper part to live in myself.   When that is done I shall be able to hold that lot at least and if I don't get any more, that lot will be worth the two hundred dollars some time perhaps.   No city interest had ever been sold last spring for so much as 500, and it is the opinion of some of the persons interested that Wood will be willing to settle for a less sum than 300.   My good opinion of Wood is gone.   I have found three persons who were waiting for me to pay Wood so that they might get the money and all of them wanted about two or three hundred apiece and all to come out of this three hundred that Fitch was to pay.

Emery and I had been over to see the man that was on my claim and on last Thurs. he came to see me to know if I would buy his improvements and I set Sat. as a day I would come and see him.   Sat. Emery and I went out there.   We found that he had got fifteen acres almost fenced and quite a log cabin.   After talking a while he offered to take 150 dollars and I offered him 125.   We could not agree and it was left in that way. In the afternoon he came over here and we had more talk.   I had between the times seen Grover, one of the men who lived here last winter and who now lives close by the claim, and he told me that if I could get the claim for 125 I had better give it.   I told the man that I would give him 125, or leave it out to three men, neighbors, but he would not do that. I talked with him all the time till almost night.   He offered to split the difference with me and I would not do that; at last we made this trade. He is to finish the fence and I am to give him 155 dollars.   I concluded it would cost me about $30 to finish the fence and he could finish it better than I could for I could not do it alone and if it was not finished whatever crop there was would not be worth much.   There is a little broken up and a crop of turnips on it.

I expect to go on to the claim in a week.   I shall cut some hay I think and I don't know whether I shall sow any wheat or not.   So you see that when I have paid 175 for my house and 155 for my claim I shall not have any money, hardly, left to settle with Wood with for I had only 400 when I got here you know and I have made only about 20 dollars since I got here, so it will probably be the case that I must have some more money.   Though I did not mean to ask for any more.   It is thought by some that I can sell my claim for about 300 now but I think after buying it twice I shall keep it.

I am in pretty good business here now.   Our sales will amount to $16 per day on an average I think and if I stay here and live on my claim, I must have a pony to ride in every morning and out at night.   I have one now in view that I can have for 50, saddle, bridle and all and it will not cost me anything to keep it and I can let it for enough to pay for him in a few months.   But I can't walk out and in from my claim.   It is 3 1/2 miles and I can have the school to keep if I want to, I expect, at least so one of

23

the committee told me yesterday and it is expected to commence next month.

Coleman says that if I get safely on to my claim again it will be worth $1200.00 and he says I am a fool if I sell for less than that but I should probably sell for that or less.

Yesterday & day before have been very hot days but today is a little better, there is more air stiring. It was so hot yesterday that large hard apples laid on a bench at the east end of our store baked almost through, a number of them. I eat some of them and they were much like apples baked in the stove but such days are uncommon though Sept. is our hottest month here.

There has been a great convention at Big Spring fifteen miles from here. They have adopted a platform and nominated Gov. Reeder for Congress. We have a ratification meeting here tomorrow night at which Col. Lane, (formerly member of Congress and Gov. of Ind.) and others will speak, perhaps I among the rest. You probably saw by the paper that I spoke at the ratification after the great Con. here. I am going in strong for Gov. Reeder though he is a Democrat, though I should rather have him go to the Senate from Penn.

There has been a free negro here for a little while back and the Pro Slaver men have been trying to prove that he was a slave and get him away. He was on a claim just north of mine and last Sun. the news came in that there had a party gone to take him. A lot of us armed with Sharps rifles went out under the command of our Orderly Sargent to protect him but the slave holders backed out and dared not try anything. If they had we should have pitched in to them with our rifles.

Tell Albert and all the rest of the folks to write to me. They have time enough. Tell Albert Gov. Reeder is a Democrat. If you will come out father and live here I will give you half of my claim. Give my respect to all inquiring friends but the most of this letter it will be proper to keep to yourselves.

Your afft. Son   Edward P. Fitch

If I find that I must have more can you raise it of that Sudbury man? I should think if not that Uncle Doctor might help me a little.

Sept. 19, 1855

Dear Father

It costs something for postage on what letters I send but not much for what I receive for I have been gone from home two months and rec'd <u>one letter</u> from you all except that note Appleton sent with that letter of Mary Bakers that he forwarded. I have dated this letter Lawrence but am writing it in my log cabin on my claim and about this same claim I am in a great quandary. I have got the claim it has cost me first 25 dollars cash last spring and a note of 75, which is now standing against me and I don't know but I may have to pay it but I dont mean to if I can help it and keep out of law. Then for the improvements now on it I have paid in solid gold $155.00

But before I go any further just let me show how my finances stand. When I arrived here the first part of August I had almost $400.00; it cost me more to come by know, from Mr. Hall for that century sermon that he borrowed and lost .25, from Mr. Alden for a shovel he lost for me 1.50 and from Stearns for what I did in the store beside my board about 20.00 = 426.00 (about). It has cost me for board not reckoned while with Stearns and for an account book and for that notice in the Herald [<u>Herald of Freedom</u>] of protest of that note about 5.00 leaving about $420.00 leaves $90.00 all the money I have got. I have a little more than earned my living since I came out and should continue so to do if I staid in the city but now I must live on my claim and all the way is to get a pony and ride from my claim into the city in the morning and do my days work and ride out or else walk the distance, and it seem as though walking 3 1/2 miles twice a day was most too much. I can go to work and cut some hay on my farm and I have got a yard all built so as to keep a pony. I can possibly walk if I keep school but not to do any other work. Now I have got to do this or sell my claim but when my claim is preempted it will be worth $1500.00 and I can probably sell it this fall for $600, it has cost me $180 and may cost 75 more and if I sell I don't know exactly where I can get another one and I want a farm and dont think I had better sell so I <u>think</u> I shall keep my claim and get a pony. Still I <u>may sell</u>.

Then in regard to my city interest I am fixed just in this way. I have built a house on the best lot in the interest and by that means intend to hold the lot and sometime it will be worth the two hundred dollars cash that I paid Wood last spring.

I made my contract with my carpenter and had my house begun before I had any idea that I should get my claim even by buying it for if I had expected to have done that I should not have built so expensive a house.   It cost me $175, and I have let the lower part for $1.50 per week and intend to have the upper part to keep my things in and to sleep in any odd night that I may stay in the city.   Mrs. Wood is very angry with me and says I am trying to cheat them and Mr. Wood is expected back very soon and will try to make some settlement probably for my withholding that money has been the means of the Tribunes not being issued for two weeks so it is of great consequence to them to get it now.   If he is willing to settle with me anything like reasonably I shall want to settle and have it done with.

If he gets me the lot that he promised me which was 43 Mass. St. instead of the one that I have built on 44 Vt., I should be satisfied to pay him the whole 300, for that lot is now worth about $400, but the one that I have build on cannot now be sold for $200, but however he settles, (unless he agrees to deed me another lot with this for the two hundred already paid) I shall have to pay him something and where is it to come from?   Thats the question?   Can you get the money of that man at Sudbury and let me draw on you for any sum less that $300 or can you get of Dr?   I should think such an anti-Slavery man as he might help me so[me].

The fact is I shall have to settle with Wood some how or other but if he will not agree to some terms that are advantageous to me I think I shall let him sue on the note and then he may get the whole and may not, But the great question for you to answer is can I draw on you if I must have more money?   And this question you must answer immediately you must not wait but set right down and write and have the letter come in this very next mail for when Wood gets here I shall want to know how to meet him.   If you say I can draw on you tell me where to make the draft payable?   at Hopkinton Bank or where, and you must write immediately. I must know within 20 days of this date.   I hate to ask you for more money for you have done all that I think you could do and yet you see how it is.   If I sell my claim I don't know where to get another; if I sell it I believe I shall sell out entirely and come to Mass to live and gain what I shall have lost by coming to Kansas but that I don't want to do.   Now write and answer immediately and then ask Dr if he can't let you have the money for me.   The fall emigration does not begin to arrive here yet much but we expect it will soon; then city lots will rise in value.

Why under the sun don't the boys or some of the rest write to me? I want to know about the farm -- whether you have any apples & Peaches, are you making any cider? And lots of things. We had some very nice peaches brought up from Missouri last week they cost us 1.50 per bush, and we sold them at 30 cts per doz a great many of them. Apples that we had at the same time we sold at .25, per doz they were very large sweet ones. There was a barrel of cider brought into town yesterday and sold for 17 dollars. 50 a gallon. Stearns & I did not make very large profits while we were in business but he has got pretty well started and if he carries on right he will make something. Tell Albert we have knocked the Democratic party higher than a kite and we are going to send Reeder to Cong. Tell him to write to me. We had a big meeting last Sat. the day the great Gag law went into force and we spoke our sentiment against the infamous laws and their makers. We all committed a State Prison offence. The Gov. came here on Sat afternoon but refused to speak and when he started away the crowd gave him <u>three groans</u>, he is a Dough face, Dough head & a Fool Knave Rascal and all.

Yours as ever E. P. Fitch

Don't forget to answer immediately.

Sept. 30, 1855

Dear Parents

  If the adage is true that what we have but little of we prise highly, it must be that 'Letters from Home' are very valuable with me for I have but few of them and if the opposite is true my letters cannot be very valuable to you and I guess that I will stop writing and prove the truth of the first proposition by writing so few that you will value them so much that you will be glad to write one for the sake of getting more.

  I have got my house done and am now writing in it. I let the lower part for $1.50 per week and keep the upper part to sleep in myself. I have got all my things here -- a chair, table & book case and I can sit here and write or read at my ease.

  I have been at work on the Hotel for the last week and more. My work has been to boil the tar or rather the Composition to put on the roof. It is made of Gas Tar & rosin & some other things. It comes in Barrels. I have to open the barrels to boil the tar or melt it and haul it up on top of the building. I have boiled six barrels. I get myself all covered with the

Tar stuff. It is dirty or rather sticky work. The overalls that I have worn will be good for nothing else when I get done.

I can have work on the hotel all along for some time but I don't know about it for today. I hear that my claim will be jumped if I an't there. I was out there one night last week and like to have frose to death. I ought to put in a wheat crop this fall but I have not the capital. I shall have to stay more on my claim and I can't hardly work here and do it with out a horse and I have no money to get one. What to do I hardly know! I recd a letter from you (father) on Aug 28 which you said was the first you had written and then I recd on the 19 inst. Numbered three. If you ever wrote no. 2 I never got it. You ought to have a paper and set down the number and date of the Letters I write; also the Date of these I receive and the time when I receive them.

Tomorrow is the day appointed by the Legislature for the Election of Delegates to Cong. and today we hear there is a large body of armed men within a few miles that say they are going to burn this town and kill all the Yankees and that they say will not take more than ten minutes! The town is in a state of intense excitement; there have been large numbers of cartridges made today. The company have cleaned up all their rifles and put new caps in all of them and are preparing to give the Missourians "Jesse" if they come here. I hardly think there will be a fight but can't certainly tell. You have no idea of the state of things that exist here and you cannot conceive of our feelings. We are going to let them have their election all their own way and not vote at all until Tuesday the 9th inst and then the Free State men have an election called by the Sovereign People so that two men will probably go to Congress, Whitfield and Reeder! and Congress must decide which is entitled to a seat. Why don't Albert write. Tell him that we shall not send a National Democrat to Congress this fall. It has been very cold here for a few days so that on low lands there has been some frost but not much, not so much but we are still haying around here.

What will be Appletons P.O. address?

Yours as ever   Edward P. Fitch

Dec. 8, 1855

This letter was written near the end of the two-week siege of Lawrence which was the chief event of the "Wakarusa War." The trouble began on November 22 when Coleman, the pro-slavery Sheriff of Douglas

County, arrested Jacob Branson on a peace warrant sworn against him by a friend of Coleman.   Near Blanton's Bridge, Sheriff Jones gave up his prisoner when confronted by a determined group of Free-state men led by S.N. Wood.   He then notified Governor Shannon that rebellion had broken out and that he needed 3,000 men to carry out the laws. The Governor called out the Territorial Militia which had two generals but no troops.   Besides the 250 Kansas residents sworn into the Militia by the two generals, his call also was answered by a large group of armed Missouri residents headed by Senator David Atchison. Most of them camped near Franklin, a few miles to the southeast.   Together with other contingents north of the Kaw and at Lecompton, they cut off all traffic to Lawrence, including the U.S. Mail.   The resulting threat to the city caused free-state supporters from the surrounding area to gather in its defense.

Dear Parents

The mail arrived last night and brot me a letter from Appleton of 32 pp but none from you and as the mail is to go back this morning I must write a few lines as it may be the last time I shall ever have to write.   As you probably know before this time, we are in a state of seige.   An army lays near our border.   The Company to which I belong slept under arms last night not knowing at what moment we might be called upon to repel an attack from the enemy.

We don't know what may come; we may <u>possibly</u> (possibly I say) escape without a battle.   A man from our Camp was killed day before yesterday and is to be buried today.

Give my love to all my friends whether I ever see them or not. Pray for us and for me; our help is in God.

I cannot write more as I fear the mail will go.   We have a number of forts throwed up which we mean to defend to the death.   My station will be Hunts Fort.   We have one cannon.

Yours Edward

Dec. 12, 1855

Dear Parents

"The War that for a space did fail etc" Scott, The Battle's fought the Victory's won. 'I still live' D. Webster. Peace, Peace! and it was Peace.

We have gained the victory without a battle. The mail starts again tomorrow morning and I have just been discharged from service in the Army this P.M. after standing the seige that we have for two weeks. It cannot be expected that I could write much until I get some rest so I must leave details for next time; suffice it to say we have gained a complete victory without bloodshed. The Gov has come round on to our side and all is right. I would not go through what I have gone through for the last fortnight for considerable.

Wait until I am rested and I will give you particulars. The murdered Soldier will be buried with military honours on Sunday next. I have sold my drum which I gave six dollars for for ten and I got the money today. More anon.

Edward P.

Thank God that we are spared. For if the Lord had not been on our side. May Kansas now say the 124 psalm.

P.S. Mr Legate who perhaps you will remember as the man who taught the centre school when Appleton taught at Lumbre St. is here. He arrived from Miss. where he has been teaching ever since. He left Hopkinton last week. He says that Appleton will not make out very well the first one or two terms for he will not know their fasions and ways. He has been teaching about 130 miles about Natches. He says they are so different from New Englanders that Appleton, he is afraid, will not do well. I am going to have him write to Appleton as soon as I know how to send to him.

The way I know anything of this is Whitteman wrote a letter that I read a week ago to day in which he said that A. was going to teach a High School in Natches, Miss

Jan. 6, 1856

The first winter the settlers spent in Lawrence, that of 1854-55, was unusually mild leading them to conclude that was normal winter weather in Kansas. The next winter was of the opposite extreme in temperature, as this letter attests.

Dear Mother

I received the letter written by the family on Thanksgiving night on the 28 ult. but have had no time to reply until now or rather the weather has been so cold that I could not write. Today is the first day for 13 days that it has been warm enough for the snow to melt. So long a spell of so cold weather I never knew in Mass. even and we are in a warm climate. I came here expecting to have warm winters and to find 'that same'. I think I shall next year emigrate to Lapland. Some idea of cold may be obtained when I tell you that apples, of which we had 24 bush frozen, we sell at 1.50 per bush and frozen potatoes at 1.25 per bush. We bought eight bush of frozen potatoes a day or two since for .75 and retail at 1.00

The cold weather commenced on Sat the 22nd ult and the thermometer has ranged from zero to 26 deg below. Several men have been frozen more or less and one died from its effects. There was a week together in which I was not really warm except part of the night. Now I am going to answer your letter written Thanksgiving eve. It is headed, First letter new series. Why is that? It is the 9th you have written to me, 7 of which I have recd. I recd another yesterday from Father written Dec 16 in which he says he has written three times since the 21 of Oct. Well that letter made the Fourth I have recd dated since that time.

You say "The family are all here but Edward. Where is he? What is he doing?" I was in the store all the time that I was not up in town listening to hear the latest news from the enemy who were camped not far distant and were intending to attack us. Late at night I went to bed with my 'Sharps Rifle' loaded and lying by my head not knowing at what moment in the night the drums would beat to arms & I should be called up to help defend the town. The military companies were guarding the town from that time until the war was over. I always had my rifle with me wherever I went; even when I went to escort ladies home I carried my rifle along with me and thus I lived for some time. My rifle was my

31

constant companion.   One evening there was a young lady at the shop helping Mrs. Stearns and our company (Com G.') was called out under arms and we had to bring large piles of wood and set them on fire to give out light to dig a ditch that we had to dig and throw up a breastwork in front of the shop after we were ready to begin to dig.   Our company were divided into two parts; one part dug, the other part watched the guns.   To the last I belonged & so I got leave to go into the shop about nine o clock. I had engaged to go home with this young lady and Mrs. Stearns but just before we were ready the drums beat to arms & we were ordered to be ready to march against the enemy who were then expected.   Every man's gun was examined and 30 rounds of balls delivered to every one who had met that number & then we stood in the armory waiting for the command from the Col.   Then I thot of friends that perhaps I might never see again but I thought also that, "Whether on the gallows high, or in the Battles van the fittest place for man to die is where he dies for Man!"   And here was that place in the forefront of the Battle of Freedom but the battle came not on that night but the mail arrived bringing me a letter of 32 pp from Appleton which I managed to read by the campfire.   This was the only time that I felt alarmed in view of a Battle.

Yours for Freedom in Kansas,
Edward

Jan. 20, 1856

Dear Parents

I commenced a letter to Mother two weeks ago and have just finished it but I can't tell what there is in particular in it.   It is so cold that I have no chance to write at all except on Sun. when I can come down to Mr. Stearns house where I am now writing.   It is a log house on New Hampshire St No 51.   For eight Sabbaths I have [not] been to meeting but one half day.   Today is the eighth and I don't know certain whether there is any meeting or not but probably none as it is so cold.   Last Sun there was a meeting but I did not go on account of sore hands and disinclination.   The other Sundays there was no meeting on account of the cold and the War.   It has now been extremely cold for four weeks with the exception of two or three days and during those two or three days the Government Surveys came along near my claim rendering its position certain.   The survey throws me in a direction which I did not expect and gives my house and most of my fence to a proslavery man, Whitlock so if he can he will prevent me from moving off either my house or fence, 250 dollars gone to the dogs.   I had had the claim surveyed by a man who said he run from the Government surveys which were new and he said I was perfectly safe and I rested on that until the day before the Gov. survey came on when I found that he had made a mistake and another man had jumped on to a vacant claim near me.   This put me into an agony of suspence and I got the surveyors to go out with me & meet the Gov. survey and from that they run to mine which was only half a mile from the Gov. survey.   If I had moved my house about ten rods in a particular direction before this last man that I speak of had gone on there, I should have gone all right but I did not.   But I still hold on and may get a claim, as part of my improvements come on this claim and were there before this man came on.   If I lose my claim now I don't know but I shall leave the country and go to California.   Many are going from here in the spring. That is unless we have a war which I think is likely enough.   I recvd a notice to appear at the Head Quarters of our company armed & equipped for inspection and ready for marching.

　　　　We hear that the Missourians attacked our men at Easton ten miles from Leavenworth on Election day (last Tues.) and demanded their Ballot boxes but our men would not give them up.   They then fired on our men which fire was returned badly wounding two Missourians. Some men were sent to Lawrence for help and two of them taken prisoners by the Missourians who say if the wounded men die they will hang our men and if they do that there will be fighting.   God only knows how it will end.   We have sent men there to see about it and they have not returned yet.   The opinion of most is that we shall have to fight in the spring.   The Missourians are concentrating a force all along our border and in the language of Judge Cato They are going to drive every d-----d Free State man out of the Territory.   We want men money and ammunition. We are just sending and have sent men to the States to raise these.   Mr Schyler raised 1950.00 in one evening in Chicago,   the drafts for which have arrived here now so that we shall be better prepared to fight now than we were before when we had no money.   Men are now engaged in making cartridges for Sharps Rifles all the time and we have sent for a whole load of powder & lead!   This moment the news has arrived that the Pro Slavery men have actually butchered a Mr. Brown one of the prisoners whom they took.   I have not heard the particulars except it is said they cut him to pieces with hatchets and soon after left hearing that men were coming from Lawrence with Sharps Rifles.   How long O

33

Lord must we suffer thus.   I hope you will raise an army in the East and March through Missouri and Proclaim liberty to the slave.

Edward

Jan. 20, 1856

OFFICE EXECUTIVE COMMITTEE
KANSAS TERRITORY, January 4. 1856

SIR:-- A deputation, consisting of Messrs, LANE, EMERY, HUNT, GOODIN, DICKEY, HOLLIDAY, and SAMPSON, have been this day appointed to visit the United States, to plead before the people the cause of Kansas, and to convey and lay before Congress the Constitution of the State, recently adopted by our fellow-citizens.   We respectfully bespeak from the friends of Freedom such attention for them as the importance of their mission demands.

They are instructed to visit and address, early   in February, the people at Burlington, Iowa City, and Dubuque, Iowa; Springfield and Chicago, Illinois; Lafayette, Indianapolis, and Richmond, Indiana; Dayton, Cincinnati, Columbus, and Cleveland, Ohio; Detroit, Michigan; Milwaukie, and Madison, Wisconsin; Buffalo, Rochester, New York City, and Albany, New York; Worcester, Lowell, Springfield, Salem, and Boston, Massachusetts; Hartford, and New Haven, Connecticut; Providence, Rhode Island; Portland, Augusta, and Bangor, Maine; Concord, New Hampshire; Burlington, Vermont; Philadelphia, Harrisburg, and Pittsburgh, Pennsylvania.

Done at the office of the Executive Committee, Kansas Territory, the day and year above written.

J.H. LANE, Chairman
J.K. GOODIN, Secretary

Dear Father,

By the above you will see that we are going to do something <u>towards</u> preparing for war for that is the object of this mission.   Emery is

34

my Lawyer and when they have their meeting in Fanuel Hall I want you to go to Boston and be there and I wish you to get introduced to <u>Emery</u>. He can tell you my business with regard to Wood for he has had it in charge. I want you to have him come to Hopkinton and Lecture. He says he should like to come & will come. Emery is a red haired man and red whiskered unless he shaves his whiskers off. He now shaves only his upper lip. I want you to go to Boston and just go up to him after or before the Lecture and tap him on the shoulder and speak to him. If you do this he will know you for I told him I should tell you to do so.

If I had the pen of an angel or somebody else that could reach the ear of every man in Mass. I would say to every one -- Beware of Know Nothingism. You cannot tell how much we of Kansas were disappointed when we heard of the defeat of the Republican party in Mass. In your defeat we seemed to see our own fall but me thinks that if you could see Slavery in Mass. and its effects as we see them here you would be more Anti Slavery. I was a KN. but I now am ashamed of the party, but I dont so much blame you there as you see the evils of popery more than the evils of Slavery. The great question of Slavery is to be <u>the</u> question before the country and K.N.ism is just going to split us up and ruin the Republican party. Amen.

Mr Emery is one of the old line Democrats but was always opposed to the Nebraska Bill. He is now a good Free State man.

I don't think you need to give much for Kansas except what you give me for I have spent enough for you and me both.

One object of the mission of these men is to enroll men to come to our rescue when the battle for Freedom shall have been begun. This is to be done privately of course, but men we must have and will.

Edward PF

Feb. 24, 1856

Dear Parents,

I received a letter from you last night in answer to the last one I wrote which was mailed here Jan. 22 and your answer arrived Feb. 22 just a month quicker than I generally hear from you. There are some thing[s] that need answering in your letter. First how should I know that my draft was honored when I had not heard from you? I shall not probably want to draw again just at present. I am in great trouble to know what to do this spring. I should rather come East that doing any thing else but that will not do. It is going to be very sickly here this spring. I think but of my business troubles hereafter.

Yes Mother, I remember that you asked me about an umbrella and old coat and I remember that I have written about it in half of my letters home and told you several times that I did just what they wanted me to do with them; vis, left them at the Coffee House for them to take.

Was Albert married before he went home? How is George now? Give my love to him and tell him I say he must be a good boy if he wants to see me again. I am much obliged to Calvin for writing to me and I would write to him if I could but you must tell him I have no place where I can write except on Sunday at Mr. Stearns home. I have been to meeting twice to-day. It is growing warmer and we have meetings more regularly and shall continue to if we are not all killed. March is near at hand and our Legislature will meet. Pierce says we are traitors so of course the Missourians are to put us down but if they try it we shall have a bloody time out here. God grant that it may be avoided. Our cannon was fired 17 times on the reception of the news of Banks election as Speaker, 16 for the Free States and one for Kansas.

The Merchants of Lawrence had an oyster supper on the 14 inst, speeches etc. & closed with a dance. I was one of the Merchant princes attended and had a good time. The Military Com[panies] or rather one of them, Com. A gave a ball on the 22, Washington's birthday, but it was stormy & they did not have a very large gathering.

March 9, 1856

I wrote so much so as not to forget what I want to say but now it is time to write again. We have had no Eastern mail for about three weeks now though the contract for carrying the mail says three times a week. They don't get it through Mo., partly on account of the muddy roads and partly because they are so shiftless down there. Consequently Eastern news is at a discount here. Our Legislature assembled on the Fourth inst. at Topeka. We have seen no Missourians yet and don't expect to at present.

I want to find out John Wheeler's P.O. address and let me know as soon as you can. And also Uncle Williams for at the end of three years I shall be as likely to be in Georgia as anywhere else. I think that plan is going to succeed but don't know; anyway I want to write to Uncle Williams and know how they are getting along.

Where does Father have to go to court? and how long? is it not a profitable job?   I was thinking that he said it was once.

It has been very unpleasant weather for a week or so but this afternoon it has cleared off warm and fine. I hope you will get the water into the house this time and have one thing done.

My house has now cost me about 200.00 cash besides a little time that I worked out and I have rec'd about 7.00 rent and am now renting it at 2.00 per week besides keeping my things in the upper part of the house.   200 for the house & 200 for the lot; 2.00 per week pays a pretty good interest on 400 dollars.   That is the best investment a man can make here now is to build houses to let; if I had money enough I would build me another but the cash is wanting.   I shall probably a little more than make my living this winter but I hope next year I shall be able to raise a crop to sell.   Has E.D. Ladd been at Hopkinton?   Did Mr. Patterson ever return and give that lecture that he did not give when I was there?   How are Uncle Doctors folks?   and Mr. Webster?   If I had sold my claim when I talked of it, I should have come home and staid this winter but should then probably have returned in the spring but it is possible I may yet come home to Mass. again within a year.   Tell the boys to write.   They have more time than I do and a better chance.   Write soon to your affectionate son

E.P. Fitch

The following item is in Edward's handwriting but has no salutation and is not signed.   It may be an addendum to the previous letter to his parents.

Now about my business difficulties.   First I have got through at Mr. Stearns as he hired me for the winter at 6.00 per week.   He said my time was out Mar. 1st and as he was not doing much just now he did not want me any longer so for a week I have been away.   I have earned just 1.00 in that week beside my board and what to do I cannot tell.   A Mr. Wilmarth who now keeps a Book store and periodical Depot has talked with me some about going in with him and enlarging the business somewhat but I dont know what arrangement I can make. He is going to move into my house with his family as soon as I can get the present occupant out; they pay me no rent and are therefore not very profitable tenants.   The reason is this: last fall when Wood found that I had a house on the lot and would not pay that note, he went and told Pike (the man who is in the house) not to pay me any more rent and he told him he would not so he has only paid me for two weeks and has been in the house since the fifth of Nov., some four months.   Wood has been gone since the middle of Nov. but is expected back soon and I want a tenant in that he can not scare and that will pay me the money for rent and, beside all this, within a few weeks a man has turned up who claims the lot that my house is on by virtue of a Deed given by Wood to him in Nov. 1854, some four months before he sold to me.   So if that deed is good for anything he and I must clash and if we do I think perhaps Wood could be made to suffer for selling the same thing over twice.

March 15, 1856

Since writing before I have seen the Deed that Mr Condit hold[s] on my lot.   It is a regular Quit Claim Deed but he don't expect to get the lot but he says Wood must give him a Deed of one as good or he will see trouble.

If I can only get Pike out and Wilmarth into my house before Wood comes back I shall be all right.

Next comes my claim matter.   You remember my writing about having it surveyed and finding my house would come off from the claim, but very soon after that survey was made another survey run the line from a government line nearer than the one that my Surveyor run from and told me that I should get a claim where my house was and told me not to move my house and as he was a lawyer (now a Senator of the State of Kansas) I though I won't take his advice, for if I moved my house and then there would be a claim where my house stood and I should happen to move it so as to come on anyone else, I should certainly lose both but if I let it alone I should get a claim.   So it was left until the Township line which comes through this city was run within four or five miles.   Then by getting a private survey from there a Mr. Longfellow found that my house came off from my claim and so on the first of Jan. he goes to my claim and puts some lumber there. Since that the weather has been so cold that he has done nothing until lately he has commenced building a house.

On the 17 of Jan. the U.S. surveyors run the township line in near my claim.   I was out there with Mr. Searl, the city surveyor, and from their line he run for me a half mile and found that my house did come a few rods off from the claim that Mr. Longfellow was on and that I claimed.

April 21, 1856

Dear Father

Your letter of the 6 inst came to hand two days ago but I have no time now to answer it in detail as I intend to do at some future time. The reasons for my being so busy just at this present time are as follows. We have had quite an excitement in town in regard to locating a bridge over the ravine between Kentucky & Ohio St., some wanting to put it at Pickney St. and some at Winthrop. We had a number of meetings and the excitement was about equal to what it was in Hopkinton about locating the Town House. It was finally agreed to leave it to a vote of the town and the election was to take place on the 19 inst. Mr. Legate whom you probably recollect (he taught the centre school the winter that I taught at Lumber St.), Mr. Christian & Mr. Sutherland were appointed judges of Election and I was appointed Clerk. I as well as Messrs. Legate & Christian went for Winthrop St. but the moneyed Winthrop St. beat by some 26 Maj. and now the other side say we allowed illegal voting but they cant prove it for it is not so. They had a meeting night before last and are to have another tonight. I expect to be hauled over the coals but I can defend myself.

When the polls were about closing Sherriff Jones came into the office where we were holding our election and found S.N. Wood, who had just arrived from Ohio here and he tried to arrest him on the old warrant issued last fall for the rescue of Branson. He got his hands on him and with another man tried to keep him but we crowded around him and took Wood away. Jones raved and swore some and said he would have S.N. Wood or kill every D___d Son of a B_____h there was there and then he went off to Lecompton. This was Sat. Sun he came back with five or six men and tried to get Wood again and also to arrest some others for rescuing him the day before. He has got the names of several persons as concerned in that I was there. I wish I had a good Colts revolver. I wish you would tell Uncle Doctor or some body that is able to send me one. Jones has gone to Mo. for help and the prospect is for another war. The Kansas Committee is in the city!

Mrs. Wilmarth of whom perhaps you heard Esqu. Emery speak died this morning and I have been busy preparing for the funeral which takes place tomorrow.

I am as well as usual but cannot stop to write more.The opinion is gaining ground that we are to have war.

Ora Pro Nobis, Edward P. Fitch

May 18, 1856

On May 10 rumors of a new invasion from Missouri reached Lawrence. By the 17th a large number of pro-slavery men had gathered at various points around Lawrence.   Mrs. Robinson reports that travel in any direction by free-state men was perilous.

Dear Parents

It is some time since I have heard from home and I am beginning to be anxious to hear from you.   I believe I did not number my last letter. I am on my claim now and don't have a chance to see every mail that comes in.   The U.S. Surveyors finally got as far as my claim last Tues. and they ran the line through my house throwing part of it on the claim where I wanted all of it but, as the person who holds that claim does not live on it, I expect I shall be able to hold but having a claim is not going to do me any good if I don't live and we don't know how soon now, we may at any time and in our present condition we stand a chance to be wiped out which is what they say they are going to do.   We never have been quite so near a war as we now are.   I think if it begins here God only knows where it will end.   Not here, at least if the North has any principles left, and not I trust until slavery is abolished through out the country.

I just hear that the commission from Congress has been obliged to leave Leavenworth and the Territory. That will probably be a good thing for us in the end but we wanted to have the rest of the evidence taken.   I am in trouble about my city property.   Wood is gone, left the country again without making a settlement with me and I can do nothing until the war is over and the thing settled.   I suppose that there is a great deal that I might write to interest you but when I get to writing I can't think of it.   But if you live in such a fevered excitement as we do here for one week you would not blame me for not writing more but I do want to hear from home oftener.   It is now more than a month since your last letter was dated.

Where is John now?   What has become of that Grey squirrel that the boys had?   I have got two fox squirrels about 2/0 as large as that one was when I was there.   I expect they will grow much bigger than that one ever will.   I sometimes keep them around the house and sometimes in a cage.   They are tame as can be.   How is George getting along, give my love to him and tell him Redard says he must be a good boy.

How is your spring work?   Farmers here cannot do much on account of this trouble.   The enemy take their horses right out of the plow teams and run them off, kill their cattle and commit such depredations that we can do nothing.   We are in a bad fix all around. What is Appleton doing now?   I have not heard from him for a great while and don't know where he is but suppose he is at Denver yet. And now one word on politics.   You Republicans were beaten in Mass last fall; now in the coming Presidential Canvass make this up.   Carry the State for the Republicans nominee whoever -- Mr. Fremont, Seward, Hale, Sumner or who not.   Kansas depends on a Republican President for the next term.   Fremont is my choice at present.   But I suppose I shall not have a chance to vote being in a Territory. Pomeroy arrived a few days ago.   I was in hopes he would bring me a pistol but it seems he did not.

Yours for Kansas Free
Edward

Can you find somebody that will give you ten dollars to send to me and I will send you ten dollars in Kansas State scrip.   It is drawing ten per cent inst [interest] and will undoubtedly be good some time.   I am all out of money but I have Scrip.   EPF

I have just been talking with Mr. Stowell and he thinks as I do that my friends in Hopkinton ought to give me a pistol and he thinks I ought to have the Navy size.   If you have not got one perhaps you had better get Navy size.   I should think there ought to be men in Hopkinton who would give enough together to get me a good pistol.   The Claflins, Adams, Woodards, Morses, Bowkers, and others and Uncle Doctor ought to give me another.   We are bound to have a big fight and no mistake before we get through here.

The mail has just come out.   No letter from home.   Why don't you write?   What is the prospect for crops this year and how much have you planted?

I had written so on before I found this was written on and now I will let it go.

I wish you would ask James Bowker how much he will take for his Land warrant for 120 acres of land.   It may be best for me to buy it.   If I knew what he asked I could tell.

How is Mr. Webster?   Has mother any help this summer?   Do you sell milk?   Who helps on the Farm?

Yours,
Edward

41

May 19, 1856

This letter, although dated the 18th, undoubtedly was written on the 19th. The excitement over the killing of the two free-state men and the fear of an actual attack on Lawrence led Edward to write again to his parents even though he had just written them a long letter the day before.

Dear Parents

The Blow has been struck, the war has begun. Two of our men have been killed, murdered this day. One within a mile of town and the other at Blanton's bridge four miles from here. God only knows who will be killed next or where this will end, not here at any rate.

We must have help from the Free States. We are not in half as good condition to fight now as we were last winter for then we were thoroughly organised. Now we are not and have got no head man to organise us that we can trust and that will take hold and again we are not as much concentrated as we were then.

The man at the bridge was shot about noon and in now dead. He was shot with a U.S. musket in the back while going away from the men who shot him. The other man was shot in the head just over the eye with a Sharps rifle. I think he was on the Cal[ifornia] road and only two or three with him. They snapped their rifles at the men who shot him but the rifles did not go off. They however wounded one of the pro Slavery men with a Revolver so that he dropped his rifle and they (our men) got it. We are in a bad fix and no mistake. The enemy have got a number of our leading men prisoners viz. Gov. Robinson, G.W. Brown (Ed. Herald), Jenkins, one of our good true and prominent men, Judge Schuyler (Sec. of State), Conway (judge of our Supreme Court) and some others of less consequence. Stewart who was killed at the Cal. road was from N.Y., Jones killed at the bridge was from Ill., both young men. I am badly armed for war and ought to have a good Revolver.

Pray for our success and also help us for probably men will have to come from Mass., even, to fight here.

Yours until death. Your aff son

E.P. Fitch

Give what is on this sheet as much publicity as possible. Tell every one who has the least interest in Kansas that now we want help --men money and arms.

May 26, 1856

"Sheriff Jones' Raid" occurred on May 21 when Deputy U.S. Marshall Fain and Sheriff Jones of Douglas County led a large posse, reported to have contained 500 to 600 men, to Lawrence. After Fain had arrested, without any resistance, the four men he had warrants for, he turned to "mob" over to Jones. The Sheriff swore the entire group in as his posse for the execution of indictments as public nuisances of the Free State Hotel and the two Lawrence newspapers, the <u>Kansas Free-State</u> and <u>The Herald of Freedom</u>. After these enterprizes were destroyed, the "posse" went on to burn Gov. Robinson's house and to plunder many other houses and businesses. This raid and the two killings reported by Edward helped inspire the next atrocity in "bleeding Kansas", the massacre by John Brown and his followers of five pro-slavery settlers along Pottawatomie Creek on May 24.

This following letter was written five days after the sacking of Lawrence.

Dear Father,

Mr Stowell, who you probably recollect seeing last winter, starts back for the East today and I am going to send this letter by him so to have it sure to go. I have not heard from you for some time and am quite anxious to hear. I wrote some time ago to you about sending me a revolver. I want you to send me a first-rate Colt revolver six-inch barrell with the moulds and powder flask all complete. If you can get a thousand of his metallic cartridges to go with the pistol, get them. I should think that somebody that you may know might might make me a present of a pair of revolvers. Uncle Doctor or somebody, but if nobody will, I want you, if you have not yet sent one, to get one and send it and as soon as you can send by some conveyance. If you can't get one yourself, just write to Mr. Stowell and have him get it and have him bring it, unless you have a chance to send it by a trusty man before. I will write his address in this letter before I close. He will come back pretty soon I expect. Come to Worcester and see him if you can possibley. If no one will give me a pistol, I want you to buy one and send or have Stowell buy it and I will pay you sometime when I get more money, if I am not killed. I have not dared to go on to my claim for a week for I have a bitter enemy in a Pro-Slavery man for my next neighbor. I am going out tomorrow but shall not dare to stay at my cabin without a rifle or gun at my bedside. I had about ninety dollars worth of things there when I left there and I should not be surprised to find them all stolen when I get back.

Last Wednesday the ruffians came into town and burnt the hotel, destroyed both printing offices and robbed the town, burnt Dr. Robinson's house. They stole five dollars out of Mr. [Charles] Stearns house that belonged to Mr. Stowell.

They have done all the mischief they could and now [Gov. Wilson] Shannonhas called out the troops to protect him for fear we should rise up and exterminate him and the Pro-Slavery party in general. The intelligence has just come in that 5 Pro-Slavery men have been killed about forty miles south of here. And it is supposed to be true about 125 Free State men from that neighborhood had come up within twelve miles of this place and soon they are going back to attend to things there. I have written four sheets the size of this full, giving an account of this war. I have sent it to Appleton and he is to send it to Whitteman, and I want you and he to take pains to show it to anyone that wants to see it, Mr. Webster or Mr. Wheeler or anyone that takes an interest in Kansas. Explain it was written in a hurry and is not a very splendid document, but if folks want to know that facts this is them just as they came under my observation.

Have you found any one who will send me ten dollars in money for ten in State scrip? If you have send on the money and I will send the scrip.

It is very warm here now, but there is generally a breeze blowing. The prairies look splendid covered with flowers and green grass. This is a beautiful country to look at and no mistake.

Kansas has now I think reached its turning point. If the North doesn't now arouse and do more than she has done yet, Kansas will be a slave state and we (the Free State party) shall be wiped out. The next thing they are going to do is to bring us a paper to sign that we will obey the laws of the Bogus Legislature or leave the territory or be hung and they are going to give us sixty days to do it in. If the North does as she ought, and goes in for letting them try to hang us if they can do it. But when they begin to hang, we shall begin to shoot. The Pierce administration must be broken down and we must have a Republican president or else we must dissolve the Union, anything to abolish slavery.

Fremont for president! Down with Douglas, Pierce and company. I wish I could be in Massachusetts a little while just now. I would lift up my voice like a trumpet against the administration and slavery and I should like to vote for president, but I hope now that Kansas will not be admitted as a state just yet, but the presidential contest fought on the Kansas question.

I am very short of money at the present and Pike lived in my house until he owed me fifty dollars for rent and paid none of it and I doubt if he ever does pay it.

Please hand the enclosed letter to Whittemore as soon as convenient and oblige (him and me) with.

Mr. Stowell's address is Martin Stowell, Worcester, Massachusetts.   Write to him and find out when you can see him for I want you to meet him very much.

Please write soon and tell me some news for I am anxious to know.   It is of the utmost importance for each man to be armed in this country.

Give my love to all my friends.

Yours from Kansas free,
Edward P. Fitch

June 15, 1856

Dear Mother,

Your welcomed letter of June second came to hand on Wednesday the eleventh inst., very soon for a letter.   Welcome I say first, because I had looked for it every mail for four weeks, and welcome because it enclosed a ten dollar bill, and welcome because you did not say as I expected you would that I must be shiftless if I could not earn enough to live on.   I should have said so myself, would I been there; and the fact is no one here is doing any business and there is not money in circulation, and therefore I can't get any.   You said nothing about the scrip, but I will send it, not in this letter however.   The letter got to me about ten o'clock in the evening.   I had been handling rails and driving teams all day since four o'clock in the morning, but the letter refreshed me very much.   I have not been in town myself until last night for a week and last evening, as I was walking with a lady (who by the way is to move into my house this week), she had a letter in her hand which I happily attempted to take away and finally got it.   When lo! it was directed to me in your well known hand, but mailed at Dover, New Hampshire.   I found it was dated the twentieth of May and I got it two days after the one dated the second of June.   In that letter I find this sentence.   "If it is Edward I shall never consent to his going to Kansas again."   Now though at times I wish I were

45

well out of the difficulty here, yet if I were there you would have hard work to keep me there I think.   I have not been engaged in any battles yet, because I have been planting and fencing ever since Lawrence was burned or rather the hotel, but I want some pistols badly and must have them.   Stowell must bring them, and if you see him tell him from me that I think he ought to be here by the fourth of July.   At any rate, there are now about six hundred or more Missourians about Palmyra, about twelve miles from here, and Colonel Sumner is concentrating his forces there. We may get into a fight this week.   If not, we shall in July.

From Buchanan and Breckenridge we have nothing to hope, and now we must be immediately admitted as a state or the Republican candidate must succeed for president, or we will be a Slave State, unless the Union is dissolved, which I go in for, now.   I hope the Northern American conventions have not nominated a candidate, but will wait and join with the Republicans and elect Fremont.

The death knell of slavery has been tolled and now comes the decisive times.   I hope if Brooks is not expelled from the House of Representatives at Washington, that the Massachusetts legislature will call home her Senators and request her Reps. to leave Washington, or Congress rather, and send an army to march into Missouri and free the slaves.   Let the Union slide.

I am so much excited that I cannot write.   Men are being found dead more or less every little while.   A man was in here yesterday with whom I am acquainted, who was robbed of his horses a few miles from here and these three men went out and went to kill him; they fired at him and he fell.   Two of the men then ran away and the other came at him to beat his brains out with the butt of his musket.   The man made out to get his gun away from him [the attacker] and he left.   The wounded man then wandered three days without anything to eat and finally got here. He has the ball in his side yet.   Such are some of the outrages perpetrated upon Free State men here every day.   Rob a man and then kill him.

How came that letter to be mailed from Dover, New Hampshire? Have you been there, and if so, why not tell how Appleton is doing, and with regards to your son's visit, I believe you feel at the East more anxiety about us than we feel here in the midst of the war, but we feel some.   I have been armed all the time for the past week.   I have been among Pro-Slavery men and near one of their camps at work, and I don't feel safe alone without arms so keep them with me all the time.

Now I am going to answer a letter of Father's dated April sixth. He says, "Your first great mistake was in remaining at Lawrence, second coming home, third paying money without seeing to the land. Now I must beg leave to disagree with him there, and I will tell you how it is. My first mistake was in not coming to Kansas with the second party or else waiting until the next spring before I came. Either of these would have been be.tter than to do as I did. With regard to staying at Lawrence, I don't think it was a mistake for I have been to Topeka twice and don't like the place and should not, I don't think be willing to stay there, if I went beyond Lawrence I should not stop short of Manhattan and there has been nothing there until last fall of any account. My going home as I did was a great mistake, sure enough, but had it turned out as I expected, it would have been well enough about mistakes. To the property, those who have land to know said it was good and those in whose judgement I put confidence in has turned out badly, I must say. However yet, I hope it will come out right in the end. If I get time before the mail goes, I meant to write to the boys. If not, you give them my love and tell them they must write to me.

From you affectionate son,
Edward P. Fitch

June 29, 1856

Dear Parents,

I received, a day or two since, your letters of various dates about June fifteenth, and one or two things in them I wish to address. First, I think that Mr. Webster had better have sent that money that was raised in Hopkinton directly to me. I have spent about $150 in cash for the good of Kansas, beside a good deal of time. To be sure I have got scrip for the money expended, but such folks as myself and those that need it most, have never received hardly any money sent here for our relief. Most of it gets into the hands of big men, and those who need it suffer for it and don't get it. My one hundred and fifty dollars I don't now ever expect to get, unless it is raised at the East and sent directly to me. Mr Stowell has not arrived yet, and I somewhat fear he will not get through. If Hopkinton folks send any more money here, I hope they will send it to me, and I will see it is appropriated to those who actually need it for there are many such here.

The $10 which you sent, came safely and was just in season. It enabled me to pay $2.75 for a bush[el] of potatoes and some other small bills that I owed. Ten more will be very acceptable; after which I shall be

47

able to get along.   I am very much obliged to Mother for her kindness in offering to send me what is given to her, and I <u>hope</u> it will be in my power to do ten times as much for her benefit.

I have quite a garden on my claim and it looks pretty well now. Our patch of corn does <u>not look</u> very well, the seed at first did not come up, and we have planted it over the last week, and hope it will be better.   I expect to begin tomorrow to work for Mr. Savage, help him put in some wheat.   I shall have an acre of wheat for a months work; he boards me and I have to harvest it if the ruffians allow me.   I may work on those terms for two or three months perhaps and <u>may put some wheat</u> on my <u>own claim.</u>   I should <u>certainly</u> if I was <u>sure</u> of getting the claim, but I may yet lose it, so I don't want to put <u>too much</u> expense into it.   The Fourth is close by, it will be an era in the history of Kansas I expect.   What will happen I cannot tell.   I hope for the best, but fear for the consequences of what may be done.   I want to go to Topeka myself but don't know as I can.

If you have a chance [to] buy or at least get to read, Mrs. Ropes' book entitled *Six Months in Kansas,* which I learn has been lately published in Boston.   I was acquainted with her some, and think her book would be interesting though I have not read it.

I am in a great hurry and I presume I shall not write half what I want to. Your letters wre not numbered, and so I can't tell whether I get <u>all or not</u>.   I keep a regular account of the number and date of all I <u>write</u> and all I rec.   I shall probably have much more to write after the Fourth. I think we are on the verge of a civil war, and I am glad that we are, for the <u>North needs</u> something to wake them up <u>once</u>, and if Kansas is lost to freedom, the <u>North</u> are to blame, and no one else.   We have done <u>what we could</u> and are about <u>used up</u>, without we have help.   I am glad to learn of the nomination of Fremont and I wish I could <u>vote</u> for him.

You must excuse looks and everything else.   When you are in the position that I am you will appreciate the need of excuse.   Please tell Appleton the news from this letter for I cannot write to him. It is very warm here yet we have a good breeze most of the time.

Your affectionate son,
Edward

I received a letter from Wood threatening to sue that note of 300.00. How shall I avoid it?   What is the way of putting property out of a person's hands?   Is there any way that he, in Ohio, can sue me here without taking territorial law!

July 4, 1856

Edward sent this letter to the Hopkinton Patriot. In the letter following this one, he tells his parents to send a piece he has written to the Patriot for publication, but it is probably not this one since this letter precedes the other by two days.

Mr. Editor,

　　I suppose that today oratories through all the country have been descanting on our glorious liberty and independence, but I think if some of them had been in Kansas and seen and known what I have here, they would have been less ready to talk of independence as at present enjoyed in a part at least of this country.

　　Things have been done here in Kansas, within the past year and under the sanction of government, that would make the Austrian Haynau <u>blush</u>, and yet we live in "<u>Free America</u>," glorified so much for being the freest government on the globe.　For proof of these facts, I need only refer to the sacking of Lawrence, burning of the hotel, destruction of printing offices, and imprisonment of Robinson, Jenkins, Brown, Deitzler and others merely because they were prominent Free State men.　I blush for my country, when I think of the enormities perpetrated by the government here in Kansas.　And yet I have read in Northern papers, statements saying that these accounts from Kansas had been exaggerated. It is not so.　The half of the enormities perpetrated here, and for which Pierce, Douglas, and company are responsible, has not been told.　But not content with seizing our leaders and imprisoning them on 'trumped up' charges of 'treason' or something of that sort, they must today put a veto on mens expressing their thoughts in speech.　The Free State legislature was to convene today at Topeka, so Colonel Sumner was sent there with his whole effective force to prevent their meeting.　He stationed his men in the street near the place appointed for meeting and as the roll of the 'House' was being called, he said he had orders from Washington to disperse them and should execute those orders.　He then commanded them to disperse in the name of the United States, and they dispersed.　He was asked the direct question whether that was to be taken as being dispersed at the point of the bayonet and he said they might take it as they liked; they must disperse.　The Senate fared in like manner.　What a Free Government this is!　What harm could these men be doing, even supposing they did call themselves a Legislature, to meet and talk over our position and difficulties?　It seems to me that this is abrogating the liberty of speech much more than is called for, and that the time for the U. S. to interfere was not when we were making laws, but when we attempted to execute them in the face of U. S authorities.

But enough of this, the end is not yet, and probably is not very near; for unless the North awakes and <u>men</u> (not fools) are placed in the Presidential chair this fall, Civil War must follow.

We have some other things to keep us stirring. We have been troubled for about a year now with rum selling; we have tried various expedients to rid ourselves of the curse, and finally, by buying out, we had but one grocery left among us, and in the absence of any law touching the case, the ladies of the town took the law into their own hands, and on last Wednesday morning about twenty-five or thirty of them made a descent on this place and took possession of the Liquor, which they spilled without mercy. They turned out all there was, and broke up the bottles and kegs. I understand that the owner threatens to prosecute them under the "Bogus Legislature" and at the same time he pretends to be a 'Free State' man. What will come of it, I don't know. The women say if they are arrested, they shall all go and take their babies along with them, and they declare that they will not be bailed out, but stay until they are satisfied with keeping them, and will be glad to get rid of them.

We had a Sabbath School celebration here today, and considering that two years ago all the inhabitants of this place were the untutored savages, I think the exercises were very creditable and would have done honor to an older town. The singing by the children was excellent and the toasts good, and taken all together we had a very pleasant time. The weather here is very warm but we have a good breese almost every day so that it is not as uncomfortable as I have often seen it in Mass. Farmers here are getting in their wheat, most of it has done very well, some fields are light but most that I have seen looks well. Corn looks finely, much of it being now as high as a man's head.

Yours for Free men, Free speech, Free Kansas, and Fre-mont,
E.P.F.

July 6, 1856

Dear Parents,

I suppose that as the Fourth has passed you will be expecting something from my pen, but I am too much occupied to write many letters. The Fourth passed without any serious accident anywhere in the vicinity. We had a Sabbath School Picnic here and had a pleasant time. At Topeka the Legislature came together at twelve Oclock and was immediately dispersed by Col. Sumner with U.S. Troops. What a Free Government we live under. I have a notion to Emigrate to Austria where Freedom is allowed.

I have seen nor heard nothing of Stowell yet, but hear that Dr. Cutter's party with which I supposed he was, has been sent back, and I suppose that my pistol has got into the hands of the enemy.

I want you, Father, to tell Mr Webster and everybody else not to send money to Kansas unless they know where it is going. I have spent nearly two hundred dollars in Kansas that I have never received anything for and I know of more who have done the same. Send your money to me. I will take some myself and the rest I will give to those who actually need it, for I know many such. I know of some families where the men served in the war, who lived on Indian meal and water all winter. And there are a great many who will actually be on the point of starvation next winter because they could not put in crops this spring on account of the trouble. I myself shall lose at the very lowest estimate fifty dollars in that way beside the advantage it would have been next year to have the land plowed this year.

Last Wed. a number of women went to the only place where Liquor is sold in this town and spilt it. The whole of it was ankle deep on the floor. There were about twenty five of them. The owner says he shall prosecute and the writs are now out for them under the Bogus Laws. They say they shall go to Prison and stay there. How it will turn out I can not tell.

That you may know how my time is filled up, I will tell you. I have to get up in the morning between four and five, take the horse, and go bring the oxen four yoke. They are turned loose on the prairie at night. Sometimes I have to ride three or four miles to get them and generally get back about breakfast time. Sometimes I milk if someone else hunts the team. After breakfast (which consists of johnny cake and a kind of milk gravy) we go to plowing; one to drive, one to hold, the third man now plows out corn with the horse. That was my part yesterday. I plowed when the corn was as high as my head when I stood erect. The fourth cradles wheat and rakes it or some such work. I rocked the wheat cradle part of two days last week. We work generally until about half past eleven when we turn out, and have dinner at twelve, and then set down to read the newspapers. Some days we do not go to work again, when very hot, until three, sometimes half past three o'clock. We have supper at five and work in the cool of the day until dusk. Our dinner is mostly hasty pudding and milk. So you see, we don't live very high. I don't probably eat a pound of meat in a fortnight nor half of it.

When I go after the oxen in the morning, I ride through grass that is as high as my knees when on horseback, and I ride a large horse as large, I guess larger, than Fanny. Wed[nesday] morning I was driving an ox and I was close behind him when he ran over a rattlesnake, who jumped at his hind leg but probably did not bite him. I had a whip, so I whipped round and got the snake to coil up and then I got off to kill him. All at once he was gone. I whipped all around, but could not find him. Not daring to go around in the grass on foot, I got on my horse again and rode him around whipping among the grass. Soon up came a snake with all vengeance and rattled away like fury. I got off and killed him, and his rattles I send in this letter. I have helped kill but one before this and this I killed alone. It was quite a large one for a prairie snake. The rattles mother can show with the other Kansas curiosities.

If you think that Hopkinton people would be enough interested in it, you might have that piece that I wrote giving a history of the sacking of Lawrence and publish it in the Patriot. But if you do, let it be prefaced by a note saying it was not written for publication. And you might take a look at it over and alter it some, as it is more extended than it would need to be to be published. Those facts with regard to last fall need not be published. If you publish it let my name be attached to it so that folk may know whether to believe it or not.

Your affectionate son,

E.P. Fitch

July 19, 1856

My Dear Parents,

Your several letters of dates of June 30 came safely to hand last night enclosing XX $ for which I am thankful. The revolver which you are to send I hope you will send by some one who will get here as I suppose you have heard before this that Mr Stowell was stopped on the MO river and his arms taken from him so that my revolver & Rifle are probably now in the hands of the Border Ruffians.   About using the Revolver if I ever get it you better believe me that if I ever get a chance at those Missouians I will use it.

"Money answereth all things" is as true to me as it ever was and that is true enough.   We are now having very dry weather and if we do not have rain soon my garden, as well as many others, will be ruined almost.

Esq. Emery arrived here last Sat. and I was with him yesterday and we tried to settle up my affair with Wood.   What we shall do I cannot yet say.

The Ladies who spilled the liquor have not yet been arrested and will not probably be.   I believe they are afraid to try to arrest them.

I believe that as long as Uncle Dr. has [done] so well that I shall write him a letter, a thing which I believe I have done once at least since I was here, but he never answered it.   My general health is good but I have been troubled for a few days with a bad boil on my upper lip.   It broke out just in the middle of the beard on my lip which had been growing for a number of weeks as it was impossible to shave it.   It has troubled me much more than it otherwise would.   I have lost some sleep but hope the worst part has past.

I am just as much obliged to you Mother for offering to send me than ten dollars as though you had sent it and I hope I shall be able to get along without it, seeing I rec'd it by the last mail.   I expected to have had twenty paid to me before this time out, of forty that was owing to me, but it has not made its appearance and now it probably will not for some time. Just after I got the other 10 I planted some potatoes and other things and it has been   so dry that they have not come up and probably will not at all.

I have had another consultation with Emery and have finished up my business except drawing on you for money to pay up.   I have got my notes up and am to pay Wood fifty dollars more and give up all claim to all the [town] lots except the one on which I have built which makes that lot cost me 240$ and Emery says it is worth 250 now.   I hardly think it could be sold for that now.   Lots are lower now probably than they ever will be again.   I have made a draft on you for $50 and Emery is to let me have the Cash on it and he will either sell the draft or take it on East with him. It is made payable three days after sight and payable at the Hopkinton Bank.

If I could only settle up about my Claim now I should be all right but that cannot be done until this land office is opened and how soon that will be I don't know.   According to present appearances I shall never get the money that I spent on the war last fall and have Scrip for unless it is raised at the East where I am known and sent directly to me.   There is about one hundred and eighty dollars of it all, and I want you to do your best to have any more than is raised in Hopkinton sent to me and sent so it will get here.   This money that is sent all ways gets into the pockets of a few, almost all of it, while we that are suffering must still suffer for the want of it.   It is not right that it should be so, but so it is.

Mon evening
        The business with Wood is all finished except my signing that draft on you which I expect to do.   I hope you will find it convenient to pay it and I hope also that I shall not be obliged to call on you again for money.   I will try not to.
        Gen Pomeroy is coming out pretty soon and he would be a good one to send that Revolver by.   Be sure and send it by some trusty man who is coming through Iowa or coming alone.   It is now 1/2 past ten or Eleven and I am two miles from home, but have a horse to ride, so I cant write more.
Yours affec.
Edward P Fitch

Please give the enclosed letter to Aunt Elisabeth, as that will save me three cents.

July 23, 1856
For the Hopkinton Patriot

Mr Editor
        Since the writing of my last (July 4th) we have had rather still times for this latitude; true some two or three men have been shot at, and, killed for going to Topeka to attend the meeting of the Free State Legislature, but such occurrences are so common here that they hardly cause a remark, except as showing how pro Slavery men are determined by all means in their power to harrass and trouble us.
        A few days ago since two men got into some difficulty and one shot the other dead on the spot.   The murderer has gone from here but is

still at large and the occurrence hardly caused a remark here, used as we are to hearing of such things every day.

A part of Senator Douglas' subduing force, the U.S. Troops are still encamped around in different parts of the country to disarm all parties of Free State men found together but to let Pro Slavery parties go on.   At least this is what they have done so far for I do not know of a single Pro Slavery party that they have disarmed, while I am acquainted with many persons belonging to Free State parties who have been disarmed by them.   They were promised that the arms should be restored to them but when they went to the Fort to get them last week they were told that they could not have them and the reason they gave was that they were afraid they would be used if given back, so they kept them after having previously promised to return them, if applied for at the Fort.

We are looking anxiously to see what is the fate for Toombs bill in the House.   If that is enacted into a law we may almost as well say farewell to freedom but we hope the 'House' will consider what it is doing and not pass such an atrocious bill; the Border Ruffians have got every thing prepared awaiting its passage.   They, in conjunction with the Bogus Legislature, have driven out or imprisoned many of our men, have stopped parties and individual from the Free States for coming in and now if the bill passes they have hundreds in Western Missouri all ready to move over the line and camp for three months, so as to be included in the enumeration of inhabitants of the Territory and to vote and then they can return to their homes in Mo. or other states and need have nothing more to do as we are not even to have the satisfaction of voting on the Constitution thus made for us, but are to be admitted with it anyhow. This is called a bill for the 'Pacification' of Kansas.   I think if it passes there will be some of them pacified with cold lead before it is done with.

Today a new act in the drama has begun to show itself.   Mr. Fain, Dep. Marshall and commander of the forces that sacked Lawrence in May last, has appeared and put up the following notice to the people here.   "I will attend at Lawrence on the first day of August next to receive lists of property liable to taxation in this county."   And under it for identification he has posted an extract from the Statutes, Kansas Territory, which says

1st,   "Every person who is liable to be taxed shall give to the Assessor a true list of all property which they had control of on the first day of Feb together with a fair cash value of the same."

2nd,   "If any person shall neglect to give in such list and the Assessor shall be obliged to go to his or her house or place of residence to procure such list he shall be entitled to receive the sum of one dollar for his trouble which shall be collected with and in the same manner as the other taxes."

3d, "The Assessor shall have power to enter any houses or land to find and assess, any property that he may find."

The people here are determined not to submit to be taxed by the Bogus Legislature but just what shall be done in this crisis has not yet been determined, as it is [threatened] that if we resist they will come with a posse and take our property and sell it. We shall see what we shall see.

Yours for Fremont.
E.P.F.

July 28, 1856

Dear Mother

"Necessity is the mother of invention." It having obliged me to procure what <u>you</u> said. If you had you would write more frequently to me, viz a <u>secretary</u>, I am enabled again to address you.

But to return to matters of fact I have been rather unwell for two or three days and have been threatened with Fever and Ague, but feel so much better today that I hope to get over it. I was intending to indite this letter and write none myself but being conscious that I could not say with truth that I was unable to write I gave it up and took the pen in my own hands, much to the detriment of the penmanship.

On Thursday afternoon I was taken with a severe nervous headache and so severe that I just quit work and sat down and did nothing and eat nothing until Sat. Fri night I lay awake all night with the toothache and Sat Mr Savage wanted one more hand to go on to the bottom to work than he had without me, and I felt very well so I went and worked all the forenoon. We were delayed and did not get home to dinner until about two Oclock when I was very faint and hungry so I eat more dinner than I ought. I came into town in the afternoon having to walk the last quarter of a mile and when I got to my house I was so tired as to be able to go no farther and my head ached very bad. I sat down and had my head bathed with cold water and then drank a cup of tea which threw off my headache. The folks here thought I should have the Fever & ague but I am much better today and think I shall get over it. I am not

56

however well and cannot write a long letter which must be my apology for this being so short.

It is, as you are aware, a little more than a year since I left home. I think you have not much cause for complaint about my letters as this is about the 24th (two a month) that I have written.

Hoping to hear from you soon. I remain with every sentiment of affection

your dutiful son.

Edward

Monday Eve.

The mail has arrived but the letters that I hoped to receive from you have not come. I have been doing nothing today, yet feel very tired and not able to write. If I am any worse you shall hear by next mail.

Yours   E.P.F.

Aug 10, 1856

Dear Parents,

Your welcome letters of dates of July 20 & 24 came to hand last Mon eve. The five dollars from Mrs. Claflin will enable me to pay for a hat that I bought last Apr and have not yet paid for.

The letter of acknowledgement for Aunt E you have probably given her before this time and on a week ago last Friday I sent a letter to Mr. Shaw. I sent it you see before I got your suggestions in regard to it but if I wait until I get the revolver before I write to the Dr. I am afraid he will never get a letter from me for I never expect to see it. I am sorry you sent it in the way you did and did not wait till you could send it direct to me by Mr. Pomeroy or some other one coming to Lawrence. I want it very much just now for I have just been loading up all the guns that we have got about the house and we don't know what night we may be attacked. We shall keep every firearm well loaded at our bedside all the time. The ruffians are gathering above us on the creek and are coming down some night to sweep all the settlers in this valley, at least so they say, so that this may be the last letter you may get from me. The ruffians are now 150 strong but they are receiving reinforcements every day. Eleven went up today to join them. My neighbor Whitlock is among them & I expect nothing less than that my house will be burned if nothing worse befalls me.

Yesterday I was down on the Wakarusa to get plums and first heard of this expected foray and today I have been over to the other side of the valley.   The settlers there are arming to defend themselves as well as possible.   The millitary company of Lawrence and the Wakarusa have both gone to Osawatomie and have been gone a week so we are not able at present to rout this force.   The troops which have been camped near here have within a few days been called in to the Fort.   I wrote thus far on Sunday and had not time to finish and have had none since until now.

Wed. P.M.   Last night a force of Free State men went down to Franklin and attacked a lot of Pro Slavery men that were there in a log cabin.   They had a cannon and a lot of muskets.   Our boys succeeded in dislodging them and capturing the cannon and a large number of muskets.   One of our men was killed and two more quite badly wounded. Today the troops have gone down there.   Col. Lane was with them it is said.   I have not seen him.

Mr. Stowell has come as far as fifteen miles this side of Nebraska line and stopped to found a town which they call Lexington.   In regard to Stowell and also in answer to your letter about Wood and some other things I intend to write more fully within a few days.   Just now we are very much hurried.   I have recovered my health again.   I was under the weather for about ten days.   I sent an article which I had written for the Hopkinton Patriot to Whittemmore last Monday.   If you ask him for it he will probably give it to you and it would do to read at the Anti Slavery Soc. meeting very well.   When you say "I believe you already know that I am President of the Anti Slavery"   you presume on my knowing considerable, considering that you never spoke of it before.

Don't show this to any body.   I write on a bed and in a hurry.

Yours truly
Edward P Fitch

Aug 25 1856

Dear Parents,

Your letters of July 27 & Aug 10 are both before me and though the time that I now spend to answer them must be stolen from other duties yet I believe [word first spelled 'beleive' and corrected to 'ie'] I will do it.   In Mothers letter of July she says "your letters are quite proper to read after I have dotted the I's and crossed the T's".   Now, Mother, if I did not think more of your letters that I look after mistakes in them I should have something to tell you about such things, for in the letters now before me, in them are a number of palpable mistakes so plain that I, who do not pretend to any knowledge of grammar can see them.   Next, you speak of the contributions etc.   I dont see why Hopkinton should not contribute to me directly to pay me what I have laid out in the Kansas wars for unless I get my 180 dollars directly from the State I never shall get it, but if you did not contribute to me alone, I can help many that I know of that are very poor.   There are two families, near neighbors to me, who have very hard work to get enough to live on.   They are brothers and they have a span of horses which they use and let be used for the Free State cause a great deal, and they <u>do</u> themselves.   Besides one of those men had no flour or milk, or butter or sugar all last winter, but lived on Corn Cake and molasses & coffee.   And the other was but little better off for food and not quite as well off for a house.   They now have hardly decent clothing enough to wear and none fit to wear to meeting.   I know personally many just such families that need actually both clothing and food.   Most however just at this time have garden sauce to eat so that starvation does not stare them in the face.   I have given much myself from my slender means to those who have been unfortunate or are very poor.   I have a number of cases in my mind that I intended to write but I have not time.   This last I have just written would do to read in you Soc. These words occur in your letter.   "Miss Paine & her Cousin visited here Sat. & from her account one would think she was in the Inquisition." Who is Miss Paine and where was she when in the Inquisition?   I don't know who or what you mean.

So much for that letter.

In Father's letter of the same time he speaks of my settling with Wood.   I suppose you know now how I have settled but you dont say a word about it.   What do you think of it?

Stowell was to bring Muzzy a Rifle or Revolver & fifty dollars which his Father sent him and was to bring me a Rifle or   Revolver.   He had stopped at a new town they have made fifteen miles this side of Nebraska line and has kept the arms there with him except Muzzy' Rifle which he sent by Eddridge.   I want the arms every day as we don't know what day we shall have to fight now.   The Revolver Dr sent ought to be here now but I have heard nothing from it yet.   What was the man's given name that had it?   Now for the letter of Aug 10.   In regard to my sickness I will say that I was not <u>very</u> sick after all being able to sit up most of the time.   I might <u>say all</u>.   I had a <u>first rate</u> nurse in the person of a young Lady who wrote that part of the letter which I did not, and my apartment was my own house where she lives.   She took the best of care of me, read to me, and did everything to make me comfortable.   Her name is Sarah Wilmarth.   (She knew Anna Herrick and heard of her death just before I got your letter.)   There are skilful Physicians here that I have confidence in that I might have had if I had wanted, but I dont believe in doctors you know.   I was packed once, and should have been again if I had too much fever.

  I had not before heard of John Wheelers movements and he has not got here yet, although I can expect him today as some of Lane's men are expected in from Topeka today.   How & for what has Maritta Phipps gone to Europe?   I am sorry to hear that Father's health is so poor.   You must not worry about me and make yourself sick that way.   We think here that you at the East worry more about us than we do for ourselves. We see danger and prepare for it but dont worry much.   The Topeka boys have just got in and Wheeler is not with them.   There is a young man by name of Ross who came through Iowa with them and he says that he is probably in the North part of the Ter. yet near Nebraska but the men from that quarter have been sent for and he will probably come with them. Who is Jim Allen & who did he marry?

  I wish you could have some of the melons that we have here at Mr Savages where I stay.   We almost always have two and sometimes three kinds of melons with every meal.   I helped eat six or seven yesterday.

  You ask 'how are your Sabbaths spent'.   I have sometimes thought of writing an account of some sabbaths that I have spent to show you but want of time has and probably will prevent.   Yesterday Capt Shombre's funeral sermon was preached.   He was mortally wounded in the attack on Titus Fort a week ago Sat. and died a week ago this morning. He was buried with military honours last Tues. afternoon.   The text was "I go the way of all the Earth.   Be strong, therefore, and show thyself a man." I Kings 2nd Chap 2 verse.   These words might well be applied to Capt. S. as he was a Christian of long standing and freely gave up his life for the cause of Liberty.   Mr Nute gave notice that he should, next Sabbath, preach the Funeral sermon of his Brother-in-law, who was murdered on his way to Leavenworth a week ago today.   He remarked that three men had, within a little more than a week, gone out of his house to their death; vis, his brother-in-law, Mr Hopps, Mr Jennison & Major [David S.] Hoyt, who was killed at Washington Creek   and for the particulars of whose murder see in sheet which I have written and sent to Whittemore.   He will give it to you in a few days.   It is written for you to read to anyone that wants to know facts as they occur here.   It is not written well at all for I am, or was, much excited at the time yet it is a true account of things.   A week ago Sun was spent in trying to negotiate for a change of prisoners and in cheering Fremont _____ arms etc.   We had a short meeting yesterday P.M. in the Hospital for the benefit of the wounded.   They are all getting along well I believe.   There is not one bit of inflammation in any of the wounds owing to the judicious use of water, which is used very plentyfully.   Mr Jennison was sent to Kansas City after lumber and was waylaid and killed on his way back here.   The particulars I do not know.   We are very short of provisions, that is bread stuff, in town now.   No flour to be had anywhere in the city at all.   I have, or we, used the last flour last week and dont know when we can get any more.   I told Sarah what your letter said about the one who took care of me when sick writing every week and told her she must write now to make up, but I guess she will not.   I have been sick with the toothache almost all the last week.   They have troubled me a great deal.   I did not sleep for two or three nights.   It dont seem to be confined to one tooth but changes all around and my whole jaw is sore and lame.   Do you have any apples this year?   I have eaten two so far I believe.   Are there any peaches?   Mr Savage & I picked a lot of elderberries and we use them for puddings and pies just as you do Whortleberries and they almost take their place.   Plums we have lots of.   They grow wild in abundance.

I was in my cornfield day before yesterday.   The corn now looks as though I should have something of a crop, perhaps 75 or 80 bush. of corn and lots of pumpkins.   My share of the field has cost me about 20 dollars thus far and I have got to harvest it.   If I had the money to get the seed I think I should sow a little fall wheat on my claim.   I shall have some on Mr Savages claim next spring at any rate

LATE SUMMER 1856

The next letter is undated but can be placed in the late summer or early fall of 1856 by its contents.   It is addressed to Edward's younger brothers, Elijah and Calvin, who were 15 and 13 years old, respectively.

Dear Brothers E & C

I am very glad that you wrote to me or Calvin at least and if I had time I would write to you [but] then I hardly know what would interest you.

61

Two weeks ago today Muzzy & I started for my claim when we got a mile from the city we found the prairie on fire and we saw it was going towards a house where there was a hay stack and we thought it would get burned.   I supposed that the man who lived there was away and so told Frank that we would go and keep the fire from the hay.   When we got there we found Mrs. Hancock taking on terribly and no one with her. Directly two more men came and the fire was coming.   We began to burn around the stack and pretty soon our fire got away from us and started we four of us and one woman started after it and we worked for two or three hours and finally put it out after it had burnt over a hundred acres, just before it got to another mans stack of hay.   If we had not got it out it would have burnt them and there was a great many tons of them.   The other fire that first started run like a race horse and burnt over hundreds of acres and only stopped when it got to the woods.   I then rode horseback about 12 miles and got caught out on the prairie after dark and staid all night at Mr. Savage who lives on the claim close by mine.   Thus ended one days adventure.   You must write again and I will try to answer it.

Edward

Sept. 21, 1856

Dear Parents,

My last [letter] gave you particulars, I believe up to the time Gov. Geary arrived here and then I supposed the war ended for the present and a week ago tomorrow I sent a short note giving you a hint of what had happened since I had at that time some six or seven sheets full all ready to send to different persons which I did not send because I thought they might not get through and I have not sent them yet but expect to tomorrow.   On Fri night a Mr Adams who came from Penn. with Gov. Geary came to Lawrence bringing the Gov. inaugural address and proclamation ordering all armed bodies to disperse. While he was here the news came that the Missourians [were] advancing on Franklin, intending to take that place and then advance on Lawrence.   My Reg & the 5th were immediately ordered to march to Franklin to keep them back for a time.   There were around 100 horsemen of them and they reported at Fish's ten miles from here that they were the advance guard of 1500 that were coming right on to Lawrence.

Mr. Adams immediately sent word to the Gov. at the same time that we marched to Franklin.   When we got there we sent our scouts down as far as the crossing of the Wakarusa where they found out that these men had gone back (as they said) to the camp of the main body six miles below but from other things we thought that they had gone up on the other side of the Wakarusa so we came back, getting home just before daylight and just at sunrise.   Gov G with 300 troops came riding into town but hearing our report they returned to Lecompton.   The Gov had an interview with our officers and told us we might keep up our military organization for our own defense until he could get things straightened and then he would prevent any invasion of the Territory. Here we rested secure but at night (Sat night) an express came in from Lane saying that he wanted help and about 100 of our best fighters all armed with Sharps Rifles went out to his aid leaving about 250 men in Lawrence and these not all armed.   Things stood just in this shape on Sunday when about 10 Oclock we discovered a flag flying on the top of the Blue Mound 8 miles from here toward Missouri.   This mound can be seen for many miles each way.   It is the highest point in Eastern Kansas, I suppose.

The flag meant this "The enemy are in sight and marching toward Lawrence."   We waited anxiously the arrival of a messenger from that point.   Soon Dr Still's son who lives on the mound came.   He said this advance guard of about 100 were near Blue Jacket 8 miles from here and the main body were some four miles behind them moving this way in wagons, on horseback and some on foot.   He said there could not be <u>less</u> than 1200 and he knew of a body of some three to five hundred just south of him who would probably join them beside the advance guard, in all something like 2000 men.   He had a first rate spy glass to look through. Soon messengers began to arrive from other points where the enemy was advancing, all telling about the same story.   At twelve Oclock a messenger was sent to Lecompton for the Troops or rather telling the Gov. the facts and asking for Troops.

We then began to think of preparations for defense.   We had a large fort on the hill but our cannon was gone with those who went to help Lane.   About 4 P.M. the advanced guard was near to Franklin and three of our men rode out to see them.   Two of their men rode to the front to meet them.   We then took the two prisoners almost under the guns of the party.   They started toward Franklin with them when one of them fired at one of our men and knocked his hat off.   He immediately turned and shot him dead.   The horse ran into Franklin.   The other prisoner got away.   There were but 15 men in Franklin.   They soon had to leave and then the enemy took possession of the town.   The first thing they did was to burn the steam saw & grist mill & one or two houses.   About 20 horsemen from here went down to see what was going on.   They were at about five P.M. driven in by about 4 times their number of the enemy's Cavalry.   They came to within the city limits and made a stand.   The enemy halted about half a mile from them.   They stood so for a few moments when another body of ten enemy was seen approaching but they did not dare to come any nearer to the hill than they were (a little over a mile) for they thought we had big guns there, so the two parties backed off and went round to come up by the river out of reach of our fort.   A small party, about a dozen with Sharp's Rifles, went out on foot to meet them and they with the horsemen had quite a little skirmish with them just before dark.   About fifty of our men with the canon went out to see if they could put some grape into them but the enemy upon that commenced a retreat back to Franklin.

We kept scouts out to keep watch all night.   I was in the saddle almost all night myself.   The troops arrived here soon after dark.   On Mon morning we saw them coming up again.   The troops formed into battle array and our men, too, and we were ready for them but they halted, in sight, but two miles off.   The Gov. and Col. Cook, commander of the troops, went down to see them and went to their camp and staid all day making & listening to speeches.   Just before night the Gov. came back and said there were 2800 of the enemy but they were going home again.   Some were going up by Lawrence toward Lecompton and some directly back the way that they came and in a few moments a number of them, 200, came up and camped close by the troops.   Soon word came up from below that they were burning houses and committing other depredations north of Franklin but the Gov. could or would not do anything about it.

Tues morning those Ruffians rode on toward Lecompton.   They began when they got 5 miles out stealing horses, stole two of Capt [Transdren].   Came to a lame man who was so lame that he had to go on crutches.   They took his two horses and when he remonstrated with them they shot him so that he died the next day.   The Gov. saw him just after he was shot and rode rapidly to overtake his murderers who he said he would bring to justice but we cannot learn that he has yet.   That day the army went back driving away with them some 150 head of cattle that they stole all around.   Some parties dispersed in different directions toward different parts of the Territory, stealing and murdering as they went.   They broke into my cabin and stole all my things -- blankets hatchet, hammer, etc   so that I have lost all the bed clothes I had, some 25 or 30 dollars worth.

Twenty dollars will not more than cover the actual loss of what they have stolen from me and fifty more won't pay for what I have lost by having to be away from my place for the last few weeks.   The cattle & hogs of Pat Meairs have destroyed my crops.   It is now generally believed that Gov. Geary is an enemy to [us] and that he has about the same as promised the ruffians that he will subdue us if they will keep away and that is the reason that they have gone off as peacefully as they have.   His acts in the last week seem to show some thing like this and when I see a little more of them I will write again.

I would like to write more now but I have not just at this hour any time.   It is very cool here, almost cold enough for [fires].

One man told me today that I must write to my friends to be ready to come out here immediately after the Presidential election for that would be our only safety to have men enough here to fight all Missouri and the troops, beside if need be we intend if we can get them, to lay up a store of provisions to stand a siege of a few weeks and then if we don't get help we must fall.   God only knows what we are coming to.

Times look dark enough.   I hope that the Proverb "It is always darkest just before day" will prove true in our case and that brighter days will come.   Why don't you write oftener.   I have not had a letter since the 24th of July.   This was the date of the last one, almost two months.   That doesn't mean you ___ surprised.

Your affect son
Edward

Sept 28th 1856

Dear Parents

I write to you at this time with peculiar feelings.   It is Sunday and today I heard for the first time since I left Mass. the sound of the "Church going bell" and how many memories it delivered up in my mind. You must imagine, for describe them I cannot.   To be sure I have heard this same bell before but it called then to prepare for battle and only once before today had it called to church & then I did not hear it.   I have this moment returned from meeting and from hearing <u>one</u> of the best

65

sermons I have heard for years from the text "Be not ye afraid of them, remember the Lord which is great and terrible." Ne 4: 14 and by a minister that I suppose Mother won't feel sorry to think that I went to hear him preach even if I was at the East no less a person than T [H] Higginson, the Theodore Parker of Worcester. It was not, to be sure, much like the sermons that I have been used to hearing in our church but it was well suited to the times and the place. He is a smart man and no mistake.

     P.M.

     I have just seen Mr Tappan, also Mr Higginson. Tappan left Boston the same time that Mr Parsons did, who was to bring my revolver. He said he was in the office when Mr P. left there & left with him and he heard nothing of a Revolver. I think you had better see the next time you go to Boston whether it was sent or not for it may have been served as that box of candy was and may be at the office yet. If by any chance it should be there you had better keep it till I tell you some way to send it if I dont come home for this sending by any and every body is not very good policy. Remember dont send it till you hear from me if it is there. Mr Higginson is going to Topeka today and will see whether he can find anything of it there. Quite a number of folks start for the East there Mon morning and by one of them I shall send this letter part way so as to have it go quick & sure. I am as well as usual. There is nothing else of the news kind that I can communicate so I will close. The rest of this letter is to be private. No one to see it but Appleton if he should be at home.

               Your affectionate son
                 Edward

Sept. 29 1856

Dear Parents

     I feel the best tonight that I have for a long time for I have just returned from the P.O. with three letters, one from Mother enclosing five dollars and written the 4th inst. Where under the sun has it been so long for I have worried a great deal because that letter did not come. It seems to have been mailed the 8th,inst, 21 days. What does it mean, for in the same mail I recd one from Appleton dated Sept 16th and one from

Whittemore dated Sept 7th while last Fri I rec'd a letter from Whittemore dated the 14th but dates aside the letters made one jump for joy. You speak Mother of my peril and say if I should be killed you would regret that you had never expressed a wish that I should return. Or what means that now I don't know, you my parents, have been for the Abolition of Slavery and now when you have a son in the war Should you wish him out? Prayers & works must go together and if you cannot fight you must send your sons to fight for you. However perhaps you can express that wish in answer to the other part of this letter if you wish. My coming will not, or need not, make any difference about your sending the things, for all such things will be well seen to by Mr Wilmarth who I shall leave as my agent if I go away and he is capable of seeing to any such thing as I am and will know of those same families of whom I spoke. You can send money if you wish in the answer to this but after that you had better not send till you hear from me again. I am very thankful to you for the five dollars you sent this time. Give my respects to Mrs. Lee Claflin and thank her for me for the money she sent me and tell her I will write to her if I have not. I think I have written to her but if I have not excuse me to her and I will write as soon as I have any time. Today has been the coldest day I ever saw in Sept. We had frost three nights last week. What I most want if I dont come East is a coat, that uniform coat will do. I guess some warm shirts, some stockings and a pair of thick pants fit to wear to meetings. I have no more time tonight and will answer more next time.

Your affec son   Edward

PART II
QUINDARO AND OTHER FALSE HOPES

Sept. 29, 1856

By the fall of 1856 the proslavery-freestate conflict had moderated and Edward began thinking of other matters -- getting married, getting aid for the numerous settlers left destitute by destruction of crops and homes during the "war", taking advantage of some of the presumably profitable investment opportunities in new towns and settlements, and having to live on his claim to hold it.

Marked private and confidential

Dear Mother,

      I always said as you will probably recollect that you seemed a nearer relative to me than Father and I to you rather than to him. I always confided my feelings and plans though I always supposed they found their way to his ears pretty quick. To you therefore this epistle is directed which I intended to have written two or three weeks ago and now am <u>very very</u> sorry that I did not then write, but the reason was the want of time. Last November while I was dodging about here doing odd jobs such as I found to turn up & just about the time that I was finishing my house in the city a Mr. Wilmarth arrived here from Providence, R I, intending at first to go to Topeka and locate but wishing to stop here or have his family stop here for awhile. He came to see me about my house but although I liked his appearance much I could not just then let him have my house but he moved into Mr Stearns house and, as I was then boarding at Mr. S. store then, I saw those that saw the family and was induced to go down and spend an evening there. I found his family to consist of himself (Mr. W) about 55 years old, his wife about 34, a daughter 22 and a son 13 but much larger of his age than Calvin. With the family, I was much pleased especially as I found all but George to be singers and not only that but <u>good</u> singers and very fond of singing. Mr [Franklin A.] Muzzy was with me considerable at that time and he is a <u>very good</u> tenor singer. My singing powers you know are not extra but I am fond of singing. After I first went there we, that is Muzzy & I, used to go down there [to the Wilmarth's] and sing about two evenings in a week besides singing some on Sunday. Just at this time I went into the store as clerk again but generally could get Mr S to stay at the store while I was out in the eve. I was at first more than commonly interested in Miss W or rather <u>Sarah</u> as I chose to call her and took her with me to one or two social parties that we had here. She also <u>seemed</u> to like my company and now I know it to be a fact for within a few weeks she showed me this passage written in her journal last Dec just five weeks after she first saw me.   She writes "Five weeks ago tonight I well remember the acquaintance then formed will, I feel, influence my entire life much. How, I cannot imagine."   And this was no idle talk for she is a girl of high, very high, moral intellectual endowments and facculties, but the real outgoings of her heart.   This was written, you see, during the time of the war last fall.   About this same time in writing to a young lady, a cousin of hers, she is telling of the acquaintances she has formed, there mentioned my name and incidently said I was from Hopkinton, Mass.   In a letter she received in answer to that, in Jan. her cousin says "About Mr. Fitch, I am glad you have made his acquaintance for Grandmother says she is acquainted with him and he is a fine young man.   His mother was old Priest Howe's   daughter and his great grandfather was the second minister of Hopkinton, so you see he is of ministerial descent.   He has received an excellent education and is a very intelligent young man!" She said _polite_, also, but _I_ leave that out for fear _you_ would not believe it. This lady that told her all this was no other than old Mrs. Herrick who used to take milk of me.   So you see that go where I will my former reputation and the reputation of my parents will follow for good or evil. This time it seems to be for good for today in talking with Mr. W. he said that last winter he found that folks he used to board with in the East knew my parents and he found that I came of a good stock and so he cultivated my acquaintance and I have very much benefitted by his larger experience I think.

   Mr. W. opened a bookstore and moved his family into a part of the same building sometime in Dec or the first part of Jan.   I was in the store almost every day and sung about as often as before perhaps not quite as often on account of the cold.   About the middle of Feb. Mrs W was taken sick-- so sick that she was not able to sit up, yet she wishes us to sing just as before and whenever she felt able she used to join us.   She was a beautiful singer and such a woman as I have _very very_ seldom seen in my acquaintances.   She seemed the most like a mother to me of any one I ever have seen except you, my own dear Mother.   She was a _Christian_ in the highest sense of the word.   She sunk gradually until the 21st of April when she left this world of sorrow for a better one as we fondly trust.   The next day but one we buried her.   I had the melancholy pleasure of directing the funeral arrangements.   We sang at her funeral the hymn "Asleep in Jesus, Years Blessed Sleep" to a tune which was a particular favorite of hers during life and which we often sang at her request while she was sick.   All the time that she was sick there were but one or two days that I did not call at least once a day to see her.   If I

71

missed once she was sure to remark it.   After her death I was still intimate with the rest until I went to my claim to live in May from which time I did not see them so much.   About the middle of June Mr W with Sarah & George moved into my house.   I was gone so much that I saw Sarah but about once a week.   The thought whether I loved her enough to try to make her my wife was often on my mind.   I had never said a word to her on this subject and from some appearances I thought perhaps her feelings were not enlisted on me as I supposed but a talk or two showed me, although she did not say so, that she was at least <u>interested</u> in me and after that week that I was sick and she took care of me, we came to such an understanding that, that gold ring that I had last year when I was at home was transferred from my hand to hers.   I am satisfied that I have found a person that can make me happy if any one can be happy on earth and I <u>believe</u> that she loves me ____ so she ____ that I ever saw does, not any better than you, my dear mother,___ "for this cause a man shall leave his Father and his mother and shall cleave unto his wife and they, etc". I want very much, as you may suppose, to have you see her and to have her see you as well as rest of my friends.   I have thought many times during the summer that if I should be married I should want to go East once more and then settle down and be steady but I did not think of going this fall but Mr W wishes to have George go East in order to have the advantage of a school that cannot be had here and as he is too young to send alone and as he must have many things done for him [there] and as he thought it was going to be a hard winter here so he thought Sarah would have to go with him and she could stay until spring and then come back.   She does not <u>want to go</u> unless I can go too and I want to go as much as she wants to have me but still I dont know as prudence would say go.   I intend to look at it on all sides and decide if possible the best way. There are many reasons, and good ones too, Pro & Con and all must be considered.   These, as far as I can, I will now enumerate and you must consider them all as well as I.

      First, both Sarah & I wish to make some farewell visits in N.E. before we settle down here and now seems to be the best time on some accounts.   We should neither of us be satisfied to settle down without once more seeing the homes of our childhood.   Besides my wishing her to see my friends and wishing to see hers myself.   If I go this winter or come back in the spring I shall then stay in Kansas for at least ten years unless I get independently rich before that time which is not probable.   If I do go this fall I shall come with my <u>wife</u> in a year or two and then I shall have two fares to pay but now I shall have but one to pay going out and

but one back if I am not married there.   And I probably should be.
Again I shall do but little, very little, probably this winter if I stay here for
business will be worth next to nothing.   But shall I do anything there?
Could you Father do business enough to keep me employed two or three
months at reasonably good wages?   Or can you get me a school to keep?
Or a chance in some shop at good pay?   Much will depend on these
things for I must not be idle much of the time.   Some of these things I
spoke of in my letter a week ago and I suppose you have given the subject
some thought.   If you have written in answer to that please write again
and answer this so that I shall be sure to get it and in order have it come
direct to me.   I wish you to put the answer to this in two envelopes and
direct the outside one to "Miss Sarah A. Wilmarth" care of Otis Wilmarth
and if you send any more money, which will be very acceptable, put that
in a letter directed to her.   It will be more safe, in fact I shall have to have
some more money before I can go East at all unless I get a Free Pass
which I may be able to do from St Louis ___.   I am not very sanguine that
I can.   I could have had one last fall I expect, but here is another thing,
unless you are perfectly willing and it will be convenient for you to
advance some more money to me I probably can not come for at this
present time I could not raise five dollars in Cash.   I have some potatoes
that the cattle have not spoilt, may have some twelve or 15 bushels and
can probably get ___ a bushel for them.   Then I have some corn which I
shall not need if I sell my pony or if let some one keep him for the use of
him.   I have got two or between two and three acres of winter wheat
growing which I can turn into [plowing] on my claim if I wish to and
perhaps might turn to money, but I don't wish to for it will be worth more
to let it grow.   I have got a lot of money owing to me here but money is so
scarce that I dont know as I shall be able to get any of it this fall. $50.00
from one man that is probably good but I may have to wait till next spring
to get it, perhaps longer, tho he promises well to pay, but the war knocked
everything all out of square.   I have lost a great deal in the war and when
I get to the East ever I intend to collect some money for Kansas and I
calculate to have a part of it to make up my losses.   Mr Higginson
brought some money to be used for the poor folks here, 100.00 of which is
to be distributed here but there are many, very many, actually suffering.
They will soon take up all that money and ten times as much could be
expended and do good if placed in the right hands.   One thing more I
meant to have said when speaking of money.   You have done so much for
me that I shall not feel willing to go East, much as I want to, unless you
are satisfied and willing to advance a little more money and wait a little

73

longer for it to return to you for I feel under deep obligation to you for what you have done and do not like to ask you to do more unless you are satisfied with my course.

Sarah wants very much if I cannot go E[ast] this fall I should come on at the first opening of navigation in the spring, which would probably be the last of Feb or first of March and come back with her early in April, but on many accounts it would be much better to come and stay all winter than to stay so little while as I would have to stay in that case, (I am perplexed in Spirit and bothered to think of all these things) for I should then have the hardship of the winter without the pleasure that I should have at the East and the going and coming would cost fully as much if not more and as at present I think would not be at all expedient. I shall now wait for the mail tonight and see if I hear anything from you by it.   It has come & the last of these letters is the answer to it.   I have not been to see Mr Parrott who is the Law partner of the Land [receiver] and I hear from good authority about my claim.   He says that I shall not invalidate my title to my claim by leaving it now as I have filed my intention to preempt.   I shall go on doing everything that must be done in order that I may go East and if I dont go it will be so much the better for being done.   I want you to write immediately in answer to this, whether you have written before or not, and send [it] right off for I shall not leave until I have an answer to this.   I was pleased at what you said Mrs Herrick said about the Wilmarth family.   She certainly told the truth and no mistake.   I presume that I shall think of many more things that I shall want to say by the time this is gone but I cannot think of them now so I believe I will stop.   O there is your last sentence in your letter when you speak of exchanging hearts.   Do you say you would know whether she is a Christian?   She is, I truly think not only a professer but a possessor of true religion.   She has been a member of a Congregational Church for six years about.   She is worthy of a good husband.   Whether I shall make her such a one remains to be seen.   I know this much we love each other dearly and we shall try to make each other happy but she dont want to go East without I go and I dont know how I should get along if I should not see her for two or three months.   Her father would like to have me go but if I cant he says stay.   He says if Providence wants me to go, the way will be provided.

Private
Sunday P.M.

Dear Parents, I wrote over the other sheet intending to send it on to Mr Higginson but he went before I got it finished.   So I have opened it to put in some more.   And now I think it will be more improbable than I did this morning, that I shall come East.   Providence seems to find more to staying and less to going but I cannot now certainly tell.   One great reason why I should not come is because Sarah possibly will not go unless I do wheras before she was going at any rate.   I guess that Mrs Herrick (the old lady I mean) has been to see you, Mother, has she not?   And if so did she tell you of that wedding that she attended just before she left Prov. and which   Mr & Mrs. Lee C, , Mrs Whiting Eames & daughter, Mrs Lathrop, Col Gibbs, from Hopkinton attended!   Also B F Herricks and wife L. and did she bring you <u>my Sarah's</u> daguerreotype as she might have done and show it to you?   I hope she did.   I have just seen an account of the wedding written by a half-sister of the bride.   And did she tell you also that the bride's name was "Irana G Farrar" and that her mother's name was Lucy Herrick!   And is she not that Lucy H. that was a school mate of yours, and that I have heard you speak of so often!   These questions interest me as this bride and her half sister <u>were</u> and are intimate and dear friends of <u>my Sarah</u>.   I hope Mrs. H has told you all about these things.   If she has not and is still in Hopkinton I hope you will see her and have her tell you.   Give her my <u>very best respects</u> and if she is not there ask Mrs. Lee C. something about it and tell her that I know by reputation some of the parties.   If Sarah does not go East this fall I shall try and have her brother come there and stay a few days with you.   He is a good boy just Calvin's age but more manly than Calvin was when I last saw him.   How he is now I don't know. Dr. C will probably bring some things that I wish to send to you -- curiosities, etc.   You don't know how much I think of my Dear Sarah and how could I bear to have her gone to the East and I not go with her, but if she stays I am contented. How I wish you could see her.   I know you will <u>love</u> her.   Write to her something in particular to her.   She will write to you soon, I think.   I suppose you will think this nonsense but it is not.   I mean what I have said tho it looks more silly to you perhaps than to me, but I know you were young once and I have heard of <u>writing masters</u> etc. too. So it wont do for you to say much.

I wish I had a thousand hands to write with all at once and then I could write as much as I wanted to once at least.

Your ever affectionate Son,

Edward

Oct. 6, 1856

Today was the Election for a new Legislature to the Bogus Laws. There were in this city of Lawrence 7 votes cast!!!! How are the might fallen. I commenced haying today, expect to be haying for a few days only.

I am as well as usual.

Yours,
Edward

Oct. 5th 1856

Dear Father

As Mr Higginson leaves today for the East I thought I would write a word or two for him to take. If you should be at Worcester at any time please call and see him. I have had some considerable talk with him. I recd last night that long letter Mother wrote about her efforts to fill those barrels and the acts of their having started. You ought to write and tell me just how they were directed and how they were sent. The letter spoke of John coming west. I don't know as I should advise him to come to Kansas this fall but in the spring I think perhaps he can find enough to do if he should come here as a surveyor and if he could get him a claim anywhere around here it would pay to keep it. The claim north and joining mine on the N.E. was sold this last week for eight hundred dollars and mine is as good a claim, some say better and mine has about half as much improvement on it as this had. This was North toward town. The claim right south of mine with twelve or fifteen acres ploughed on it and twenty fenced was bought by a Free State man for five hundred dollars, a good log house on it and a poor one beside. If I had only known that it could be bought for that price I should have bought it for Mr. Wilmarth. I should liked to have had him have it very much. It was owned by a Pro Slavery man. My house comes partly on it. The probabilities seem now to be that I shall not come East this fall but I cant tell. I shall endeavor to do what seems to be best but as Mr. Higginson said in his lecture last night Kansas is the hardest place to tell what is going to happen one week ahead that he ever saw, so I say and I may come yet.   Mr. H gave us a good lecture on Slavery and the crisis in Kansas last night.

Did Mr. Conway have anything to say about me when at Hopkinton?   I am not much acquainted with him but am some.   I should think he would remember me.

And now I think of it, use what influence you have and ask Mr Webster to do the same --   not to have any more money given to Stowell from Hopkinton.   Wheeler may say he is all right for he can put a good face onto almost anything but I know many things about him that Wheeler dont and I know he had better not be trusted with any more money from them.

Another thing I am sorry that your large contributions are going to the state com. unless they have some better agents here than they have had, for the money, too much of it, goes into the pockets of those who do not need it.   I have been thinking that I would send a paper East to Hopkinton stating that I had spent nearly two hundred dollars in this war and for which I had <u>war scrip</u> which would not be redeemed to me at present, at least unless my friends raise the money.   If I could have that money it would be of immense advantage to me next spring.   If I come East I intend to raise money enough to redeem my scrip.   Somewhere among my friends, if I don't go, I should think it might be raised in Hop[kinton], Weymouth, by a little exertion and if they wish I will send on the scrip and have it deposited in Hopkinton Bank so that when it is eventually redeemed they could have their money back or a part of it at least.   What do you think of it?   What is to be done with that $500.00 that you are now raising in Hopkinton?   I wish they would give it to me. My <u>actual loss</u> in the three wars we have passed through cannot fall far short of 400.00.   That is my private loss, for everything I had almost is gone for the good of the cause.

Wheeler has been as near here as Topeka and I hear he has gone back.   Ask his Father what I shall do with that Indian   blanket if I ever get it.   There are some letters here for him too.   I shall send this by Mr. Higginson and I will write again <u>very</u> soon.   I hope you <u>did not and will not</u> have a <u>Tea Party</u>.   I should about as soon you would do nothing for us as do it in that way.   It seems to me very incongruous.

You aff son
Edward

Oct 12th 1856

Dear Parents

      I have recd no letter from you since I wrote last but hope to receive by tommorow's mail an answer to my first letter in which I spoke of coming East this fall.   I dont expect to come however for Sarah has concluded not to go but to send George under charge of a Mr Farren who is going to New Haven.   So if she dont go <u>one great,</u> and <u>the greatest</u> reason for my wishing to go is obviated and other things seem to look more like staying also.   I am as well as usual.   We did what haying we shall do this year the last week.   I have got my corn all stacked up.   It is not very good.   The frost came just a week too soon for it but I shall have some corn.   I dug my potatoes on Wed.   I had about 15 bush. [bushels] from one bush. of seed and they are very good potatoes too.   Have you heard from John W. since he left from where you wrote to him?   Tell him I wish he would write to me and let me know what he thinks of the West. Where did he get his Theodolite?   I am very thankful to Mrs Davenport for that coat and pant if it ever gets here, for the pants I need much the most of any kind of clothes and next a coat & some socks.   Then some blankets.   How is George & the boys getting along?   Why do you keep that William, the Torment as you call him?   Where there are other boys to be hurt by his influence is not the place for him.   Why have him. . . .

      I have not heard anything from that Revolver that the Dr sent yet and think now that I never shall.   Things are peaceable here now. (How long they will remain so I cant tell.)   We have a Com[pany] of Soldiers camped here all the time, foot soldiers they are and not Cavalry.   The Gov I dont think much of. <u>He thinks he is a smart</u> man but many others think differently.   I tremble for the result of the Election in Penn this week.   If the Reps are successful, I am afraid they will relax their efforts and the Democrats will redouble theirs and they will yet carry the state for <u>Buchanan</u>.   What we shall do if he should be elected I dont know, but we must fight any how.   Is there a Buchanan man in Hopkinton?   If there is tell him for me that if he votes for Buchanan, some of the blood shed in Kansas will be found at his door.   How any man of common sense can vote for him in the face of his turning in to the Cin. Platform I can't see.   I dont like your going for Gardiner for Gov at all but perhaps it is the best thing you can do.   I should like to speak at one Fremont meeting in Hopkinton this fall.   I think some of writing a letter for you to read at one but I have so much to do that I dont know certain as I shall.   Remember me to all who inquire for me.   I will __. Has Aunt Howe been up there?

How many children has she living?   and how do they do?   How are the crops on the farm this fall?   What are the boys doing?   Have you ever paid that draft?   You never wrote a word about it.   I wish you would.

Your aff son
Edward

Oct 16, 1856

Dear Parents

  If this letter ever gladdens your eyes it will be brought probably by George O. Wilmarth, a young man of my acquaintance in Kansas who being at the East and being about the age of Elijah & Calvin I thought could not spend a week more pleasantly any where perhaps than at Hopkinton with my friends.   I therefore send him to you trusting that his being a friend of mine will secure him a grand reception and a pleasant stay with you.

  He has with him for you, Mother -- a Daguerreotype of a Soldier in the Kansas wars of 1855 & 6 which I hope is natural enough to have you know who it is meant for.   You will see I had the Sharpes rifle and revolver sent from Hopkinton and another revolver. Those, with my Cambridge box containing some fifty rounds of ammunition, were my load generally on the march.   Sometimes a blanket was added.   Tell Mr Webster that it is the picture of a Sabbath School Teacher in Kansas.

  The other, which is also for you, is the exact likeness of one who is dearer to me than anyone else on Earth.   I think it to be a most excellent picture and it is so natural that I think that you would know her if you should meet her in the street.   I also send by him an Indian flute which you can put among your curiosities.   I got it of a young Delaware Indian, son of <u>Sicoxie</u>, one of the chiefs of that nation.   Their land is across the river from Lawrence.   It is just as he made it and left.   I heard him make some sweet music on it which I could not imitate at all.   When the reed is properly fixed it will blow nicely after it has been blowed for awhile to get moist.

  He has or will have I expect a map of Kansas with him by Whitman & Searl of this place, which is very correct and he can tell you the location of many places that you have heard of or not.
If his aunt who has the care of him is willing I should like to have him stay a week or so with you.   I think with Elijah & Calvin he can pass the time very pleasantly.   He is just about Calvin's age but appears more manly

79

than Calvin did a year ago which is not so very strange considering the different circumstances in which they have been placed during the past year. He was in the war, stood guard considerably with his Father and others. He tried hard enough to be at the Battle of Titus Fort but was a little too late to see the <u>fun</u>.   He can tell you all the minute particulars about the war which I presume you would be glad to hear but which would be too much trouble for me to write, and you will find him willing to answer all   questions relating to this subject.

I will try to have him take a likeness of his Father & Mother for you to see as you will perhaps be interested enough in them to look at them at least; but it will be so much better for you to talk to him that I will stop and introduce formally Mr George Otis Wilmarth to Mr & Mrs John A Fitch.

Yours as ever
Edward

Have Whittemore see George at any rate. E

Oct. 17, 1856

Dear Parents,

I wrote to you last on the 12th inst. at which time, if not before, I spoke of receiving that last five dollars that you sent.   I have received all your letters. I believe the reason why I did not have one for so long was that one mail that had one of your letters was delayed a long time for some reason or other.   I have been very busy at work moving a house this week and have had no time or I should have written a letter for you to read at some of your Fremont meetings.   I have got a good deal to do and but little time to do it in.   Wed night I recd a letter from you dated the 2nd of October in which you speak of what is being done there and say that J.J. Marshall sent me 20.00.   I have heard nothing of it yet but hope I shall.   You say the money is sent to the State Com. & c. I have not much faith in those Committees, some of them, for they take too good care to feather their own nests first.

I should think Hopkinton folks might sent me a two hundred dollar draft when they know that I have spent almost that amount in Cash besides all that I have lost here, but if they won't, they won't. I suppose I dont want you to give <u>any money</u> if you can help it but send to me all that you can spare of it.   If I could get that 20.00 from Mr Marshall it would be a great help to me just at this time.

You say you had rec'd my letter of Sept 21st in which I spoke of coming home. You say the farm is big enough if I would come and live there. I never could be satisfied, I dont think, to come back there to live. At any rate if I should give up Kansas and come back I don't think it would be three years before I should be in <u>California</u> or <u>Australia</u>. I mean just what I say exactly. But things have taken such a turn now that I should not come home this fall on any account. Perhaps a year from this time may be different. You speak of my selling out here. Property is now at its lowest ebb, and I should rather buy than sell. We shall not have to fight the U.S. troops at present but we may have to yet. When we do count me in.Sarah, <u>my dear</u>, decided something more than a week ago not to go East, at any rate not unless I went and as Providence did not seem to point to my going she concluded not to go. Mr W. was intending to keep Bach. as we say here-- stay at his store all the time. Now of course he will not but will remain in my house.

Tonight I rec'd your letter dated Oct 7th and directed to <u>Sarah</u>, in which is a list of articles in the barrels and a note from Elijah, but you send no intelligence of how the barrels were sent. What route nor how they were directed, to whose care, but I hope all these things will be all right in time.   How far did you pay freight on them and how did you expect me to pay the charges on them?   I hope Lee Claflin's draft will come for I know now of some person who is in want of some money to pay for seed wheat and other such things.   I will account for it.   I don't know but I ought to take some of it to pay the charges on those barrels.   I am somewhat sorry that I cannot see you as you much desire me to but it does not, at this time, seem to me to be possible to come.   It lacks three days of being three weeks since I wrote the letter which this was the answer to. The letters went very quick.   You can send money & direct either to Sarah or myself just as you please.   It will be safe no doubt.   George starts for the East tomorrow morning.   I tried to have my Daguerreotype taken over today so as to show the pistol & rifle better but could not do it because the artist had a lame arm so.(I should not have written this if I had thought when you see George you will know all about it.)   I want him to come and stay a week or so with you and have given him written directions how to get there, etc.   He has some things for you and I want to have you take him to Westboro & the state Reform School if you can. Have him see Whittemore anyhow.   He is <u>my brother</u>, for my sake make his stay with you pleasant.   He can tell you many things that I can't write. I recd tonight a letter from Mr Webster in which he seems to not think much of my coming home this winter. It was a good letter and I must

81

answer it and I will soon.   I have been hoping he would write for some time.   We have had frost here every day this week.   The cattle got into my corn today and destroyed some of it.   George may write to you.   If you go to Boston you can find him and have him come out with you.   I wish I could hear of the result of the Election in Penn. now.   We hang much hope on that being carried for Fremont.   I hope you are doing what you can to elect him.   Give Buch a wide berth and Filmore, too.   Both of them are worse than nobody.

Yours in Bondage,
Edward

George has a letter of introduction with his name on the outside so that you will know him when you see that.

Nov. 2, 1856

Dear Parents,

  I recd night before last your letter dated Oct 17th in which you tell me how those barrels were directed but you dont seem to know <u>how</u> they were sent.   I have heard nothing from them yet but I should think that it was about time to have them get here.   I am going to Leavenworth tomorrow with a team and may find them.   Hope I shall but I am not at all sanguine.   In a letter which I recd about three weeks ago you say that J.J. Marshall has sent me 20$ but I have not seen it nor have I seen that check for 25 that you said Lee Claflin was going to send.   I could use it to good advantage if I had it now for on Monday last the fire ran through here and burnt the <u>house and hay & corn all</u> up of one of those families of Reynolds that I wrote to you about. They are now entirely destitute but the folks around here will help them some.   There were two other houses burned at the same time.

  I am as well as usual but much hurried with work so that I have no time to write letters.   I am very glad that Father is still alive,   as I see he is by about 3 or 4 inches square of his writing-- the first I have seen from his pen for two months.   It is rainy today so that I cannot go to meeting and I have some time to write but I must go over to town to see the <u>folks</u> if possible.   We formed a Glee Club here on Fri eve. and <u>intend</u> to meet once a week all winter.   Whether we shall or not I can't tell.

I am very glad that you sent that quilt to Sarah for I think that you will have a first rate letter of acknowledgment for it.   That is, if it ever gets here.   Col Blood is not now in Lawrence so I have not seen him but shall see him as soon as he returns from St. Louis where he is gone to purchase goods.   It is doubtful whether I get the things that were designed for me unless you Mother as <u>Chairman</u> of the <u>Com</u> (or Father) or as Pres. of the Soc. write to him [through] me and ask him to deliver the barrels to me which I should like to have you do.   Day after tomorrow will decide the fate of poor Kansas.   What will it be.   Will Fremont be elected.   Alas I <u>fear but hope</u>.   You ask whether you had better sell your farm at 1,000 sacrifice and come out here.   My answer is decidedly NO!!   not as things now are but if Fremont is elected and other things go right and you could sell for what your farm is worth in the spring I might say come.   I hear that the Land office may be opened this month.   I hope it will for then I shall know about my title to my claim and I have had the offer of help to build a house if I wish next year and if every thing works well I shall try and build in the summer.   If not I shall put it off.   Another thing if the land office should be open in a week or two I <u>might</u> get to come East this fall.   I want to very much but duty at present says No.   I don't know of any claims to be taken yet within less than eight or ten miles of Lawrence and not many good ones in that distance but there will be chances to buy close by and get good bargains to.

I have really got out of material to write and I dont know what to write.   I will leave this and get Sarah to fill it if she will.

Yours
E.P Fitch

Nov. 17 1856

Dear Parents,

I just sat down to scratch a line or two to you so that you will not think me dead or in prison but I am very busy and have no time for extended remarks.   The bbls [barrels] that you were so kind as to send me have, three of them, come to hand, No. 1, 2 & 3.   The other I have not seen but expect it tomorrow or next day perhaps.   No 1 arrived a week ago today.   The others today.   I have distributed quite a lot of clothing where I think it will do some good.

We are still in doubt as to the result of the Pres. Elec. but most now think that Buch [Buchanan] &   Breck [Breckinridge] have gone in. We are sanguine however of making Kansas a Free State at any rate.   You cant begin to have any idea of the interest we take on the returns as the reports come in each day.   One day we are sure Fremont is chosen; then we feel well. The next day we find that the Old Buch's chances are the best and by the next day every body says the election has surely gone into the house. [House of Representatives]

Gov. Robinson arrived here yesterday.   He thinks that Buch. is Elected but says Kansas will be free at any rate but he says we have only been playing for this past year and now we have got to work.   What that work will be you can judge.   Write me all the news about Mass Elec [Massachusetts election] and send me a good paper that has it in for I get no Mass. paper now except the Ploughman.   Just as soon as I get time I intend to write a long letter but cant now.   Give my love to all.

Yours in haste.
Edward P Fitch

Nov 21, 1856

Dear Parents

I recd a long letter from Father by the last mail enclosing a draft for 25.00 from Lee Claflin.   I wrote a few days since and intended to have written a long letter by this time but don't know as I shall make out this time.   I went to one of the stores here today and they agreed to pay the draft so I shall get the money, probably today or tomorrow.   Appleton wrote to me that I might draw on him for 25 which I shall probably do. The 20.00 which you said was sent to me from Framingham has not arrived and perhaps will not but I hope it will.   The present draft, or the cash that I can get for it, I can find good use for very quick.   Some of it ought to stick to my own fingers but whether that would exactly meet the wishes of the donor I dont know, but I know of families that it will help to flour and sugar and such things and families that stand in need of such things too.   I will try and make it tell & do some good and shall be glad to receive more from the same source.

I have not seen Mr Nute and do not know exactly how we shall manage that that was sent to us but think that if you had sent it to me alone it would have been better as Mr Nute, being a Unitarian is a little more apt to look for that kind of men to help.   At least so I have heard and I only say it as a report.

Three of the bbls of things sent by you have arrived and I have distributed quite a number of things for which I have recd many thanks and for which I in my turn thank the givers.   The pants sent by Mrs

Davenport are a little too long for me but can easily be fixed.   They are very nice and I am very thankful for them.   The coat I have not found.   It must be in the other bbl which I have not yet opened (nor seen No 4).

Gov Geary appointed yester[day] the 20th as a day of Thanksgiving and the ladies of Lawrence got up a dinner to which they invited him, the proceeds of which were to be used to give a dinner to the Free State Prisoners at Lecompton.   The dinner took place yesterday about 5 P.M.   Gov. Robinson was here but Geary was not.   The reason for his not being here we understand this morning was that he was arrested by order of Judge Lecompton while on his way home.   This is said to be a fact but of its truth I am not certain.

The Dinner was quite a good affair, about 100 sat down to the tables.   A blessing was asked by Rev G. W. Hutchinson after which all ate a genteel sufficiency of roast Turkey, baked pig,   Chicken pie & such like fixings.   We then adjourned to the hall where we had speeches & toasts and a good time generally until between nine & ten when the floor was given up to those who wished to dance, while the sober staid portion of us went home.   I went to the dinner almost solely on account of introducing Wheeler into our society here and I staid for a while after dancing commenced to look on.   This occasion was a very pleasant one.   The speakers or at least those who spoke on politics, Gov.   R.,   Lieut Gov. Roberts and others, seem to be very hopeful for the future of Kansas and say we are bound to have a Free State any how and if we cant have it with Buch[anan] & Breck[inridge] we will have it in spite of Buch, Breck, & Geary, too.   They say, and I hope, it is true that there will be such an Emigration in the Spring as has not been seen for a long time from the Free States. That and nothing else will be our Salvation now.   We feel sorry of course that we, or rather you, did not elect Fremont but as it cant be helped now we'll make the best of it.   Free Kansas we must & will have.

My List of Letters is not where I now am and so I cannot number this and I did not number the last I wrote.   Yours was not numbered but I shall keep account of this and number the rest just as though these had been numbered.   I saw Dr Hunting a day or two since; he says that no Revolver had ever got to him and he has made inquiry around there at the P.O. and stores but has heard nothing of it.   He does not know Mr Parsons personally but says he supposes he is near Fort Riley.   I am going to write to him about it and have the Dr carry it up with him.   He wished to be remembered to you.   I wish that I could come home this winter and it is not utterly impossible but I may yet, but very

85

improbable according to present appearances.   How did it happen that 50.00 was sent to Wheeler.   If it is for him, I am in much more need than he is.   He has made money at least part of the time he has been West while I have not but lost all.   I have never found out yet whether you had that draft of 50.00 that I gave Wood.   Are you all well at home.   How is George & what is he doing?   Where is his mother?   I found his name and town in his shoes all right.   Give my love to him.   Ask him if he has forgotten me.   Most of the Free State men that I have talked with since the result of the Election became known with certainty seemed to think that we must stick it out and make a Free State.   Some are disheartened but most are hopeful.

Your Aff
Son Edward

I have no more time to write but must close in order to have this go in the next mail.

Yours, E.

Nov. 21, 1856

The next letter was written by Edward to his brother Appleton who appears to have been in Dover, New Hampshire.   By the time this was written the "reign of terror" in Kansas, which followed the Pottawatomie Massacre, was beginning to recede, largely due to the energetic efforts of the new Governor, John W. Geary.

Dear Brother

   I rec'd a day or two since a letter from you dated Nov. 6 and in it two doll[ar]s which you say nothing about.   So I suppose the letter must have been opened and the bill put in.   I wish they would do more the same way.   We had Thanksgiving yesterday in accordance with Gov. Geary's proclamation.   The Ladies here got up a drive and the tickets were two dollars so that bill just bought my ticket.   The proceeds are to be used to give a dinner to the Free State prisoners at Lecompton but I acted as door keeper and gave them a part of the time and so did not have to pay anything.   I rec'd a letter some time ago giving me leave to draw on you for 25.00 which I think I shall do in a few days but whether I shall come home or not is uncertain.   We intend to make Kansas a Free State in spite of Buch, Breck   Geary or the D____l if the Lord is on our side.

   I went to Leavenworth a week or more ago, was out in a hard storm.   Brought a load of stoves but broke one of them and had to pay

8.00 damage.   The pay for hauling the load was 16.00 and it cost me 4.60 on the way to feed myself and the team so the trip was not very profitable. I was gone 4 days and part of another.   I am going to keep Thanksgiving next week at Mr. Savages where I stay at present.   We shall have a kind of family party and I shall think of home much, especially if we have it on the same day that you do in Mass.

I wish you had written a little if not more to my Sarah for she would probably have been glad and I am sure I should and perhaps she would have answered it.   (try and see)   The bbls of clothing sent by ladies in Hopkinton to me have arrived, or at least 3 of them, and have been distributed to some extent among the destitute and those who have thus far rec'd them seem very thankful.   I hope they will do much good.

Buch & Breck have gone in.   We are sorry that you did not elect Fremont but are glad that poor benighted N. H. has done so nobly in the struggle.   (did you vote)   Gov. Robinson, Lieut. Gov. Roberts & others with whom I have talked seem to think that we shall have a change which if not for the better cannot be for the worse.   When Buch comes in God grant that it may be for the better but he knows best and his will will be accomplished.

How does it happen that you are to lecture at Teachers' Institutes! Are you among the profs!   Saul in among the prophets sure.   What are your prospects for another year, shall you teach?   John P. Wheeler has been here with me the past week or so.   He thinks of opening an office in Lecompton soon.   I am not in hopes that I can enter my claim within a few weeks and prove up my preemption.   If so I may come East this winter.   Shall you be at home to Thanksgiving?   I wish I could be there!

I attended the Sabbath School Concert last Sun. eve.   The exercises were principally singing by the children interspersed with verses recited from the Bible and some questions by the Supt.   It was very interesting.   There were probably 60 or 70 children present.   We have from 60 to 80 scholars in our Sabbath School every Sabbath.

I have no more time but must close.
Yours truly
Edward P. Fitch

Nov. 30, 1856

Dear Parents

In the last letter I recd from you was enclosed a draft for $25.00 which I dont know whether I have acknowledged before or not. I think I have however. I send with this an account of the manner in which I have disposed of it which you will please hand to Mr Claflin and I hope he will send me $25.00 more. I should not care if it was $100.00. I will warrant it would be thankfully received. It is hard for me to have money pass through my hands and none of it stick when I have lost so much myself and I am as poor as any one and if I get that that was sent to Mr. Nute & I, I will have some advantage from it myself, I'll bet. I have got those two bbls [barrels] of clothing that were last sent from Hopkinton directed to Mr. Blood and I have given away many of the things. So I now have recd six bbls in all and it has been no small task to see to it all and I have had to pay the Freight on them from Leavenworth to here. You wrote some two months ago that JJ Marshall had sent me $20.00 I have never seen anything of it. I wish you would ask him how he had it sent for I cant understand about it. If I only had it now it would help me amazingly for I want to buy me a stove but have not quite enough money yet. Appleton wrote that I might draw on him for $25.00 which I shall do at my <u>earliest convenience</u>. You see I went to Leavenworth and drayed a load of stoves and broke one of them a little, not enough to hurt the stove at all except the sale and he charged me Eight Dollars so the only way to save it is to buy the stove and it is a large size $40.00 stove first rate kind something like the one you have got in the kitchen. It is just what I wanted only one size larger. I broke it about the first of month and had Fremont been elected I should not have hesitated at all about buying and as it is I must have a stove and this seems to be the best course.

I have not yet seen Mr. Nute in reference to that money sent from Hopkinton but I shall in a few days. Give me the particulars how it was sent. Was the 50.00 sent to Wheeler the same that his Father wrote to him about? Did he and Capt Daniels give $50.? or was 50 to be sent to him and have they sent 50 more? The Com. [Committee} through whom it was sent are slower than Death and it will probably get here, if at all, about next July. I was very lucky to get all my bbls and should not have got them had I not been right on hand all the time. I have not yet disposed of any of the ministers coats for want of time but George

Harrington's wedding coat fits me so well that I have a great mind to turn minister and wear it myself.   Sarah has got her bundle but the quilt for the Methodist ministers wife still remains at my house.   What kind of a coat was it Mrs Davenport sent.   I found none marked as hers but there is a kind of brownish Chequered Coat that fits me very well that I think must be the one. I have it at any rate.

What kind of Thanksgiving did you have?   We had Thanksgiving the 20 inst   We had a dinner and a good time out last Thurs., your Thanksgiving.   I went to work on the bottom without any dinner at all and I went to one of my neighbors and got my Thanksgiving dinner. Most of our Kansas men who have been at the East Electioneering for Fremont have come back and all seem to feel encouraged at the prospect for Freedom.   I have heard the statement within a few days that Buchanan had declared in favor of free Kansas but did not give much credit to such statements as Mr Buch cant make it a Slave State if the men of the Free States do their duty and send us help enough money, clothes, & men.   The Free State men who were prisoners at Lecompton have all escaped or been discharged except a few that have recently been taken for robbery, etc. near Osawatomie.   They have been cutting up dreadfully, down there lately, robbing and murdering.

The Committee that have charge of this clothing sent from the East are not giving very good satisfaction.   It is said and with some truth at least that they do not treat applicants very well.   The Com at Chicago re-marked some things and planed off the original mark so that many things were lost.   They could not get the markers off of my bbls because you marked them so much but the bbls sent to Mr Blood could never have been recognised by him except by the numbers for they had both been broken open and parts of new heads put in but I made out to find them and get the whole.

I shall keep some the pants myself.   One or two pairs fit me very well.   Those that you made for me do not fit very well and I dont know as I shall keep them.

Your aff Son
Edward P Fitch

Dec 3, 1856

Dear Brother

I have written to you I believe within a few days and now write again to tell you that I have drawn a draft on you for $25.00 at the Strafford Bank, Dover, N.H.   A copy of which draft I send you.   The reason of my drawing on your charity is this: I want a stove and must have one and I had not the money to pay for one.   I went to Leavenworth two or three weeks ago and brought a load of stoves for Allen & Brothers. One of the largest size and the best kind I broke so that they docked me eight dollars on the hauling.   I have now agreed to take the stove.   It is not broken so as to hurt it at all, only the sale of it as it just broke off part of the hearth.

I don't think that I shall come to Mass. this winter tho I should like to very much but I cannot without running some risk of losing my claim and I have had trouble enough with that you knew.   I believe that there was another man on my claim that was going to contend with me for it at the Land Office but today I have made an arrangement with him to divide; he takes eighty acres and leaves me eighty.   I amy much better satisfied with the eighty clear of incumbrance than with my chance for the whole.   I am in hopes by shrewd management to get 160 acres yet but may fail.

The draft was written in this way

25,00

Pay to Lyman Allen on order Twenty Five Dollars by virtue of deposit of

Appleton H. Fitch

Edward P. Fitch

To the cashier of
The Strafford Bank
Dover, N.H.

So you will have to deposit the money in the bank subject to my order.   I am very much obliged and very thankful to you for this 25,00 as it will do me a great deal of good.

Time fails and I must close.   Sarah sends her respects to Brother A.   Please write to her.

Your aff brother
Edward P. Fitch

Dec. 8, 1856

Dear Brothers Elijah & Calvin

     I am very much obliged to you for those letters that you wrote to me on Thanksgiving.   I guess that I will tell you of my trip to Leavenworth that I took nearly two months ago.   Mr Savage and I wanted to make a little money so we concluded that we would go to Leavenworth and get a load of freight.   He had one horse & two yoked oxen so he borrowed his brothers horse and wanted me to take the oxen and as the horses would travel faster than oxen he wanted I should start one day at noon and he would start the next morning and then we should get to L. about the same time and could help each other load and come home together.   But we finally concluded to start together on Mon. morning the 3d of Nov. but when that morning came it was stormy and we could not start and during the day all our cattle ran off to the woods and did not come home at night as they usually did.   It stormed till Tues. noon, the day of the Pres. Election.   Then I started to find the cattle so as to start right off that night.   I hunted until dark but could not find them. The next morning as it was fair but cold Mr. S. started with the horses.   I went to find my team again and I rode all day until about two o'clock and could not find them there. I thought I would give up going and was just going to start away on some other business when the oxen came home. Then I was in a quandary to know whether I should start or not.   I concluded that I would, so getting ready as soon as possible I started and got to town where I was to cross the river just at sundown.   I found that Mr   Morgan & Mr Enos were to start the next morning.   Mr M. was a neighbor of ours.   I left word with the Ferryman to have them hurry and catch me in the morning as I should not go far that night for I never had been to Leavenworth and did not know the roads.   I went on and camped all alone in the woods with the wolves and coons all round me.   I made a good fire and laid down side of it and slept by fits and starts until morning when I found that one of my oxen had got unyoked and was loose.   But he was quite tame and so I caught him easily.

     Five miles from Lawrence I came to Sicoxie's creek, so called because Sicoxie lives there.   He is chief of the Delaware Indians or one of the chiefs.   The Interpreter lives here too.   His name is Pechalka.   It is quite an Indian village.   The Chief has a very good house and he keeps people that come along overnight.   He was over here at Lawrence one day and wanted one of our men to recommend his house to those traveling to Leavenworth.   He said "Me got fine big house; Sleep a heap of white mens."   The Interpreter also keeps folks and his house is said to be the best, but as I have stopped at neither I cannot tell.   I saw the chief's son just starting to Lawrence.   I am well acquainted with him as he and his brother used to come in to the store last winter a great deal. His name is "White Turkey."   That is his English name.   His Indian name I can pronounce but cant write.   He has got a very pretty squaw wife.

Five miles farther on I passed Ten Mile Creek where there are two or three Indian houses. Five miles farther I came to Ton-ga-noxie's Creek where Tonganoxie lives.   He is a chief of some importance among the Delewares here.   I stopped for an hour eat my dinner and waited for Morgan & Enos who overtook me at this place.   Passing on we passed the grave of Roberts who was killed by the ruffians & burned by US troops at the roadside.

Three miles brought us to The Stranger or Big Stranger as it is called to distinguish it from the Little Stranger to which we came after 5 miles more of prairie.   As it was now dark we thot of camping for the night.   Thus far we had come over the Indian reserve but now we were on land open for settlement and at this Creek a man by the name of Starns had built him a large house.   Mr. M. & Mr. E. spoke for lodgings in the house but I intended to sleep in my wagon.   Three other teamsters came from Leavenworth and two of them also got room to sleep on the floor. About the time we intended to retire (great retirement I must say, six men two women and two or three children slept in that one room together), it began to rain so I was obliged to give up sleeping in the wagon.   There was a kind of open shed that is open at the sides with a roof over it & under this roof on the ground I laid my blankets and rolled myself up in them and tried sleep.   But neither Morpheus nor Somnus could I coax to my bedside but Boreas came without asking.   The rain blew in on to my head so that I had to cover my head up to keep it off and my teeth ached like fury and there I staid thro that night.   It seemed an age almost till morn.   Before morning it began to freese and I got to sleep.   When I waked up it was about sunrise.   Everything was frosen up solid and the ground covered with snow & ice and still snowing.   My bread and meat that I had left in the wagon was frosen hard so I took breakfast with mine hosts, such a breakfast as is generally found in a Squatters house, vis: Corn dodgers & side bacon & molasses.

After feeding our team we started on for Leavenworth eight miles distant.   It was very cold and the wind blowed furiously.   We got into

Leavenworth in the midst of a storm of snow & sleet. We went to the warehouse where I was to get my load and the first thing said to us was take a glass of old <u>Bourbon</u> which we went and drew. He gave me a glass which I very properly--declined --

NO -- accepted and then you might have seen that strong disciple of Temperance Edward P Fitch drinking a glass of Brandy !!!!!!! The reason why I drank was I had the toothache the night before and most all of that day and I thought that Brandy might help it. I drinked two or three swallows and left the rest tho urged to take it all as it would warm me up. I then went to work and got on my load which consisted of stoves, some of them were very large and heavy weighing nearly 300. We all got loaded and started back about 1/2 past 2 P.M. We drove as fast as our load and the road would permit and stopped sometime after dark at Wallaces 2 1/2 miles this side of Leavenworth. There we had a warm fire to sit by and in comfortable room. It was as cold a night as we have had this year. We drove all our cattle into a small yard and fed them with corn and then set down in the house. The family consisted of three grown up young men and two daughters, one the wife of one of the young men, and their two little children. They were quite intelligent people and I spent a pleasant evening in talking with them. They were Free State folks.

Early in the morning we started toward home. Had got but a few rods when Mr Enos hind axle broke off so he had to go back to L. [Leavenworth] to get another put in. Mr. M & myself came on. We drove hard all day and after dark came to Tonganoxie's where we intend to stop. We asked him if he had any pen where we could put our cattle in. He said "<u>big pen</u> Down there". We asked can we have any hay. "Yes, heap hay, help self." We have to do every thing ourselves at these Indian houses. They wont do anything when they can get any one else to do it for them. There were something like fifteen of us teamsters that stopped there that night. We had one room to ourselves about 12 feet square with a good floor and well plastered and a large fireplace full of logs. We slept on the floor and about the middle of the night two drunken Indians came in yelling and shouting. I sung out to them and asked them what they were about. They said about their own business. One of them trod on me getting in to the fire and the other was so drunk that he could not find his way out. They said "were drunk we be" "bad whiskey" Then they tried to sing. I guess it would have made you laugh to see them.

In the morning (it was Sabbath morning) we started by sunrise for Lawrence 15 miles. Had to double our teams up one bad place.

93

Otherwise got along very well till we got to the bottom at the Kansas River here.   The mud was half hub deep and it was very bad getting through. We got into Lawrence about sundown, one of my oxen came near getting in to the river in crossing.   When I came to unload my load I found one stove broken somewhat and I had to pay 8 dollars damage and I have since bought the stove.

On Christmas day I was over the Wakarusa and saw a splendid & fine looking Deer with four branching horns.   He would weigh two hundred pounds I guess.

Thus far and no farther can I go so I must come to a period or full stop or change in the sentence.

Your affectionate
Brother   Edward

Dec 10, 1856

Dear Father

Appleton told me some time since that I might draw on him for 25.00 at the Strafford Bank Dover N H and as I wanted a stove and had no means of getting one I drawed on him.   I have explained as much as time would permit in the enclosed letter.   If A. has not made a deposit there payable to my order and if he is gone where you cannot hear from him in a very short time I dont see any better way than for you to send $25.00 and deposit it in the Strafford Bank subject to my order and have Appleton pay you.   I am sorry that I drawed it but it cant be helped now and you must make the best of it.   I have not more time to write more now but will write at length by the next mail.

Yours truly
Edward P. Fitch

Dec. 12, 1856

Dear Parents

I rec'd a letter from you dated the 21st of Nov on Monday and today have rec'd the others written at Thanksgiving.   I have been intending for some days to write a long letter and will endeavor now to answer both of those letters as well as tell you what news there is.   I rec'd today a letter from John W., the first letter I have had from him since I have been in Kansas.   He was in Ill. says he is making from 20 to 25 dollars per month.   If so he is doing better than I am at present.

I have settled up my claim matter in this way.   I have agreed to divide with Kitchenman thus giving me a clear right to 80 acres and that I consider now better than the chance that I stood for the whole, so that now I probably shall not have but 80 acres but if I had known as much about the Preemption law six months ago as I know now I might just as well have had 160.   I may possibly get it now but I hardly expect to.   I enclose a map of the claims around here with some remarks.   I am now feeling better about my claim than I have for months before.   I would not go through the anxiety that I been through about my claim for the best claim around here.

I made this arrangement with Kitchenman this last week.   If I could have made it a month ago I should probably been in Mass. now but I thought it best to stay and see my claim through whether I went to Mass or not, but my making these arrangements now will prevent its being necessary for me to be on it this winter as much as I should otherwise have had to be.   If I get him to preempt I shall not have to be on it at all except when I have a mind to, but I should not complete my ___ quite as soon as otherwise.   We have been having some cold weather and much mud thus far this winter.   Our corn is yet in the field, much of it in the stack.   We are husking every day.   Wheeler is here with me yet.   He has been and still is quite unwell.   He thinks of going to Topeka as soon as he is able.   I wrote that I need 300. to invest in town property in Quindaro if you will furnish the capital I will invest it for half the profits.   It will I think be quite a paying concern.   The title to the property is perfect and undisputed but according to Mrs. Mary Ida Torry, moderate are better than rapid gains and perhaps I am better off than if I had a share in Quindaro.   How does your aparatus work bringing the water to the vineyard.   Do you have running water there all the time?

I was over to town last Monday night and rec'd your letter in which you spoke of the E.A. [Emigrant Aid] folks writing to Mr Nute to find out about those bbls and on the same evening I saw both Mr Nute and Mr Arny and told them that the bbls had all arrived in safety.   I also gave Mother's note to Mr. Blood tho he had previously let me have the bbls or rather I had got them from the Com. Rooms, but that money that J J Marshall spoke of I have heard nothing of, nor that that was sent to Mr Nute & myself.   Wheeler has come but that has not.   What is the reason of that?   Mr Arny is going to look after both of those things.   I have bought some flour on the credit of what I expect to receive from Lee C. I bought it now because it is low and I know of many who need the article and I intend to give them some.   I wish that I had two hundred dollars to help the poor with this winter.   I think I could use it to good advantage but if you wish to send any more money, deposit in some Boston Bank and send the receipt or give me liberty to draw on it, placing it subject to my order at the Bank.

I rec'd a letter from John and I have just been answering it.   He will probably stay where he is this winter (he says he is making 20 to 25$ per month) and that is more than I can make here by a long shot.   Will E. W. stay at Westboro?   Do you get any pay for your time spent in going up there?   And what other business have you that takes you away from home so much?, for Mother says you are gone a great deal.   Mother wants to know where my 33d letter is.   It was sent from here by George Wilmarth and may come to hand yet if it has not already.   I rec'd the one sent to Sarah W. allright.   Perhaps you will have a chance to send those socks to me sometime.   Watch your chance.   What was the Church Fast for?   and what was [Mrs. Norton's] Tea Party for?

Now a word about those last bbls.   After I heard that they were on the way I went to see Col. Blood and told him the circumstances.   He said that he would willingly give the bbls to me knowing that they would be well applied in my hands.   But he being in a store did not know any thing about when the bbls would come.   So on Sunday the 23 ult. I was at the Committee Room and I found there the fourth bbl that Mother sent and found one numbered "132" but no J. Blood on it, for the head had been lost but another put on, but I knew the bbl. I then came the   next day to the committee and asked them to let me look for that bbl and in looking for that I found another that had lost all the head except one piece and that piece happened to be marked "131" so I made a head for that and got it.   They proved to be right two bbls so they are safe but if I had not been at the room by accident when I was I never should have got them, for there was no sign of J. Blood on them except a B on one of them.   Those bbls were very valuable indeed and many poor folks here will bless Hopkinton folks this cold winter for their aid and comfort.   I have not yet given that comforter that was intended for a minister's wife away yet, for I have not found a Methodist ministers wife who will say she needs it.   However I have not made much inquiry yet but intend to soon. I am very much hurried helping Mr Savage get his corn husked.   I hope we shall get over our hump soon but if it continues cold we shall not get along very fast.   I expect that I must close this letter and sign myself
Your aff Son Edward

96

Dec 12, 1856

Letter notes it was written from Spring Hill Farm near Lawrence at N.W. quarter of Section 12, Township 13, South range 19.

My Dear Mother

  I intend this to be private from any except Father. As you probably are aware I have always been opposed to marrying for money and it has always been my intention to marry (if I ever married) a fortune <u>in</u> a wife, not with a wife. I believe I have found that person who would be a find to anyone that is lucky enough as to win her affections, but she is not entirely without portion. She has <u>herself</u> and <u>her own</u> almost all the household furniture necessary for housekeeping (like the man that was going to be married because he knew where he could have a bed for a dollar a year) and her Father has offered to help me build a good house on my claim next summer if I wish to. Mr W. is not rich in the common acceptation of the word but he has some property with which to make himself comfortable the remainder of his days. It is stipulated that he shall have a home with us and as long as I have a home, he will.

  You say in your last letter but one, Mary Baker is in town and it will be strange if your affairs do not get abroad but in saying that you cast reflections where they do not belong. Mary is one of my best friends and I about as soon trust her with anything that I write kept a secret as any one in Hopkinton, yourselves not excepted. Not that I would tell her things that I should you, but if I did I would warrant them not to get out. You no doubt will laugh at this and say, well it is all over town now so you will have to give it up, but not so fast. I expect the fact that I expect to be married to a Providence lady is now current news for it has got to me from persons that I never told but it did not go from Mary B. nor E. W. nor Sarah Fitch, the only three to whom I have ever written that such was the case out of our family. But it came from friends of Sarah's to Hopkinton and then to me from them, but I shall tell the fact to some and if any of my cousins should come there and ask you to let them see those Daguerreotypes that I sent home let them see both mine & Sarah's for no one will be likely to ask to see <u>two</u> who does not know that there are two there.

  I am very sorry on many accounts that I could not come to Mass this winter and on some accounts glad I shall be some better fixed for next summer by staying here but I shall not be as well able to go East next Fall as I am this but it is all for the best I suppose. I thought of you on

Thanksgiving day, I should liked to have been one of the family circle at that time but could not. This is the second Thanksgiving that I have been away and it may be years before I am with you at Thanksgiving again but I hope it will not be many. I am not forgetting my old friends tho. I am forming new acquaintances all the time but still dear to my heart are the scenes of my childhood as fond recollection presents them to view. That plum pudding, if I only had a piece just now, how good it would seem. I have very few luxuries where I am now, even butter I have not tasted for weeks and very little sugar or molasses either. I sigh for a home of my own. When I was with you I looked upon a home as a matter of course but having been deprived of a home for two years it seems a real blessing to have a home.

But all those bbls have arrived and from them I have got many things that will do me much good. I was destitute of many clothes until they came but I have taken some of them. I did not find any coat sent by Mrs. Davenport but I took a checked coat and a black coat that are good ones and I have the coat that J.S. Brown sent, an every day one. I kept _____, stockings and am sorry that I did not keep more. I have kept some of those best new pants sent to and two prs of good ones beside those sent by Mrs _____. I have some shirts also which I very much needed and some overalls. I am sorry that you did not send twice as many pants this last time and so had four bbls full. I could have found enough who needed and would have been glad to get as many more but you & Hopkinton have done pretty well. If you would only refund to me that $180 that I paid out in the war last fall I should like it better however. I think that that $141. ought to have been sent to me instead of Mr Nute and it would have been vastly better to have deposited it in Hopkinton Bank and then have given me or Mr Nute liberty to draw on it than to have it sent by the Nat. Com. The 50.for Wheeler has come but the rest has not. What does that mean. The 25 that Lee C. was never so as to have it benefit me some as well as others and if I got hold of that that was sent to Mr N's I shall use some of it to pay for seed wheat for folks here this fall and have them give me as many bushels next year for it so that will help them and benefit me. I have given a great many things from those bbls to the Savage's folks, but there was pollicy in that. They are my neighbors and he will let me have his team and will help me in such ways very much so that is a reason why I give them a good deal. They were needy too, having lost a great many things coming on. They expect an increase in the family before long and I have given them many things to clothe the expected stranger. They are nice folks, just such as I would like for neighbors. Sarah will not accept anything out of the bbls as she says they were meant for those who were needy and she is not, or rather there are many worse off than she is. [And now] that I think of it, did you not mean that she should have that quilt that was in that bundle for herself?   I know you did but she will have it that you meant for her to give it to some poor person.   Tell us how it is.

I have given the coat and vest sent by Daniel Eames to a Methodist minister and he promised to write to you & suppose he will. His name is George.

Your affectionate son
Edward P Fitch

Dec. 17, 1856

To Those Gentlemen and Ladies who so generously responded to the appeal for help, from the suffering poor in Kansas.

Friends, In the good Book we read "Blessed is he that consideroth the poor," and if <u>that</u> is to be fulfilled to the letter, you in Hopkinton will certainly come in for a share of that blessing,   for to your consideration, many of the poor in this troubled country will be indebted for many comforts that they will enjoy this cold winter.

When I wrote of the suffering that I know of here, it did not occur to me, that I would be made the instrument (knowing your Liberality) of ministering to the comfort of so many of them, as it has been my pleasure to do, but right nobly have you answered the appeal for aid, and you will accept the heartfelt thanks of our of very many citisens of Kansas, for your liberality and kindness.   <u>As you were promised</u> that if your donations ever came <u>into my hands</u> you would be advised of their disposal, I feel it my duty to render to you an account of my stewardship. I have been so much driven with my own business that I have had to crowd the dispensing of your charities into a small compass of time, but I have <u>tried</u> to make <u>every</u> article tell   for the comfort of someone who, without it, might have suffered, and I trust I shall have succeeded so well, that if it is ever necessary for you to repeat the effort, you will be encouraged to do so by my report of benefit that your charities have been this time.

I have kept a Record of account of <u>what</u> had been given and who has rec'd the different articles and as the donors names were inscribed on some of the things I shall be able to tell the names of where and when those things have gone, but it was not possible for me to keep an exact acct, so that some things even that were <u>marked</u> I cannot tell the location at present. I shall try and give some account of some of the families that I have helped <u>most</u>, drawn from such sources as I think reliable.

In almost all instances the donations have been rec'd with marked expressions of thankfulness and in only one instance have I yet found that there was any doubt of the worthyness of the individuals receiving aid.

For almost all cases those <u>to whom I have given, I have</u> myself been acquainted with during <u>some part</u> of my residence in Kansas and I have tried to give to those only whom I <u>knew</u> to be needy for this, I think, has been one great trouble in the distribution of things by the National Com. Many would go there and get things who did not really need any aid, when many who really needed could get none. But I suppose that they have done the best they could, under existing circumstances.

The bbls which contained the things you sent, and I <u>refer only to</u> those four, which were sent by my Mother, were a long time in reaching me and at one time I thought that I never should see any of them, as the marks were taken from them in Chicago, and they were sent on with different <u>marks</u>. The first arrived here Nov. 10, and the 2nd , 3rd, Nov 17 and the last on the 24, and up to this time I have disposed of most of the articles, contained in them, I have a few still left, because I have had no time to find, <u>or rather to carry them</u> to those who I know to be in need of them. If I had five times as much sent to me I could find <u>enough who need</u> and would be <u>thankful for them</u>. But what I have not I cannot give away.

I will now give some sketches of families that I have helped with your charities. Mr. Savage's family consists of himself, wife, & three children. His oldest, a boy of seven, is afflicted with Chronic Rheumatism, and is so bad that he cannot <u>sleep</u> nights more than half the time, but requires someone to nurse him; during the day he gets around quite well, with the help of a crutch. Mr S has been here through all the troubles, and has had his share of the losses to bear with the rest and had it not been for the troubles with which we have been surrounded he would now have been in a fair way to live, but as it is he has to live from hand to mouth as best he can. He is a hard working good honest man but poor. To particularise, he has had no butter for family use for many weeks, an article which I think few of you do without, and much of that time he has had neither molasses nor syrup in the house. To him I gave the Overcoat sent by Den Freland, <u>an under coat</u>, pr of pants & pr of shirts. To his wife

I gave a dress and some undergarments, to this sick boy I gave a pr of Boots and a coat sent by G. C. Webster.   Gave also a flannel night dress and some stockings.   He was very thankful and very often speaks of the nice comfortable things he received and your liberality.   To the other children I gave boots & some small articles.   The whole family both speak and seem to feel thankful for what they have rec'd.   Mr S wishes his special thanks to be given to Den. F for that overcoat.   This family came from Vermont.

Mr. Lindsey is a man who came from Ind. in the spring of '55   to Kansas.   He has a family of three small children.   They have had much sickness in the family; Col Lane cheated them out of some of their earnings and tried to bust the character of Mr. L. to save his own.   They have been robbed by Border Ruffians yet they are still here.   I gave Mrs. L the dress sent by Charlotte Freland and some undergarments together with some clothing for the children for which they are very thankful.

Mr Elmore Allen came to Kansas from New York during the winter of 54, 55, and settled four miles from Lawrence.   He has lost his crops by fire, and three horses by means of the war.   His wife & children have been sick a great deal.   I gave him a coat sent by Mr. Raymond that he was much pleased with and some small articles for his wife and children.   I have promised his wife more, as soon as she can come.

Mr. Smith came here from Maine in the fall of 54 & has been sick most of this time, has had three houses burned by the Ruffians and one by prairie fire. I gave him ___.

Mr. Paul Jones came in the spring of 55 from Ind. to Kansas.   He settled on the Wakarusa, and was one of the 14 who rescued Branson from Sheriff Jones last Nov, or rather Nov 55.   The rescue of Branson was the immediate cause of the war last fall, for being concerned in that he was taken to Lecompton and kept there for some time without sufficient clothing, and was exposed so much that he has not been able to do any work this whole past summer (except a very little), thus leaving the whole support of the family to come on his children, of whom there are four, of the ages 13, 15, 16 & 18 years, the oldest a girl; their mother has been sick for a long time.   I was there within a week and he told me that he had but a very little flour in the house and when that was gone, he did not know where he would get more.   He had corn but cannot get it ground.   I gave him & each of the boys a coat, and some under garments, also dresses and stockings to the Mother & daughter.   I have bought some flour and shall send it to them, in the course of a few days.

101

Mr <u>Mears</u> was another of those concerned in the rescue of Branson for which <u>crime</u> he, like Mr Jones, must suffer. The Sheriff [Samuel Jones] harassed him all last winter , and all the fore part of summer, so that he could not get his crops in, but has never been able to catch him yet, but it kept him from getting in a crop, so he is without means. I gave him pants & a coat, also a dress for his wife, sent by Mrs. Perry, and some clothes for his children, of which he has three, all small.

Mr. <u>Sam Reynolds</u> came from New York to Kansas a little more than a year since. He has had a hard time with sickness and the war. He has always been on hand to fight when needed. He has a family of three children and last winter he had no sugar nor flour all winter but lived on corn bread and molasses & coffee. I gave him a coat sent by Mr Baker and some smaller articles, some boots or shoes for all three of his children.

Mr. <u>J.F. Reynolds</u> came here in the fall of 54 and has been a hard working man; had a house and some corn harvested this year but in an unlucky day it caught fire, and <u>house</u>, corn, and <u>all</u> were burned. I gave him coat and pants. His wife had been provided for by others and he is now in a fair way to get along.

<u>Mr Ela</u> was <u>one</u> of the pioneers of the Neosho settlement. He has been sick much. To him I gave the coat sent by David Eames and some other articles.

Mr Burroughs is a young unmarried man from Conn. who has been one of our brave defenders in time of war, and in time of peace has been sick so much, that he had not been able to earn his clothes. I gave him a pr of boots, pants and shirts. He was very grateful indeed for them and said when he was able he would do as much for some other poor man.

Mrs. <u>Pratt</u> came from Boston in June 55 to join her husband who had been here since 54. She had <u>three</u> small children to bring. The journey was too much for her, and she has not enjoyed good health since. Mr. P was among that ill-fated party that was taken prisoner at <u>Hickory Point in Sept.</u> and have been kept prisoner at Lecompton <u>ever since</u>. She was in a <u>very destitute condition</u>. To her I gave a sack sent by Mrs Webster, and a skirt of a ___ sent by <u>Sarah Eames</u>, also some stockings & shoes for herself and children. She was profuse in her expression of thanks, for the articles which she really needed.

<u>Miss Jane Davis</u> is a Welsh girl, who has supported her Father and Mother principally by her labor this past summer. They are quite aged. I gave to them the Basques & skirt sent by Frank Gillinghast, now Mrs Pierce, and a more pleased girl <u>I never saw</u>, or a better fitting dress.

102

She was <u>perfectly delighted</u>, and the dress fits admirably. Mr Kitchenner a round Englishman, I supplied with a coat & some other things. He was in Lawrence and his life was threatened the 21st of May, and has been sick most of the summer. His crops were all destroyed.

That coat which was twice Mr. Underwoods wedding coat, <u>now</u> clothes the back of a young man from New York, who has been unfortunate and is <u>or was</u> sadly in need of clothes. Rev. Mr Clough is a Methodist minister who has had much sickness in his family. He has, and now preaches when he is able. I gave him a Coat sent by Daniel Eames & a Vest from Lowell L Claflin and some other articles of warm clothing for his wife and daughters. He has had some experiences among the Border Ruffians, and his son has had to flee the country.

Mr. Palmer came from Mass to the Territory, and sent for his family to come this last summer. His guns were all stolen and his <u>tools</u> also (he is a gunsmith) on the Mo River. I have for his wife and children some clothes which they have not yet rec'd.

I have thus given you some account of most of the families that I have helped. I have some more children's clothing to give away yet, and I expect to have some time to see to it this week but I am not sure. I could not tell more particulars about single things without taking too much time, and wearying your patience to hear them.

In conclusion let me express for all those who have benefitted by your <u>liberality</u> (among whom was myself for I have two coats and a vest that were sent, one by Artemus Johnson) our   heartfelt thanks and our prayers that your charities be returned in blessing on your heads <u>fourfold</u> for "They that give unto the Poor, lend unto the Lord."

And that the richest of Heaven's blessings may rest upon you all, is the best [wish] of your absent [son], the almoner of your

Bounty to the poor of Kansas
Edward P. Fitch

Dec. 29, 1856

Dear Parents

It is Monday. I am confined to the house, an invalid, but you will not wonder this time who is taking care of me. As you will probably guess that I am not writing well lying down. I took a violent cold last Fri night and on Sat. and got wet through. And yesterday and today my face has been swollen up very badly. I thought this morning it was Erysipelas but the Doctor says it is not but proceeds from my tooth.   But my tooth, tho some sore, has not ached any.   It is some better this afternoon.   The swelling seems to be going down.   It was swelled so much this forenoon that I could hardly see out one of my eyes.   I have the worst cold that I have had since I came to Kansas.

I rec'd a letter a week ago from P.T. Jackson of Boston saying that he had recd twenty dollars for me and authorized me to draw on him for that amt which I have done and sold the draft and got the money.   I suppose that is the 20.00 that J.J. Marshall wrote about.   He does not say where it came from.

I hope that you Hopkinton folks will raise some more money   for Kansas and when you have raised it deposit it in Hopkinton Bank and give me authority to draw on it.   I will put it where it will comfort the heart of poor Kansas men and & women.

Wheeler has gone to Topeka where he has an office building rented where he will make his headquarters for the winter.   We have had some very cold weather but today is pleasant.   Christmas was a fine pleasant day.   The Stubbs had a ball here but I didn't go.   I dread the cold weather very much. If I ever move from here, it will be to a warmer rather than a colder country.

Yours with much love.

Edward

I have today ordered to your address a copy of the Herald of Freedom -- a New Year's present.   Edward   Jan 1/57

Jan. 11, 1857

Dear Parents

I don't suppose that you can form any adequate idea of the suffering that is experienced here during this cold weather but to help you form an idea I want to just have you compare the modes of building here with that of the East.   There you board your houses over first and then clapboard <u>them</u> over that.   <u>Here</u> we take <u>shakes</u>, which are nothing more or less than clapboards <u>split</u> out of oak and of course they cannot have a very true edge nor be jointed very close.   Then our frame is put up and these shakes nailed on to the posts fitting them as close as possible but it is impossible to fit them so but what the wind will have free passage through.   Those who can afford it and can get the lumber will get sawed

104

weather boarding instead of shakes, but this being green will always warp a great deal. Then the roof is often covered with shakes too and they will let the rain in all the time that it rains. There is not one house in a hundred that is plastered and only a few that are lined with anything. Some may be lined with cloth but cloth costs money and that is a commodity not easily obtained in this country. This then is the sort of houses that most of our Kansas folks live in - just one thickness of shakes 1/4 or 1/2 inch between them and outdoors the snow will blow through one of these houses just about as easy as it will blow out of doors.

A week ago today I was told of a family that were sick and I was asked to go and see them. I went and found the man sick abed where he had been for three weeks and most of the time he was out of his head. He had the billious fever. His wife and six children were in one room with him. They had nothing to eat in the house except a little flour and sugar. She had all the clothes she <u>had</u> on, not having another dress that she could put on while she washed the one she had on and they had no wood, tho it was cold, except a few sticks.

I helped them to wood for that night and on Mon, the next day, I got them ten dollars worth of things or rather gave them three dollars and a half to pay for a load of wood that they had brought and got them six dollars & a half in provisions and groceries. Tea Rice beans soap mollasses etc.

I went there again today and found the man much better and I guess he will get along now. I gave the woman a dress and several articles of clothes for the children. They were very thankful. They said that they did not know what they should have done had it not been for me and the provision that I got them the week before. When I came to see the man I found that it was a man that I knew but he did not know me. I found another family about two weeks ago that were out of flour and some other common articles. I got them a sack of flour & some sugar and coffee for which they were very thankful. All the trouble with me is that I dont have money to supply the wants of those that I find destitute. If I had a hundred or two dollars to help such poor folks with I should like it but alas! I am poor myself and cant do much for them.

Fri eve Jan 16/ I have just read your letters Dated Jan 4th. They have come through pretty quick. I recd by the mail tonight also a letter from Lee Claflin enclosing a draft for $25. which I shall use for the benefit of the poor here. He says that I may appropriate 6.00 of it to myself, the rest I can find use for very well. That money that was to be sent to Mr.

Nute & I, I haven't heard a word of.   What does it mean.   Wheeler was here last night and has gone on to Topeka today.   He has been all around the north part of the Territory since he was here last Dec.   He has found much suffering where he has been.   He tells me   he got lost one night on the Kickapoo reserve and got almost frozen to death.   He walked 250 miles & laid out 4 towns within <u>four weeks.</u>

       Look at Gov. Geary's message in the Herald of this week.   It is a very able paper.   The bogus Legislature are down upon him and he has sent to Leavenworth for troops.   You will probably hear from Sarah before long about the quilt.   I have not yet given that overcoat to a Methodist minister but I shall do so within a week or two.   I am as well as usual.   It is quite cold with a little snow Saturday.   It has been a terrible rough day today.   The snow has blowed terribly   we have only been out enough to fodder the cattle.   I think that I shall answer your letters during the next week sometime.

Yours
Edward P Fitch

Jan. 18, 1857

       Last night was the coldest night of the season.   This morning the thermometer stood at 26 deg <u>below 0</u>   We don't have any outside coats in <u>this</u> <u>country</u>.   I came very near freezing my feet last night.

<u>Edward</u>

Jan. 19, 1857

Dear Father

       I have been attending to some business in town all day and have now concluded to answer your letter that came by the last mail especially in regard to that money and some other things you said.   Shall you get Whittman a place at the Reformatory?   How is Mr. G., the new Supt.? Does his honor <u>pay</u> you for your time spent there?   John W.'s P.O. address is still [Siskilwa Bureau] Co.   He is near there engaged in map business he tells me.   I have not heard from him since I wrote before. Appleton I have not heard from since he left Hopkinton.

You ask about the state of religion here.   I regret to say that it is low, there is not much attention to anything of a religious character. There are in fact but few religious persons here in comparison to the population.   We have meetings every Sunday to be sure and prayer meetings every Sunday & Wed evenings, but there doesn't seem to be that deep feeling of interest that I wish there was, neither in my own heart nor the lives of others.   Our Church is small and weak but I hope we shall grow in strength and grace.

Now about that Quindaro Stock.   When I wrote about that it was from the fact that about that time the stock was very high having gone up from 150. to five hundred dollars.   If I had at that time had the money I should have liked to have bought two shares at the start and would have sold one when it would have paid for both and the other when they got pretty well up.   Quindaro is on the Missouri River 7 miles above Kansas city and immediately opposite to Parkville Mo.   It has come up very suddenly and shares are now selling at 5   & 700 dollars.   The title to the land comes from the Wyandotte Indians but the title is not yet perfect so some say.   At any rate if I had bought stock then when I wrote to you I should sell it now soon, as I think that it will go down sometime as rapidly as it has come up.   If I had the money I should invest I think in Wyandotte City which is three miles above Kansas City Mo and directly at the mouth of the Kansas river.   It has a good location for having the trade of the Territory as the Trade will not go to Kansas City again and we do not like to go to Leavenworth since they destroyed so much stuff for our merchants there and murdered our men and them prisoners.   The Trade must go to the river somewhere and either Wyandotte or Quindaro must be the place and in all respects except the mere landing place, I think W. has the advantage of Q.   The town there contains about 640 acres and is divided into shares 10 lots each and will be ready to open the sale of shares in a short time, three weeks at least, perhaps less.   Then shares will probably open at 500$ though perhaps they will at 300.   I cannot tell certainly which until next Monday when I expect to know all about it. The trustees of the city are Lieut. Gov. Roberts, Mr Jenkins one of the Treason prisoners, the two Walkers, one of them is Chief of the Wyandottes, and two other men whose names I do not recollect.   In all probability   there will be two or three steamboats plying on the Kansas river between this place and those places next season.   I should like if the shares open as low as 300. to get two shares then and sell one when it will bring enough to pay for both, or keep both one for you and one for me. The former would be the better way I think as then if it even failed it

107

would not be much loss tho I dont see any prospect of its failing at all.   I don't think that shares there will rise as rapidly as they did at Quindaro but they will be more sure.   You say if there is to be no more war, and it is to be a Free State.   I dont think and I don't know of any one that does think there will be any more war and as to its being a Slave State I don't think there is a single chance for it to be a Slave State.   In fact I heard a Pro Slavery Lawyer of this place say yesterday that he did not think there was the slightest chance of its being a Slave State and he is a Lawyer practicing in the Bogus Courts.

But beside all this chance for investing in Wyandotte there is a good chance to invest in Lots in this city now and make 50 per cent on the money invested in three months.   I have got two lots now within a short time that I can make a little on but they are cheap lots and I shall not make much.   I get them in the way of boot by swapping stoves, and shall probably make 10 or 15 dollars on the trade which is considerable for the capital invested but if I had two or three hundred dollars I could buy good lots here now that would rise much in value before spring and should sell then as I don't think that the title to part of the town is perfect.   Another way to invest money here is to buy Delaware Trust Lands.   That is a sure thing gives you the title direct from Government and they cant help rising in value.   I saw Sen Pomeroy within a day or two and he asked me if I heard from you and if you had any idea coming out here.   I told him you had not said much about it at present or lately but that you asked me once if you should sell out at a sacrifice $1000, and come out here and I told him that I told you no!   Sen P. said tell him to sell at its value and come on and if he should sell at 1000 discount he would make it up in a year or two.   He and all of us look for a very large Emigration in the spring.   Then there is another good chance for a paying speculation that I know of. There are four new towns just laid out and the Trustees have agreed to sell some shares at 50. per share.   I can get a share in all four for 100.$ It will be secure property but will not rise very fast probably would pay 20 per cent.   There is a city called Palmyra half way and directly between here and Osawatomie that is a good place to invest and sure but will not pay so fast as Wyandotte.   These are all sure;   my experience has taught me to look for sure titles.

About the title at Wyandotte   the land belonged to the W. Indians.   They have become by treaty citizens of the U.S. and have a right to sell their lands and the lands are now being set off to the different individuals of the tribe and the Trustees have bought this land of the ones to whom it is set off.   Some of the Trustees in fact are the Indians themselves, that is the Walkers.   The title to Quindaro is the same except that they have bought property of minors and when they come of age they may make them trouble.   I am troubled some for fear that because of my speaking of Quindaro that you have seen Gov Robinson & bought a share.   Then if you have I advise you to sell as soon as possible when you can make 50.$ Dont sell at a <u>loss</u> because they will go up some more but eventually it will be weak <u>without doubt</u>.   Shares will be sold at Wyandotte in a week or two.   I think now that I shall speak for two shares at the opening price and then wait to hear from you.   Then if you do not think best to furnish money I can either let them drop or sell them and perhaps make a few dollars without making any outlay.   If you will furnish the Capital I will invest for half or I will buy for you or if you will Lend me the money I will run my own risks.   I want D. to bring this subject before Uncle Doctor and tell him that if he will let me have money I will invest it for him for half the profits and there are sure ways enough of investing it to pay well here.   I dont know much about your Eastern land speculation but this I think is safe.   Property here must rise at any rate.   I wish you could turn your farm into money and come out here. My lot that my house is on I could sell now for about 500, I expect,   and it has cost me 250.   You know in the spring I expect the lot and house will bring 800 but I dont expect to sell.   I am going to write to Wood and see what he will redeed those lots to me that I had before, for.   If he would do it for $250, the sum I failed to pay before, it would be a paying operation to buy and sell them right out as I took the opinion of a Land agent on them a few days since and he made them out worth 450.$ now at present prices.   Unless I could get a note that was sure, however, I would not try to trade with Wood.   If you can make anything out of this desultory statement of facts you will do well.   I am so much confused by things around that my mind is not very clear and I cannot write well.

Edward P Fitch

Jan. 21, 1857

Dear Mother

      It is now ten O'clock and I have just been out with Sarah who is to watch with Mrs. Ladd tonight and have now sat down to answer your letter of January 4th.   I gave that coat of F.   Harrington to a Welsh Congl [Congregational] minister by name of Lewis and with this I send the letter that he wrote to you.   I thought once that I would copy it but finally I thought you might like to have it in his own hand writing.   The Lewis house was burned the same night Judge [John H.] Wakefield's was. I was up there with our regiment at the time or rather a few hours before it was burnt and also a few hours after.   The other man that I gave a coat to has not written yet.   I am going to send that quilt that the girls made to the Revrend Denison of Manhattan, a Methodist minister and a good man but poor.   I bought a lot at auction tonight and gave 88.$ for it.   The circumstances are these.   Mr Wilmarth owns the lot 111 N. H St and the last summer he ploughed and fenced Lots No 107, 109, & 111.   The lots are in a first rate place for that st[reet] and I wanted to get one that joined Mr Wilmarths.   I tried to buy 113 but it had just been sold for 150.$ I then went to Mr F. A. Hunt who owned 109 and tried to buy that but he would not sell but tonight he was going to sell some things of different kinds at auction and to help the sellers he put in some city lots and this among the rest.   I bought a lot a few days ago for 15$ and sold it today for 22$ and I had part of that money that was sent from Framingham left and Mr Wilmarth was owing me some on the rent of my house and he advanced enough to pay the rest for the lot and I bought.   The lot is easly worth 100.   and by spring will be worth probably double what I paid but I do not intend to sell it if I can get along without but keep that and sell the one my house is now on when I can get enough for it.   It takes every cent of money that I have got and some that I have not got to pay for this but I have worked one day and shall work some more on the ice where I got 1.75 per day so I can earn a little spending money.

      Now for your letter.   If I had supposed my letter would have been read at the Lyceum there are some things that I would have left out for that is making me pretty public.   That quilt that was sent to Sarah you will hear of pretty soon, probably my next letter.   She has not been convinced until now that it was meant for her and beside she has been busy taking care of the sick and has not had much time.   Besides she thinks that you are expecting more of her than she can perform for she says that she cant write a letter especially to be read at the Sabbath School.   What has become of Rev Mr Thayer formerly of Ashland?   You say you hope I will write often and Father says that my letters are always welcome.   I am afraid that bye & bye they will make you "twice glad" as the saying is, glad when they come and glad when they go away or dont come, but I hope you will write often however for I like to hear from home.   You speak of Aunt A. & Sarah F coming down there as an unusual occourrence & I hope you will not visit the iniquities of the Mothers upon the daughters but will treat Sarah well for my sake.   She is my friend and I hope _____   as such. I told her to go there and ask you what she did and I expected that long before this time you would have received per George Wilmarth, Sarah's brother, my likeness & Sarahs but we heard from him a few days since and he had not been to Hopkinton and would not go at present.   He is in Attleboro attending school and will not come until his school is out.   I hope you will not leave the impression with any one that inquires to see those pictures that I have been making a fool of them; you did leave that impression on Sarah.   You ask how long before you can say you have a daughter; probably the last part of April will be as soon as that event will happen.   I am not entirely ready to be married yet and I don't think it is best to be in any hurry about it.   I have talked the matter over a good deal and the prevailing opinion is that the time will be not far from the 20 of Apr next but the time cannot be certainly fixed yet.   Then I swapped stoves and got a stove two sizes smaller than the one I had and got two lots by paying 15$ I sold one lot for 22 and was offered 27.50 for the other today but would not sell it short of 30.   I think that I shall sell it to pay for the one I bought.

I have written about that Pistol that Uncle Dr sent me but can hear nothing from it.   I am going to send up there by Mr Pomeroy in a few weeks and see what he can find out about it.

I wish some rich man like Dr Howe would send me a thousand dollars to speculate on this winter.   I could make something out of it but I suppose that I am better off without it.   When I get some Wyandott stock however I shall feel better.   If I could get what is owing to me I should like to but folks wont pay here if they can help it.   Don't _____
.

Your affectionate son
Edward

February 1857

On Sat the 24th day of Jan 1857, the women of the city of Lawrence Kansas met together for the purpose of devising some means to put a stop to some of the drunkenness that prevailed here. They thought that the best way would be to spill all the liquor that they could find in town. They first visited a liquor shop kept by a Mr. Rowley, where they found quite a lot of Whiskey and other Liquor, which they spilled on the floor, as there happened to be a floor to the room. Then they went to a Bakery kept by a Mr. Fry and found a lot of ale which they spilt. Mr. Fry, after they got out, was so very brave and valiant, said he would shoot any one that had any thing to do with it that was any man. He flourished his revolver around but did no harm. The ladies visited in succession some six places where intoxicating drinks were kept and spilled all that they could find. After they had got almost through, one of the sellers said that they had not found his liquor and they began to suspect that he had some hid in the store of one of the small retail merchants of this place. They searched his place and under a bed found five bbls of whiskey hid away nicely. This they very soon made to weep tears of firewater out into the streets. After they had got through some of the sellers who were mad as they could be, let some of the drinking men have a team and they went down to Franklin and brought up about half a bbl of whiskey which they passed around the streets and let everyone drink (that wanted to). Such a <u>hideous, yelling, hooting & 'sick'</u> you never did see. It seemed as tho all the fiends from the bottomless pit were let loose for a time but just about night they had all got dead drunk. I never saw and hope never to see again such a sight as I saw then. Boys from 10 to 15 years old so drunk that they could not stand alone but tumbling down on the street and lying there until some of their friends took them home and put them to bed. There were more folks drunk in town that day than I ever saw drunk before and had it not been that Capt Walker persuaded one of the town men to tip the bbl over all hands would have been drunk. Loud threats were made that all the houses in which those ladies lived who were engaged in spilling the liquor should be burnt before the next morning and that the Herald of Freedom Office should be torn down. But the next morning found them all standing and safe.

Feb. 13, 1857

We are having fine spring weather like the last of April in Mass. Spring has opened. Boats will soon be running up the river and we shall soon be able to plow. The frost is not out of the ground yet but soon will be at present appearances.

Edward

Feb. 3, 1857

My Dear Dear Mother,

What would I not give could I see you today. I am so much troubled about many things. How I want to talk with you for I cannot __ impossible. My mind has been much exercised within a few weeks about the future, some means for getting some things to start with. I am troubled never so much I continually think if I only had Capital how much I could do and then I think how kindly Father offered to furnish me more when he has done so much for me already. I don't know what to think. And then in view of getting married! I never thought before what a world there was in setting out in life. I have been able to live along thus far, or rather to stay, for I have not <u>lived</u> and shall not till I have a <u>home</u> of my own and <u>one</u> to share it with me and the thought of the responsibility that this new relation will involve, I am almost driven to distraction. I can't tell you the reason for my feeling so -- writing out if I could only <u>see you</u> I could tell you all.

I have thought much within a short time of leaving Lawrence, selling out everything here and taking the money to start with in another place. There are some advantages and <u>many</u> disadvantages to be derived from such a course. If I could only see a little into the future and see how certain things were coming out I could tell what to do. Property is valuable here now, but if I get only 80 acres of land I can't sell any of it to get money to carry on the rest because I want as much as that myself. If I had 160 acres then I could sell 80 and have something to use on the other 80. That of course I cannot now do so it may be best to go somewhere else. I think that I can sell my house and lot here for $800 in the spring. It has cost me $450 and I think I can sell my half of the claim, or my 80, for about the same amt. I have a lot that I bought a week or two since for $88. which I have been offered 137. for and think I shall sell it today for $143, may not. I swapped stoves and got about as good a stove as mine was and a lot to boot. Sold that lot for 22, took the money to buy the one

113

I gave 88 for.   I bought a lot yesterday for 50, sold it for 55 and did not have to pay for it till it was sold and then had the deed made to the one I sold to, so that cost me nothing.   Made a 5.   If I had Capital I could trade in lots in a small way and make a hundred Dollars in [a] month or so.

There is a new town just about starting in Linn Co. about 60 miles from here here I have some notion of going.   By putting in 300 I can have 1/8 of the town site of 920 acres.   I can probably get a claim near and if I can sell out here at the price I wrote and go there and grow up with the town I might in the end be better off than to stay here.   If there was a chance to get claims near Wyandotte I would go there but there is not. There is a good chance within 15 miles of here at Palmyra, but I don't know as I could get a claim to suit me there.   Mr Wilmarth wants much to go to [find] some place where he can get an interest in a town as he has none here and property is so high that he cant purchase much and he will probably go away from here if I don't.   Wheeler has something to do with some town north of here and I dont know but I may go up there.

Feb. 13, 1857

I sent another letter to you yesterday dated since this was begun and now I have given up going down south with Wheeler, but I shall in all probability go up North to look at a location there and if it suits me I shall sell out here and go up there.   I have bought some shares in some towns north and depend on selling lots here in town to pay for the shares as I have two months time to pay for them.

You asked me sometime since how soon you might say you had a daughter, probably after the 19th day of April has passed you can say so, and have it a fact.   That is the day set if nothing unforseen intervenes, but of course that is not to be told of.

Private

Father   I recd the money by way of Mr Nute yesterday Feb 21st.   I rec'd those two letters that you wrote partly at Boston this past week and shall reply to them at length soon.   I think of going to Quindaro and Wyandotte tomorrow and may invest that money there.   If I draw on you I will write again before the draft goes.

Mr. Savage where I staid last summer was blessed with a daughter since yesterday, Feb 12, 1857.

114

Feb. 27, 1857

Dear Mother

      I intend on this sheet to write what news I have to tell and answer your letter which came last week dated Feb 1.st   You may be sure that I shall not trade with Wood much more unless I am sure that I can get good bargain in spite of him.   I intend to be careful how I manage money intrusted to me and shall try and not be any worse off than I now am, but no one can tell what a day may bring forth.   You speak of having some in Lawrence and some in <u>one</u> other town.   I have some in Lawrence and shall probably keep a little here and I have some property in four other towns beside Quindaro.   The Trustees promised all a lot that staid [stayed] here but I never got mine and dont suppose that I <u>ever</u> shall, may possibly get it yet.   Wheeler has used some of his fifty dollars among the poor in Northern Kansas and some around here .   Mr Nute paid me that half, $10, a week ago.   I shall attend to it.   I gave a poor man some yesterday.   He had been to Utah and come back here last fall and was going to locate a claim on the Neosho if he could get one.   You will not probably hear from Mr Nute except through me, for he has had 3500. pass through his hands and he cant have time to write to all the donors who have sent to him.   He reports to the State Com. that forwarded the money to him.

      I started from here Monday morning for Quindaro, rode pretty fast,   arrived at the Delaware Baptist Mission at half past two.   There were twelve of us.   Gov Robinson, Mr Grovenor, Mr Hunt, Whitney and Attorney Emery, five of us, stopped at the Mission over night.   The rest went through, I should have gone through   but my horse gave out and could not stand it.   The next day my horse could not go so I walked to Q and got there about two Oclock.   That night a Boat came up there and left some passengers.   We were pretty full before but like an Omnibus were not quite full and made room for all.   The next day I walked back to the mission and yesterday rode to Lawrence again.   I shall go down again by & by but shall have a good horse.   I offered 100. for a horse the other day but could not get him short of 125.   and today I offered 110. for another one but 125 was the price and I could not get him less.   I suppose he is worth that 100. but I dont like to put quite so much money into a horse but I dont know but I may buy him yet.   If I live on my claim this summer I shall need a horse for I shall have all my water to draw more than half a mile.

I may sell my claim however and go to Quindaro and put up a store.   That is, go in with another man.   If I can have the chance that I expect I can and could keep my claim too, I should go into a store there right off.   I have not time tonight to answer Father's letter but shall do so by the next mail I think and enclose copys of the drafts on him.   I want him to get the money from Boston and have it ready to pay.   I shall draw a three days from sight [draft].

From your ever aff Son
Edward P Fitch

Feb. 27, 1857

I arrived back at Lawrence last night from Quindaro after a absence of four days.   After looking the subject over I am convinced that Quindaro is going to be a place.   I have therefore invested there.   I think now that I should rather have property there than in any other place in Kansas just now.   I should rather have it in Lawrence only there is a flaw in the title and we dont yet know whether we have got any title or not.   If we had a sure title here, property would immediately be worth double what it is now but on account of the title I dont know but I shall sell all my property in the city while it is up this spring.   But if I had a Deed in a sure and valid form from the right authority for this lot where my house stands I would not sell it for $3000, The title to property is poorer in Lawrence than in any other town in the territory.

The principal advantages of Quindaro are First it has a good landing.   The levee is I believe some more than a mile long and is a good part of the way rock.   It is high and for the whole length the river is almost perfectly straight.   I dont think there is another place on the whole river that is straight so far.

2nd its position.   It is on the Missouri just above the mouth of the Kansas and bears about the same relation to Kansas that St Louis does to Missouri.

3d   The fact that the title to the land is indisputable. Gov Robinson tells me that the title is as good as can be got. It is in this way: the Wyandotte Indians by the last treaty become citizens of the U.S. and as citizens have a right to sell their lands.   The have been distributed to each Indian by Commissioners sent from Washington for that purpose and they have sold the land to the Quindaro Co.

4th The Company own a lot of Timbered land right opposite to the city of Quindaro, in Mo which will of course give them the timber and not only that they will be able to keep what they dont want away from that side.

5 Parkville Mo is opposite the upper end of the town and they will have a ferry between them.   6th it is a Temperance town.

The chief reasons why it is better than Wyandotte are it is higher, better landing and they can have a ferry which they cannot have at Wyandotte and Wyandotte is a <u>Whiskey</u> town.

They have the largest mill in the Territory at Quindaro 120 horse power three boilers

Gov R says there will be some $50000. invested there this year beside what the Company are going to invest.   They have got the largest Hotel, except one, in Kansas almost done and have a large number of men at work grading the streets and they are putting up the steam mill, two or three large ware houses and other buildings.   The company are selling shares on these terms: the buyer to pay $750.00 and agree to put 1000 dollars worth of improvements on within a year but I found a man who was in want of money now and bought his share and Simpson told me that the three first lots of that share as it is now drawn are worth now $1000.00 which is more than the whole cost me.   I shall make the arrangements about the pay tomorrow, I expect, and shall draw on you for the money with which to pay.

I shall draw on you for $700.00 payable at the Hopkinton Bank to T.L. Whitney or his order.   You are to take 500. of Mr Fitch's money and the rest from Barnards unless Mr Fitch has a mind to send the whole. When the <u>Trust land</u> sales commence again I think likely enough I shall sell out this stock and buy Trust lands but dont know certain.   The best of the Delaware Trust lands have been sold but the Iowa lands will be sold soon and will be good property.   I dont think there is any danger of losing money by investing in Quindaro.   I can have another share, my choice out of four for 700, two hundred down and my note for two months for the 500.   Then at the end of two months if you dont have any more to send I shall sell my house and lot here to pay it or sell the interest itself.   I have not positively agreed to take this one yet but rather think that I shall. Mr Grover owned this interest and would not take less than 800. for it but he had one of Mr Hunts some time ago and now he is obliged to let Mr Hunt have one of his or pay him for it so Mr Hunt chooses this share which he refused to sell me for less than 800 and he sells it to me for 700. There is one lot in it which is worth 300., he asked 500. for it alone, and

117

two others worth 300, for the two and then 1 more for the other hundred. I have looked the matter over and dont see how I can lose by the operation of this stock.

Edward P. Fitch

Feb.   28th 1857

Three days from sight pay to the order of T.L. Whitney
____   dollars   at the Hopkinton Bank,   Hopkinton Mass
          and charge the same to the acct of

Edward P. Fitch

To John A Fitch Esq
Hopkinton Mass.

This is a copy of the drafts that I sold today on you, one filled for 500. and the other for 200.   500 from Fitch & 200 from Barnard.   Mr. James Blood, I believe, has them of Whitney and he will not send them on for some little time probably.

Feb. 28, 1857

Dear Father

I am now going to answer your letters. Of course the first thing you speak of is those land warrants.

At present I think that land warrants cannot be located on the lands here and in fact I believe that only warrants issued under the law of 1855 can be located here.   At any rate after a while I can no doubt locate a Land warrant for 20 acres within ten or twelve miles of Lawrence and I will let you know in season about it if I want to do it.   The other I can locate to suit that Irishman I think but cannot do it at present.   I have a place now in view that I think would suit him and I intend to see about it by & bye.   I will write again in regard to it when I can do any thing about them.   About Kitchenman preempting another qr. sec [quarter section]: he is not exactly willing and I am not willing that he should.   That is I want him to preempt his half because I intend if possible to get not only half of the one we are on but half of the one of mine that Longfellow

118

jumped last winter.   I dont know as I shall be able to get it but I shall try for it so if I had to preempt Kitchenman for him I could not get it at any rate and the way that I expect to be sure of the 80 that I am now on is to live on it.   My not getting my title so quick was if K   preempted for me. I should not get my title for a year after he did because he has no right to convey it away before that time.

About Quindaro I have spoken before the land is high and healthy and the title good I expect.

I advised with Gov Robinson and others about investing there and looked the matter over as thoroughly as possible. I hope that I shall receive authority to draw for some more soon as there are chances to invest if I only have the money at the right time.   What is done in that time must as you say be done quickly.

You speak of Lee Claflin wanting you to go to Kentucky etc. and want to know what I think of it.   I think just this that if you leave Mass you had better come to Kansas than go to Ken. by all means.

And if you could sell your place for what it is worth and Mother is willing to come I dont know but the best thing you can do is to come.   For instance if you can get 6000. for the farm you, I believe, could put that 6000 into property here that would double in three years at the farthest. I know of a claim that I would advise you to buy now if you was here. The price is $2500.   it is a good claim has water and a little wood on it. The 2500 includes one or two horses, oxen, carts, hay, cow,s and everything.   The man wants to sell and in all probability can sell for 3000 in a month from this time.   It is a bargain and no mistake and if you was only here I should advise you by all means to buy it.   It will make a splendid farm.   I should like right well for you to sell out and come here to live.   Elijah would come in a minute I should think and whether Calvin would or not I dont know.   Then you could put a part of your money into Quindaro and when the title is perfect you could buy town property here that would pay first rate but I would not advise anyone to buy much here now as the title is not secure.

In regard to the money that Mr Fitch pays you and I invest, you can tell him that the property that I have put it in is sure I think and will pay at any rate.   It will pay for a while and then I can take it out of the city property and put it in Trust lands or something else. The best of the Delaware lands are sold that is of that part that they have given up and the next first rate investment will be the Iowa lands that belonged to the Iowa Indians or else the Kickapoo lands.   I think that I shall not lose the money that I have invested.   I bought a share in Quindaro gave 700.[$]

119

and Simpson, the investing agent, says that the three front Lots are worth 1000, and Gov. Robinson thinks they are worth ____. I can have another share for 700; 200 down and 500 in two months on my note if I buy that. At the end of two months on my note, if I do not have authority to draw on you to pay up, I shall sell either this lot & house where I now am in Lawrence or sell the share itself or some lots in it to pay. I have not certainly agreed to take it yet and dont know certainly as I shall. Mr Grover had the interest when I was at Quindaro and asked me 500. for one lot in it.

About the quarrel between the Central and National Committees, I dont know enough about it to write anything. I believe the Kansas Central Com. are the ones to blame in the matter and on account of this quarrel I shall lose 100, likely enough. That is I shall not get my scrip redeemed as I probably should have done had Arny staid [stayed]in office and his resigning was caused, viz. a newsman, by the Conduct of the Committee here.

I bought a horse today and gave 125.00 cash. It is a very good animal from all accounts or any way she is a splendid saddle horse easy gentle and smart. I went four miles on purpose to buy her three weeks ago and offered 100. but could not get her and today I bought her for 125. She is eight years old I believe is very dark brown or black rather. Kitchenman told me today that my claim was going to be jumped if I did not go onto it immediately and I am going on Monday.

Yours truly
Edward P. Fitch

March 5, 1857

Dear Father
I rec'd a letter from you yesterday dated the 16th ult. in which you say that you suppose we are looking for a busy season. So we are, but I think that when you say that I am thinking of making money more than of my friends at home you do me an injustice for I think that I have written about two pages to you there for every one that I have recd. Sarah had a letter from Appleton today saying that he was in Chicago.

I want you to be prepared to see a draft of two hundred on yourself for I expect to draw on you for that amt to buy hides with within a few days so be on the lookout for it and ask Lee Claflin how I shall direct the hides to him and whether I shall get them insured or not.

I have found a man who I expect will go into it with me.   He is a buttcher and understands hides .   He has gone to Missouri to buy cattle now and when he comes back I shall see what can be done. I may not use the money and shall not draw until I see him.

But I expect to draw in a few days for the ballance of what Barnard was to send,vis. $200.   I think I shall draw for that this week or next certain.   I bought a lot day before yesterday for 30 and sold it for 50 within an hour.

You speak of those <u>imaginary</u> town that Wheeler has laid off and say you may take two shares for E & C at 25$.   A share in those towns cannot be bought now for less than 75.$ but I believe he has laid out some more and perhaps I can get a share or two at that price for E & C.   If I can I will and draw on you to pay.   They will be valuable when they come of age and I think it would be a good investment for you to make for them.   I have been trying to get some shares in Manhattan.   There is a good place; it will not pay as fast as Quindaro but will be sure.   If I can get two shares there at $100 I want to do it.   Dont know how to pay for them but shall try and make it come round somehow or other.   I have given my note now for some property and may have to sell my lot in Lawrence to meet it yet; but I guess I shall get through.

I am very busy just now trying to build a house on my claim so as to live in it after I am (etc & etc" as you say).   Remember we shall expect you the 19th of Apr. which will be the day I suppose.

I have a terrible cold and a bad cough.   I think it is a little better now.   It has troubled me for about four weeks.   Mr Savage sold his last lot in Lawrence a day or two ago for 1000$.   I bought a lot of him about six weeks ago gave 20, sold it yesterday for 47 dollars and a half.   I have not had to sell any lot for less than I gave, and dont expect to.   If the title here was only perfect Lots would be worth much more than they now are. I gave 88 for a lot some time since and expect to make a hundred dollars on it clear but may not.

I have written to John to come out here this summer, hope he will come.   I can secure surveying enough for him to last him all summer at any rate and I think I can get him on to that Rock Road from Quindaro but dont know.

Yours as ever

Edward P   Fitch

I shall draw for two hundred soon, perhaps tomorrow   E P F

121

March 29, 1857

Dear Parents

    I rec'd by the hand of Mr Barnard yesterday the first letter I have seen from you for about six weeks and was very glad to get it as well as to see him and get those things that you sent by him. I was expecting him & Mel Claflin as I had the day before seen Wheeler and he told me they were on the way so I was not so much surprised to see them as they thot I should be . Mr B. has delivered those things all safe. The socks are rather small but I shall find them useful. I think the vests will do me or some one else some good. That nice vest will probably save my buying one for the 19 of Apr.

    I suppose you have wondered why I have not written for so long. I have been so busy that I could not get time. I am building a house on my claim and plowing getting ready to plant. We are going to plant some next week, or this rather, probably earlier than you will plant in Mass.

    Barnard & I are going to Quindaro & Delaware, Wyandotte and Leavenworth some time this week I expect. He has said nothing to me yet about that money. I shall write about it when he does. I shall pay him the two hundred if he wants it right off. I have sold my house & lot in the city and invested the money in Delaware.

    Mr Wilmarth is going there to live and I dont know but I shall go too by & bye. My house & lot cost me about $500. and I sold for $1000, $500 of which comes in the shape of a share in Delaware and the rest cash which I have used to buy more in Delaware with. I have part of an Original interest there and shall have share to sell myself. I expect my claim I shall not sell, at present at any rate, probably not at all. You speak of not depending too much on Gov R. [Robinson's] statements about Quindaro etc. I dont depend much on any body's but take all together and look at all sides. I have no condition of puting on 1000 of improvements to my share but the Com. requires it of those to whom they sell now.

    The lots in Quindaro are 26 feet front and about 130 deep and these are ten in a share, 1 first class lot alone the rest drawn two or three together.

    My lots in Quindaro are R St. 31 Corner, P St. 6 & 8, K St. 42 & 44, I St. 89 & 91, S St. 83, 85, 87. I have bot no hides yet but think that perhaps I shall soon. I talk of going in with a Mr Rease who is a butcher here and buying some, he being a judge of hides and I furnishing the money.   We will share the profits equally, he doing the work.

I have no more time to write.   Mr Webster sent a letter in which he says he supposes I have given up this being anything but a slave state. You can tell him that we have no more idea that Kansas will be a Slave state than that Mass. will be.

Yours
Edward P Fitch

April 6, 1857

From the first few sentences of this letter we may surmise that Appleton has moved from New Hampshire to Chicago.

Dear Brother

I rec'd a letter from you last December in which you said "don't write to me again until you hear from me again" and I have had no letter from you since, until three days ago when I recd one in which you say that you have written several times.   I have no time now to answer your letter as I must put this in the P.O. just this minute and I start for Quindaro in company with Mr. Barnard tomorrow morning early.   Shall be gone four or five days.   Will write from there if possible.   I dont think it possible for me to get those views taken that you spoke of.   I have been to see the only persons that I know of that could do them since our only daguerreotype artist left some days since.   I have sent to Lecompton today to see if they can be got there; if they can I will let you know by the next mail and will send them on as soon as possible but I don't expect that I can get them.   We had an artist here but he has now gone to St. Louis and will not be back for some time.   I want you should be here on 19th of April as that will be my wedding day if nothing breaks.   I mean that Sarah shall send you an invitation in this.   If she does not then consider this as an invitation.   I am getting along first rate, have sold all the property that I had in this city and have only my claim round here now.   I have some city property in Quindaro and some other places.   I sold a lot today that I paid $112.50 two weeks ago for, for $150.   That was the last I owned here.   I got $1000, for the lot and house that I owned so long ago, the house I built.

Yours
Edward P. Fitch

123

Brother

Edward insists upon my adding a few lines to your letter. Altho I told him I could say nothing to interest you. I had hoped to receive an answer to my letter before this, but will excuse you in the "multitude of business" which seems to be pressing upon you. I shall be sorry however, if your engagements are such that you cannot visit Kansas this summer. We shall always be glad to welcome you when you can find time to favor us with your presence. We should be particularly pleased to have you in Lawrence on the 19th of this month. Perhaps you can guess why if E. has not already told you. Could you not possibly come? Let us hear from you often. And even believe me.

> Yours affec.
> Sarah A. W.

APRIL 13, 1857

Since I wrote before I have in company with Mr. Barnard been to Quindaro & Delaware City. We left here on Tuesday morning and got back on Fri night. Mr. B. got quite tired riding horseback and has been rather unwell since we got back but is better now. I could not get those views that you spoke of for Mr. Gihon the only man that I could get them of left the territory some time since. I sent to Lecompton to see and found that he had left.

About the routes I don't know as I can tell much. One route is from Albany to Buffalo by the N.Y. Central R.R., then by steamboat to Detroit, if it is summer so that boats can run, or else from Albany to Niagary Falls and then by the Great Western R.R. through Canada to Detroit, from there to Chicago by the Central or Southern R.R., then down to Alton or St. Louis. Then the best route is to take the R.R. to Jefferson City and take the boat from there to Quindaro or Leavenworth or Delaware either of which are good points and all in the Territory. The R.R. has boats connected with it that run up the river. Tickets can be obtained at St. Louis of Simmons & Leadbeater through to any point on the river in the Territory for Ten dollars at this time. (Sarah bothers me so that I can't write but then as you may know I am quite willing to be bothered in that way so it is of no consequence) But after this week when she is with me all the time I don't know as I shall be able write any more so you can consider this as my farewell address.

As to when you can get the information that you wish on this subject I can not tell you.   If I could compose my mind long enough I could tell you more but it is impossible for me to sit down and write any length of time.   I am so nervous.   If you want to get the Kansas news you had better subscribe to the "Lawrence Republican" which is to be started here in a few days.   It will be a good paper.   I think I am going to take it instead of the Herald of Freedom myself and I hope it will kill the Herald out.   You want to know what I am doing with 7 or 8 hundred dollars. Well I am speculating some.   I bought a share in Quindaro which is a new town on the Missouri river which I think to be the second Chicago of the West.

I am glad that you are prospering so well as you seem to be there with 1000$ a year.   I think you ought to be able to lay up considerable and if you wish to put some of it where it will be bringing you something you had better send me two, three or four hundred dollars as the case may be and let me buy you a qr. section of land.   The Delaware Trust lands are to be sold at auction in June and I am going to attend the sales and buy a qr. sec. for myself if possible, and I expect likely that I shall buy some for other folks too.   The terms of the sale are cash.   That is if I bid off a qr. sec.   I have to pay in gold for it the same day or it will be sold over again the next day.

None of the lands will be sold at less than five dollars per acre. Wheeler has been over the tract to be sold quite extensively and has taken down minutes of the most desirable locations and I shall take advantage of his knowledge to help me about buying.   I think it would be a good thing for you to have 160 acres of land and the way for you to do if you want me to will be to authorize me to draw on you for as much as you can spare and then if I can buy a qr. sec. for that price or less I will buy in your name.

Sarah has just recd your letter of the 8th inst and will probably reply to it soon.   She says that when she gets out into the country to live she shall have more time to write.   She is just now very busyly engaged in getting ready for next Sunday.

I have no more time and must close.

Yours
Edward P. Fitch

125

April 13, 1857

Dear Mother

I have this evening recd a long letter from you and an inch or so from Father.   I have not time to write much.   I am very busy in preparing for the great events of next week and I have been very busy getting spring work done.

I intend to answer your letter at length sometime soon but I cannot now.

I have not paid Mr Barnard that money yet but shall do so soon I expect.   We went down to Quindaro together Thu. last week.   He bought a share there.   I have not bought another share and dont think that I shall.

And I think that I shall not enter much more into speculation in city property for I am now as deep as I can wade without drowning.   And I am sure I don't want to draw Father down any more than he is.   I wish he and you would come out here and live.   It is just the best country under the sun.

Elijah would be delighted to come here where he could ride my pony over these prairies at the rate of 240.   I have got a splendid pony, a pacer.   I sold the one I gave 125$ for for 127.50$ because she was not heavy enough to work much.   And have now got a pony for a saddle horse.

Your aff. son
Edward

April 20, 1857

Dear Father

If Mr Fitch of Boston has got any more money that he wants invested or any body else, or if you have got any that you want put where it will pay, I want you to send [it] on to me by the first of June and I will use it to buy some of the Trust lands that will be sold on the twenty fifth of June or there abouts.   The reason that I want it sent so long before is that it will take some time to get it changed into gold, the only currency that will pay for land.   Mr Woodbury arrived here within a few days and brought a bundle for me.   Yesterday was my wedding day so I cannot write any more.

Edward.

May 23, 1857

Dear Parents

'Firstly' we will suppose that my wife is sick--: well its a fact-- She is quite unwell, threatened with a billious fever I think.   I hope she will get along without but can't tell.   I am going to see the doctor about it this P.M.   I believe this is the first time I have written to you since I   was married.   Well the eventful 19th has passed and I am a Married Man!!! Wonderful, ant it?   It seems 'kind of curious'.   But no less strange than true.

I have no time today to enlarge upon any subject for I am very much driven with my spring work and have to stay and take care of Sarah some of the time.

I wish Mother you would tell me what present from J.J. Marshall's wife you thought would grace my wedding for I have racked my brains to find out but can remember nothing that she ever gave me.

I suppose that George Wilmarth has not been to Hopkinton yet unless he is there now but he will be there soon I expect and I want when he comes that you should send me by him a copy of Grandfather Howe's Century sermon.   The only copy I had was lent and lost and I want one much. Now be sure and do not forget this and then I want you to see if he can bring Ed Whittemore's brass horn, "B flat Barritone Tuba" or rather "Sax Horn".   Whittemore said he would send it to me if he had a chance and if George can bring it I should like to have him.   I dont know as he can and that is the reason that I want you to see to it and see whether he can bring it or not.   I want it because I now belong to a "Brass Band."   We played in front of the Morrow House last evening and are going to town to play at a Concert this evening.   I now beat the Bass Drum but should blow a Horn if I had one.

And there is one thing more important than all the rest and that is if George W. has not been vaccinated when he comes there I want you to see to haveing it done immediately on his arrival there and have him stay until it gets through being sore and the effects are entirely gone.   The small pox is quite prevalent here now and on the Missouri River too and he would be exposed to it coming up the river and it might be too late to be vaccinated when he arrives here.   It has been done once but he might take to varioloid if it is not attended to again and his folks wish it done. I was vaccinated yesterday and I shall not let my wife go to town again until she, too, for it is very dangerous so many have got it here.   Please forward the enclosed letter immediately unless he is now at Hopkinton so that it may get to him if possible before he leaves Attleboro but see that he is <u>vaccinated</u> at any rate.

I have written once or twice to you Father to have you send me a copy of the account between us so that I might know how much I owe you.   And I wish you would send it. My planting and fencing drives me hard and I have no time to write.   I have not heard from you for some time.   Wish I could.   Please remember and send the sermon.

Yours in haste
Edward P Fitch

Dear Parents,

Edward has left a small space for me to fill.   As he has told you I not very well this week but hope it proves nothing serious.   We were very glad to receive a letter from you on Weds, -1 or two since -- and some day I am going to send you as you requested a particular description of our home. I only wish you might visit it and <u>see</u> for yourselves what a pleasant place we have tho' our house is none of the largest.   I believe E. told you nothing about Mr. Barnard.   He has gone to Sumner, a town on the Missouri about 30 miles from Leavenworth, where he will probably remain most or all of this summer.   Mr. Wheeler is there and they seem to think prospects are very flattering.   If my brother has not yet reached Hop, if you will be so kind as to forward the enclosed immediately to him, you will greatly oblige your affec daughter

Sarah

We had a letter from Appleton last night.   I should judge he was quite well now tho' he says he has been sick since leaving Kansas.   The letter sounded just <u>like him.</u>

JUNE 8, 1857

From this letter we gather that Edward and Sarah moved to the cabin on the claim south of Lawrence shortly after their marriage.   Sarah's father also lived there part of the time even though his business was in downtown Lawrence.   Edward, at least during the summer, appears to be devoting all his time to farming his claim.

Dear Parents

As a married man I dont know how to write hardly and you will perceive that I have not tried much lately for I have only written one letter to you and one to Whitteman since I was married.   I have been so busy getting my house into some kind of shape and getting my plowing and planting done that writing letters has been out of the question.   I have not done planting yet nor plowing for that matter.   I have two acres of potatoes corn and garden growing and about an acre more of corn planted that is not up yet.   Sarah has been sick for two weeks and I have had her to take care of as well as attended to my work out of doors.   She is better but not entirely well.

Dear Brother Appleton
        I dont know but you will think that we have forgotten you entirely, and you have some cause I will allow for thinking so but I have been so busy since you were here   getting my house done and moveing and planting that I have written but just two letters since that time and those were on business that could not be postponed very well.
        We wondered and wondered for a long time why you did not write but at last to our great joy we recd your letter.   I got my house done so that I moved into it the first day of May and since that time I have been ploughing and planting and have not got done planting yet.   I am I dont know how much obliged to you for that money you lent me for it has enabled me by borrowing a little more to get along until now and without it I dont know how in the world I should have got along.   For the future I must trust Providence.   I have hopes of being able to get $50, that has been owed me for more than a year soon.   If I do I may be able to get a cow which I want much.
        Sarah has been sick for two week[s] so that she was not able to do anything and I had the work to do and take care of her to[o].   She is better now but not entirely well yet.   I am going to send you a couple of numbers of the Lawrence Republican.   You will see a notice of my marriage, a notice of our band and of the Chicago Magasine in it.   On them, Brown has never noticed those I gave him.   I have not yet got any one to subscribe for it.   I have not had time to try much.   I want you to send them to me regularly and I will try and pay for them by & by.
        The "Lawrence Cornet (not Brass) Band" meets twice a week to practice.   We have got so that we play a few tunes pretty well.   I blow the Bass Drum at present but think some of taking a Baritone Sax Horn soon. We played in the Church at the time Henry Wilson was here and Daniel Foster, John Pierpont, Dr. Howe of Boston & Gov Walker.   We expect to

129

play one afternoon this week for a picnic.   If we do we have 25$ and expenses paid.   We have one offer for the Fourth of July, 50% and expenses 12 miles from here.   If we do not play at Lawrence we shall I think go to Quindaro.   They are getting along finely there, building very fast.   Barnard has gone to Sumner where Claflin was when you were here and has gone into brickmaking.   He and Claflin have bought part of an original share there and think they shall make well on it.   Barnard was here about four weeks ago and I have not seen him since.   We are not having a fine shower here, the largest raindrops I ever saw.   It has now turned to hail and the stones are about as big as sparrows eggs.

Mrs. Savage that you saw, you recollect, is very low and is not expected to live from day to day.   Disease of the heart, she is very low indeed.   If you cant send that Magasine and wait till I can pay you I want you to send me at any rate the number that has your article and tell me if either of these contain one of yours and if so which is it, for I cant certainly tell that any of them are yours but I think one sounds some like you.   My family is pretty large now.   I have four besides myself and wife. Father Wilmarth and Mr & Mrs Messenger from Providence and their daughter, a girl of eleven.   I hope that I shall have more time to write in future and I will try and ____ to you at least.

E.P. Fitch

Sarah filled out Edward's last page with the following:

Dearest Brother Appleton
        After long waiting, our hearts were rejoiced by receiving a letter from you.   I was sorry indeed to learn you had been sick but hope that you are now entirely recovered.   By the way what good sister has come to you?   Judging from the initials I supposed it was not one you mentioned here.   I am glad if she is really as good as you say -- but excuse me Appleton I seriously think you need one wife vastly more than a half dozen sisters -- don't you?   I wish we could welcome you to our little prairie home.   It is very pleasant, I think tho having been quite sick for two or three weeks I have not yet got things to my mind.   I am expecting my brother George sometime the last part of this month and I wrote him to be sure and find you in Chicago if possible and presume he will do so. Write often to us, Brother, and be assured that here you are ever affectionately remembered by your sister

Sarah.

June 15, 1857

Sarah has been worse again for a day or two since and I have not had any time for a week to finish this letter and should not now only the leader of our band is sick and we dont play tonight.

My family is large and occupies a good deal of my attention. We have Mr. Messenger & wife & daughter staying here with us, also Father Wilmarth when he is here which is not all the time. My planting is not quite done yet but is very near; should have finished today only I have not seed enough and have got to go to town after some before I can finish.

That vest was a very nice one and fit me just as you left it cut. I guess I shall have to write Mrs. Marshall a letter and send her a card tho I have none to spare.

We are having pretty warm weather here now with considerable rain. I have got a lot of sweet potatoes growing; dont you wish you could have some.

Your letter (Mother) of June 3d came to hand nine days ago enclosing a draft for $50 sent by Uncle AH. I am much obliged to him for it tho at first I was of a mind to send it right straight back again. I am very much obliged to you for your kind endeavors to get money for me to invest in Delaware lands but I shall not be able to do anything that wa[y] I fear, for in the first place I cant buy less than a qr. Sec. [quarter-section] and I have got to be a squatter on that to get it for 200$, and as long as I am not I may have to give for the qr. 5 or 6 hundred dollars so you see two or three hundred will do me but little good. Then again that hundred which Doctor Howe lends me as it is sent in draft will not yield me cash over 98 and perhaps only 96 dollars; (I rec'd a letter tonight from Appleton enclosing 50$ in draft etc.) so your labor will not do me much good I am afraid. I should like to know what "account of Kansas life" you had to read to which all my friends "listened breathlessly"? I am very sorry that you did not have Sarah's daguerreotype to show to the folks and to see yourself but I hope you will see it before you see this, but if George comes there after you get this, if you have got any good apples or any of any kind send me two or three by him if possible.

I don't know as I exactly understand about the hundred dollars that I have recd the drafts for. I understand it in this way. I am to use the money as I please and pay it back to the Doctor when I can. If that is not so, if I am expected to put it in any particular place, then I dont want it. Write immediately and explain a little more fully. As to giving a note dated the first of June, it is now the middle of the month and I only have the drafts and it will cost from 5 to 7 percent to get the drafts changed to gold and if I buy land I must have gold.   The money sent to me and Mr. Nute I acknowledged some time last winter Jan I think.   I have bot <u>no</u> land for E & C, had no orders to do so unless I could get it at a certain price which I was unable to do.   I have a share in Florence which I will sell them for $50.   Wheeler says it is worth 100$ now.   I bot a share in Moneka for $50; have drawn the best lot in town worth 150$ now and there are four other lots in the share.   That share in Florence consists of nine lots.   I have sent you some copies of the Republican lately.   See the difference in the remarks of that paper and the H of F [Herald of Freedom] about Gov. Walker's Inaugural.   I think that the subscription list of the Herald will be shortened here where it is known and folks will take the Republican.

Write the particulars about that money immediately for I _____ about it as I shall not use it till I hear.

Your aff. Son
Edward

June 23, 1857

Dear Brother

Your letter of June 15th has just come to hand today and I have "sit up" (for to go answer it.)

I rec'd a sheet of paper with two or three lines written across it and your name at the bottom <u>four days ago</u> and enclosing a Certificate of Deposit on Chicago for $50.00 on some insurance Co I think.   I dont know for I sold the Cert yesterday and got the money.   I find by refering to your letter which enclosed the draft that you say draw on you for 50, at the Marine Bank, Chicago and invest for me.   Well there is no way of investing so small a sum as that that I know of now so that it will pay. There is nothing going on here <u>now</u> in the way of speculation except the land sales and here nothing can be done without some hundreds of dollars at any rate.

The mail before I rec'd your letter enclosing _____ I rec'd one from Father enclosing a draft for $50 on Boston which he said was sent me by Dr. Howe and that he would send word to you to send me the $50 that you was going to send him and I was to send him my note for $100.00 so when I saw the fifty in your letter I took that it be the other fifty of that hundred but I dont understand from Fathers letter just what I am to do with the money and so I dont know but I shall send back the hundred dollars without using it at all instead of my note.

I have written to Father for instructions in regard to it.

And now tonight I received your letter _____ and I don't understand what it means for you say that you have written two or three letters since you was here and recd none.   Now we have rec'd two (one of eight lines) and we both have answered the first one.

Then you want me to send you a recpt for $51.50 which I have never recd.   I recd $50 from you for which I will give you a recpt and also give my note to Dr. Howe that is if I keep it.   You say I have not _____ and if I have and that is what you want it for how am I to get back my $1.75 that I paid for <u>express on those magazines</u> _____.

You say further "please tell me about my stage fare as far as Leavenworth and from Quindaro as I left that matter in your hands." Preposterous!   What matter did you leave in my hands?   And what do I know about your fare to Leavenworth or Quindaro except that Father Wilmarth paid your fare to Leavenworth and you paid him?   And what do you want to know about it?   As to leaving anything about it in my hands, I know nothing about it.   If you will explain so that I can understand I will try and explain what you want to know!

Sarah has been sick for more than a month so that she has not been able to be up much of the time and I have had so much to do and to take care of here so that I have had no time to write letters, and have only written to you and one or two brief business letters home since I was married.   I have finished planting but have not got my fence made yet. Mrs. Savage our next neighbor is dead you know she was quite unwell when you was here.   She died last Wed. just ten years to a day and almost at the very hour that she was married.

There was a young man buried under arms at Lawrence on Sat last and <u>we "the Band"</u> played at the funeral; performed Danl. Websters Funeral March.   Major Hoyt
 who was murdered last August just before the battle at Fort Saunders will be buried tomorrow with military honors.   I dont know yet whether we shall play or not.   We don't yet know whether we shall play for some celebration on the Fourth or give a concert in the eve here.   If we play at any celebration it will be at Bloomington probably.

I want you to send me that Magazine regularly and I will pay you when I am able if you can't do that send me the no. that has your account of Kansas in it at any rate.

Yours for information
Edward P. Fitch

PS.   Sarah tells me to give her love to you and tell you that she has answered your letter and she hopes you will get it.   She is not able to write herself or she would at least fill the sheet.
Edward

I shall try and get this into the return mail if possible so that it may reach you without delay. -- E.

July 21, 1857

Dear Brother

George arrived here a week ago last Fri. four days from Chicago, and he says you are raving about that money affair.   I have not rec'd but one letter about the money tho he says you wrote two and the one letter that I did get no one could understand for there was but one short sentence in it and it spoke of four 50$ or of sending $50 in four ways while only one $50 ever came to me.   I have sent my note to Dr. Howe for $100, 50 of which you sent and the other 50 Father sent.   You say that I have paid $1.75 on the Mag. call it so from now on toward the magazines. Well in the first place I have not recd any magazines yet except those that you gave me. And I think that 1.75 will pay well for these two without paying 1.50 more for which you want me to give you a recpt for and what it means I don't know.

I wish you would write and explain yourself in plain English for I can't understand anything else.

Gov. Walker is here at Lawrence with 400 troops to keep us from organizing a city government.

Hurrah for the Pacificator!!!!!

Shannon & Woodson are surpassed!!

I am likely to have bad luck this year.   The tobacco worms are destroying my potatoes and the grasshoppers my beans and this dry weather my corn.

Yours till we have some rain.
Edward P. Fitch

I have not written much because I did not know as you would be at Chicago during vacation.

Aug. 9, 1857

Dear Parents,

     It is so long since I have heard any thing from you that I domt know whether you are dead or alive hardly.　I have not had a letter since George came from there and that was more than a month ago.　I suppose that you are deep in the meadows haying now, and almost through at that. How is hay this year with you?　We have none here except on the bottoms.　It has been so dry that grass nor any thing else could not grow but within a week we have had three fine rains and things look more promising.　I have cut a little hay but shall not be able to get enough from my claim.　I am afraid to keep my horse and cow this winter.　I dont know as I told you I had a cow but I have　and she has a calf about five or six or seven days old.　We have milk enough to use but do not make any butter, indeed I hardly know what butter is for I have had only three pounds since I was married and that I got when Mrs Messenger was here. I have got so that I dont care much about it thanks to your making me do without so much when I was small.　I gave 25 dollars for my cow and calf. There would be considerable hay on my claim only for the fact that there have a large number of cattle ranged here all summer so that in the place where two years ago at this time the grass was as high as my head there is now not enough to pay for cutting.　The cattle have thinned it out so much and eat it off.　Hay on the bottoms where the cattle do not range much is very good and folks that own bottom claims are selling the grass at from 1.00 to 2.00 per acre.　Hay will be very high next winter and spring.　There are a good many mowing machines used here now.

     The 2nd Vol of the Herald of F. [Freedom] closed with the last weeks no. and I shall not renew my subscription.　I dont think _____ has sold out to Gov Walker.　I take the Lawrence Republican which is by far the best paper in the Territory.　We had a State Election last Mon and voted on the Ratification of the Topeka Constitution.　The Constitution got more votes in this district and Quindaro, Wyandotte and Leavenworth than were polled for Delegates to the Lecompton Const. Convention in the whole territory that looks almost like a Free State Majority.

     You will see in the H of F. this last week when Brown speaks of the Apportionment for the 2nd Territorial Legislature he dont dare to say much against it till he sees how his master Gov. W. [Walker] will regard it. It is the most damning piece of villany ever perpetrated by any men or set of men.　It is fixed so as to give Missourians a chance to carry the Election much easier than they did on the memorable 30th of March

1855.   The Lawrence Republican exposes the inequity of it in its full extent and handles the matter very ably indeed.   The Editor of it, T.D. Thacher, is a first rate man, has been or was going to study for the ministry, belongs to our Church and is Assistant Supt. in our Sabbath School.   I had no black ink and was obliged to take red.

AUG. 16, 1857

Where is Appleton?   I have heard nothing of him since George saw him in Chicago and, John, do you know anything of him?   I have written once or twice to ask Father how the money acct stands between him and myself but I dont see as it does any good to ask questions for I get no answers.   I have been breaking prairie on my place for the past week and expect to for a week or more to come.   We are having plenty of rain now and things begin to look first rate.   I had the first water melon from my garden today. Last year we had them a fortnight earlier than this

AUG. 17, 1857

My Dear Mother
          Edward has left this page for me to finish.   He is so busy now that he hardly finds time to write a word.   He & my brother are now out busily at work 'breaking' up the prairie just west of the house.   I sometimes fear his friends will think that some way or other, I am accountable for his negligence in writing since he was married -- but it is not so.   I believe he has been too busy to find spare time this summer -- & perhaps you may know how hard it is when one has got a little out of the way of writing, to begin.   We are very well now -- I am so well as ever. Some time since I wrote you quite a long letter - and as we have received no answers -- fear you have not received it.   Please write as often as you can find time -- for we wish to know often of the welfare of our dear friends at home.   If you only lived within half a mile this afternoon I would come in to sit with you awhile -- in spite of dark clouds & wet grass and would chat of a thousand & one things that cannot be put on paper. I feel just like it -- but with so great a distance between us -- I must be content with paper & pen talkings I suppose.   Love to all-- Write soon & often -- & accept much love from your Daughter

Aug. 23, 1857

If you have got a paper that has got the new apportionment for Senators and Reps in Mass. I wish you would send me a copy as I want to see how it is done.   E.

Dear Parents

      I put a letter in the office for you on last Mon and found one from you at the same time which seems to need some answer.   I have been plowing all the week and today am about sick so that I have not been to meeting.   We are having a fine rain this afternoon.   I expect to go to work for Mr Savage tomorrow and work for him a week or two helping him get in his wheat.   I dont think I shall sow any wheat this year but plant all my land with corn next spring.   We regret very much that George did not stay there longer as he will not have such another opportunity for a long time.

      There seems to be one item of news (not good) that I have failed to communicate and that is the Death of Mrs Savage.   She died the 17 day of June, just ten years from the day she was married and almost to the hour for she was married after dinner about one Oclock and she died about twelve (noon).   I sent a letter to you that same day but it was all written in the forenoon before I knew she was dead.   She was one of the best women that I ever knew and we miss her very much.   Mr S. feels very sad indeed.   If you would write him a note of sympathy I think he would feel grateful.   He thinks of going East to Vermont in about a month.   His Father & Mother are staying there keeping house for him now.   If he goes East he intends to carry his little girl and leave her there with her Aunt.   I think you are brave to talk of wanting a place in the shed for your stove when you have a whole house full of rooms that you have not had a fire in.   I should be rich if I had two rooms.   All the place we have is one room 12 x 16 ft.   We have moved the table out of doors once or twice to eat but as there is not a tree within two miles it is not very pleasant.   The heat is great enough here and we want a place for the stove very much but I am not rich enough to have one yet.

      I am very glad to hear of those ministers that are coming out here and I hope we shall find one that will do for us for we need one very much. Unitarianism is flourishing here but that about Mrs. Nute I dont know to be true and guess it is not.   In regard to Gen. Pomeroy, he has lost the confidence of many of the people here.   He lost it from the time when on the 21st of May he told Sheriff Jones where the Cannon was and not content with that he went and hauled it out of its place of concealment with his own hands.

About the 20,000 I cant tell.   I have heard from pretty good authority that he has been unable to account for some of the funds placed in his hands.   The fact is he is careless about his account and pays out money without taking rec'pts and dont know where it goes.

About that Land Warrant I have acknowledged the rec'pt of it as much as three times.   I am sure, but it will do me no good for I can not use it for a long time unless I use it on my claim in which case it is worth to me $120. being what I can get one just like it for.   I shall be able to use it by & bye after we have preempted our land here.

I wish you would dry a lot of berries and send me some if you have a chance.   They would be a treat to me and a cheese too. You will have a chance to send them
some time no doubt.   I want to hear from Appleton as I have not since the first of July, and John I have heard nothing of since I was married.   I wish the boys would write to me and tell me the news for I have not heard any news from Hopkinton since George came.   Is Dean Morse living? If you see him Remember me to him.   Is Father Supt. of the Sunday School now?   How is Georgy?   and does he go to school?

Your aff Son
Edward

Aug. 24, 1857

Dear Mother

As usual, Edward has left his letter for me to finish.   Your good, long letter came to us last week just as we put ours to you in the office.   I cannot tell you how glad we are to hear from you -- and I hope you will let no opportunity for writing us pass unimproved.   I only wished you lived within such a distance that we might reasonably expect a visit from you at least, semi-occasionally.   Then you could see how we live -- what a little house we have -- but no description could make you see it as it is.   As E. has said we have but one room, with the chamber over it of the same size--Large enough for two beds -- with the sundry trunks, boxes, chests, -- etc. in which we dispose our clothing, bedding, etc.-- closets & bureaus are things yet to be -- When I look back sometimes to the days at the East, & think how I used sometimes to complain of "want of room" -- that I then almost had a palace -- Why such contrivances as we resort to put things out of the way, & yet to have all look neat & orderly, & be convenient -- I think my "bump of Calculation" must have increased considerably since I came to Kansas.   At least it is sufficiently exercised. I shall feel, if ever I do have a good sized house, as tho I could <u>appreciate</u> it, I shall have to finish very abruptly -- for Mr. Savage is waiting to take our letter to town.   Please write often.   Love to all.

From you aff. Daughter
Sarah

September 6, 1857

Dear Brother

A few weeks ago a young man by the name of Roy formerly of Chicago, died here and was buried by the 'Stubbs', the 'Lawrence Cornet Band' ("of which I am one") furnishing the music for the occasion. Today his brother the Rev. Mr. Roy, Pastor of the Plymouth Church Chicago preached here.   I had an introduction to him and asked him if he knew you.   He said he did not personally but had heard of you.   I wanted to know if you still had your school, as I had heard you were turned off. He said that you were turned out but had been restored which I was very glad to hear.   Now why won't I get those magazines?   I have only had those numbers that you gave me.   You said you would send it to me a year and I want it.   I have not found any one or but one that wanted to take it but there are a number that will buy it every month.   How much can Father Wilmarth have them for if he takes ten or a doz. copies every month?   He wants to know right off so I want you to write to me and tell me.   Send me mine and send me six copies of the last number right off and tell me how much they will be.

Your[s]
Edward

My Dear Brother

Edward says I must write some to you in this letter & yet he hurries me so that I can hardly collect my thoughts enough to know what I want to say to you.   Why do you not write to us -- at least "once in an age"?   We have written & written & not one word have we heard from

139

you for I cannot tell how long a time.   We suppose you have been spending your vacation as pleasantly as possible in jaunting round to some new part of the country -- but conclude you must have returned to Chicago by this time & will soon commence your school again.   Please write as soon as you can find time for indeed we would love to hear from our brother often.   The band with which Edward is connected are to give a concert Thursday Eve.   They play very well, <u>So every one says</u>.   E. is going over to town to practice this afternoon.   George is going to town, too, so I shall be entirely alone for a few hours.   <u>We are as happy as can be</u> -- I wish you would make us a visit in our little home.   Wouldn't you like to have some of <u>my butter</u>?   I am getting initiated into all the mysteries of a "farmers wife" I never made any butter before in my life but <u>it is good sometimes</u> –

Love from Sister Sarah

E. says I must tell you that the Free State men are to vote at the October election -- some fear trouble -- but I fervently hope not.

SEPT. 14, 1857

Dear Parents

No one can fully realize the blessing of a 'home' unless they have been deprived of one for some time, and that I have been.   I drifted about, at the mercy of every wind that blew for more than two years with no home but now I can sit down by my own fireside under my own vine and fig tree with none to molest and make afraid.

How pleasant it is to sit down with your wife 'around you' as 'Paddy surrounded the Woodchuck' and feel perfectly at home, contented, and happy, this I can do and when the wind blows and it rains as it does tonight and all out doors is dark and dreary we can sit round our table a[s] happy as kings.

I don't hardly know when we last wrote to you but it was long since we heard from you or it is long now.   Yesterday morning Mr. Savage started for the East taking his little girl with him.   He intends to leave her there, he expects to be gone between two & three months, and I have a kind of oversight of his farm while he is gone so I have two farms on my hands now.   I shall have about 40 acres of corn to help cut and see to beside the cattle and all other thing[s] and I have got my house to lath and plaster to get ready for winter.

The Band gave a Concert last Thursday night at the Cong'l Church; had a good audience out and had a very good time.   Did not make quite so much as we hoped to but did well considering it is a new country and we have not practiced long.   I heard the best sermon that I have heard since I left Hop[kinton] last Sunday 'week' preached by Rev. Mr. Roy, of Chicago, Pastor of the Plymouth Church, on the Suffering of Christ from the text "Perfect thru Suffering", Heb 2nd 10th.   It was communion day.

Sarah has commenced making butter but the detail I will leave to her more ready pen to enumerate.

Your ever Aff son   EPF

Sept. 17, 1857

Dear Parents

I sometimes think you will hardly thank Edward for leaving in every letter a space to be filled by an unfamiliar hand -- but I will try to make my scrap of a letter as interesting as possible to you.   I see E. has laid out a subject for me -- in my experience in <u>butter</u> - making.   This cannot as you may think be very extended as my very first experiment was made some three weeks since -- I presume I am about as awkward as one of your "green Irish girls."   E. knows a good deal more about it than I do -- but I am determined to learn to make <u>good butter</u>   -- I only wish I had some good mother here to <u>show</u> me just once -- Perhaps however a few (or good <u>many</u>) failures may teach me better than anyone could. Someday when I see you I must tell you of my first attempt when I churned 1/2 <u>a teacup</u> of butter -- We have but one cow but we think her an excellent one -- Our cow & calf -- with a pig - pony - six hens & a cat - comprise our stock - Quite an establishment.   Don't you think so?

However, I believe in a "little farm well-tilled" *   or a few things well taken care of - as better than more when we cannot afford it - Isn't it so? - Next week I expect our house will be plastered.   E. has been to town today after laths, etc. and is very tired tonight & has gone to bed - as have also George & Mr. Muzzy - all seem to be asleep - so I am keeping vigil all alone - But it is quite late so I suppose I ought to stop & follow their example.   We have not heard from you for a long time - hope we may have a letter soon - Love to all - from your Aff. daughter.   S. F.

Sept. 27, 1857

Dear Brother

  I am glad to find that you are still alive, as I suppose, having rec'd a few pages of the Chicago Mag with your autograph, the first atom of news I have had from you since George was there in July, though Sarah and I have written <u>twice</u> certainly and I think more times to you since that time. I have never seen any more of those magazines but I want some and if you have not sent any I want you to send immediately. First, one copy of all the No's from March to Sept. A lady told Sarah today that she wanted it for a year beginning with the first number. She will probably pay me when she gets the two that you gave me, then I want the May, June, July, August & Sept. for a man that wants them a year but is only willing to take them and pay for them as fast as they come. Then I want six copies of the Sept. No. and I want to know at what price they will be sent to Mr. Wilmarth if he takes six or eight ever[y] month to sell, I want (of the March No 1 copy

(...... April - 1 -
(...... May   - 3 copies
(...... June - 3 .....
(...... July - 3 .....
(...... Aug - 3 .....
(...... Sept - <u>9 .....</u>

       23 copies

I want these sent to my address through the Post Office as that is much the cheaper way of getting them here. If you have sent some _____ let them go as far as they will toward filling this order and send on the rest right off. You are loseing subscribers here because I have not had more of the numbers before this. Send all these to me and I will tell you how to direct the next ones before the Oct. number comes out. Can you not get them by taking so many at a low rate? As they are for me to sell most of them? if I sell at .25, as I must I can't give that. It is an order from the trade realy as they go into Father Wilmarths Book store If in order to be a Trade order it must have more, make it six copies of every number since April or even more if it must be rather than not have them and want them right [now] for I have been putting off those that signed for them by saying that I have sent for them as I have twice before and every time I go to town somebody is asking if those magazines have come yet. Let me hear from <u>you immediately so as to know what to depend on</u>.

I am very busy fixing my house up for winter, cutting and building on an addition at the west end.   I am drove to death.   I have got about 40 acres of corn to cut with George and 'Grandpa' Savage to help me and it is all fit to cut now and my house not done yet.

Rev. M. Roy preached for us again today and he starts for Chi. tomorrow.   If you ever see him speak to him for my sake.   He says he wrote the article published in the first no of the mag. on Lake Superior and hopes you will yet write one on Kansas.   Perhaps I could get some illustrations of Lawrence at least now, as our daguerreotype artist has now returned to the city.   Mr. Roy is very much pleased with Kansas. My health is very good as so is Sarah's at present.   Do you know any thing of John now?   I have not heard from him since last spring or winter.

Write soon.
Your aff. Brother Edward P. Fitch

I wrote so much of this _____ intended to send it but could get no chance till four days after when I recd your letter of the same date, Also Sarah recd one at the same time.   They are not at hand now so I cannot reply in detail.   You say the Chicago Mag has "gone up".   If it ever comes down again, send me some copies.   I have been hard at work the last two weeks and have been all in a heap all the time.   We have had our carpet up three weeks.   We have got the room lathed and plastered but the closet nor addition are not built yet.   We have got more than half of our corn out now and I have some faint hopes that we shall get it all done before frost comes but I don't know certain.

The Election of last Mon. & Tue passed off quietly.   The probability is that the Free State men have a maj. in the Legislature.

That Miss Tappan that you saw at Rev. Mr. Lum's is to be married this week Tues. night and Sarah says I must go to the wedding-----.

Oct. 18, 1857

I still have faith to believe that you will get this some time or other if I keep on writing.   I don't know now where your letter is so cant answer but we had our first frost here on the night of the 14 inst.   My corn was all cut.   On the night of the 13 Sarah and I went to a wedding that Miss Tappan was married to Mr Hanscom.

143

Oct. 4, 1857

Dear Father

You are apprised by the papers ere this that the Free State men of Kansas have agreed to vote at the Territorial Election tomorrow. I think as I always have that it was impolitic to vote at all but now that the party is going into the Election I am bound to vote at any rate, if possible. We have got to go to Lecompton to vote and all the F.S. [Free State] men are going in a body from this part of the district. From here we have got to start at daylight. We all go armed as it is feared that there may be disturbances, but I hope not. The Gov has issued a Proclamation in regard to this Election which is the meanest concoction of lies and black-guardism ever put forth by any man or set of men. I am going to send you a copy of The Republican with remarks on it. Brown, you see, licks the spittle off of Walkers fingers and dont dare to say much about it. It is said the Missourians are coming in, in some places now to vote. If it is so there will be some fighting, I think, but it is getting late and I have to be up before daylight to get started. I go with two horses and any three or four beside myself.

Oct. 11, 1857

Sun Oct 11th The Election has passed and probably the Free State men are victorious. They are if the returns shall be taken as they are and not tampered with but I am a little afraid yet.

I have been just so busy as it was possible for me to be cutting corn for the last ten days and we are not near through yet. We have about twelve or fifteen acres more to cut which will take four or five days.

We have had no frost yet. If it holds off a few days more we shall get all the corn cut before we have any which is a great object. I have got my room plastered so that it looks better and I hope will be warm this winter. I expect to be drove up about two or three weeks more and then I hope to have a little more leisure. How does your sugar cane grow? Mine did well what I planted. I shall try and have more next year. I gave away a large part of the seed you sent to me because I had no place to plant it. I have not heard a word from you since I dont know when. I believe it was the first of Aug. when Mr Morse was there. That I think is the last letter I have had. That's more than two months. Wed I was at work when a man came to the field and introduced himself as Mr Morse.

144

Said he saw you and he made me quite a call but did not bring his wife with him.   He came again next morning and got my horse and is gone with him some two hundred miles more or less to see where to locate. He has gone to Emporia first.   He will be gone nearly a week.   I suppose meanwhile I must ride on foot.   Keep a horse and walk!!   I hope you have got the letter that I sent in haste two weeks ago and you will have before this sent those things that I wished for, but if by any means Barnard did not or could not bring them I will provide another way for them to come and if you have not been to Attleboro after those things Sarah will send a note in this which you can forward to Mrs French and she will send the things by Express as you may direct her to in a note which you can write yourself to her.   I have just this summer thot that those things were only mentioned in a confidential note to Mother but I'll bet she told you so it is all the same.

I want you to get the things together that I wanted and whatever else you have a mind to send and send them by Express to Mr J. E. Hood, Republican Office Springfield Mass. and at the same time send a note to him stating that you send the things and that they are for Mr Joseph Savage to take with him to Kansas for me.   Mr Savage is brother to Mr Hoods wife.   I want you to put the things in a box, not a barrel, because he cannot bring a barrel with him as they do not allow them to go as baggage, a boot box is as good as any thing I think.   Have it hooped with iron as Appleton hooped the one I brought with me.   You can get a small one it should not when full weigh more than 50 pounds.   If Aunt Clark or any body else has an Overcoat to give me as good as the one she (I think) gave me when I was East I should like it.   That one was stolen.   The box must be at Springfield by the first of Nov. certain or Mr Savage will start for Kansas without it, which would be a serious disadvantage to me.   I have delayed writing this too long altogether since I wrote the others but it cant be helped now.   Please send on what I want just as soon as possible.

Oct. 14, 1857

Mr Morse has come back today with my horse.   I met his wife at a wedding last night and was very much pleased with her.   I think she is a very nice woman indeed.

I have just sent a letter to Mr Savage telling him to send a line to you stating when he will start from Springfield.   I want you to be sure and have the box there in season for him to take.   Be sure.

Oct. 18, 1857

Dear Parents

Your letters of various dates from Sept 27 to Oct 4th came to hand last night after I had pretty much given up all hope of hearing from you again and I am very glad to hear from you and know that you got my letter. (Do you sell milk yet?) Well I have been to two weddings in my life. The <u>first was my own</u> and this other I attended last Tues night. Had a very pleasant time indeed. Two of my intimate friends, members of the Church here, they were married at Mr. Lums where the bride lived, Mr. Lum having had her in his family for quite a number of years.

Mr Grover one of my next neighbors was married on the same evening. His claim is N.W. from mine. The reason why I wanted to know how much I owed Father was so that I could know how I stood with the world when I was married. I am very thankful to you Mother for taking time to pick and dry those berries for me. I hope I shall get them sometime. We had our first frost here the 15 inst. All our corn was cut before that so now I have got through with my hardest drive for this fall and shall be a little more at leisure. I have enough to do to keep me at it all the time but it will not drive quite so much as it has for some time past. I have written again to Mr. Savage about taking that box and he will probably write to you. If by any means he fails to bring it, send it by Mr. Johnson and tell him to send me word when he gets to Sumner and I will find some way to get it down here. And if he carries it send me the dimensions of the box. I should like a pr. of good boots but as you have not my measure you could not well get them. Those that I brot with me are pretty much gone. I had a letter from Appleton just as he was recovering from his sickness.

As to John, I wish he was settled somewhere.

Sumner may be a good place, think likely it is. I am going up there one of these days to see the Hopkinton men that there is there. Why did you not write to me, when Barnard first got back, that he was there. It would have done me a great deal of good. I think I shall see to the locating of that warrant soon. I shall take a trip to Mo. for the purpose on horseback. I shall get Wheeler to go with me if possible.

Your Edward

Sarah can fill this tomorrow before I go to the office.

Oct. 19, 1857

My Dear Mother -

     I am going to use the few moments before my dinner will be ready to put on the table in filling out this sheet to you.   It is quite late - about one o'clock - but E. has been gone all the morning in search of some <u>truant hogs</u> of our neighbor Mr. Savage - and I delayed preparations for dinner hoping to have all warm for him when he should return - but all is nearly ready and he is not yet in sight.   It is no easy matter to find such creatures on these wide prairies - and if they get in the bushes of the 'bottom' I do not see how they can be found.   Your long looked for letter arrived Saturday eve.   We had feared some letter had been miscarried, so long a time had passed with no word from home - but your time must be fully employed.   I only wonder where you find time to attend to so many things - and by the way, I must thank you for your kindness in preparing those berries - You were too kind to do it all yourself - and if we receive them, I can assure you, they will seem all the nicer for thinking how much pains you took to gather them for us.

     In your last letter before, you spoke of Rev. Mr. Morse who was to come here.

The next day after he arrived, he inquired his way here.   (he was stopping with one of our neighbors, it seems - a relative of his wife) and staid quite a little time.   He seems a very pleasant man.   The next day, he came to get E's pony, to go on an exploring tour in the south part of the Territory. On the Sabbath (last Sabbath) I was introduced to Mrs. Morse - and liked her much.   And Tuesday eve. spent at Mr. Lum's where she was also present and became very much interested in her.   We found we had many mutual acquaintances and this made us feel at once like old friends. Wednesday Mr. M. returned about noon   - took dinner with us - and then went to make arrangements for his immediate removal to Emporia. I have not since heard from them but presume they have gone by this time, as he was in some haste to return that he might be making preparations for <u>winter living</u>.   He has procured a claim near the town - & there recovered from his sickness - I hope he will spend his vacation with us next time - But my paper warns me to stop - and <u>dinner</u> needs attention.   Write often as possible.

              Yours as ever   S.F.

Oct. 22, 1857

Dear Brother

  I am going to commence one more letter to you hoping that you will sometime or other get it. I have been driven to death with work all the fall until now. I have a little more leisure and the evenings growing longer so that I hope to have more time to write to you and others too. I don't have a letter oftener than about once a month now from all my correspondents together. I wrote thus far and then could not find the letter you wrote so stopped till now Oct. 28th. I have your letter and will try and reply to it. The first thing seems to be in regard to John. Well!! I don't know what to say about him. Sumner is quite a place and he might do well there. Wheeler is there and he may help him along. I don't know of any thing that he could do here at present or at Quindaro. As to the Shawnee Reserve it is now pretty much all taken at this end, that is the good claims, and down below the Missourians have marked every qr almost. Rather a poor chance for a claim there. I have my Quindaro share yet, It is low now.

  In regard to the money you say that "these are two explanations of the money affair.: Well if it is I have never seen the other and can not fully understand this.

  1st you sent me 50$ well! I am willing to give you a recpt for that, but not for 51   or 55 till I know what for.

  2 You sent me 50 in Check. I must sell the check to get the money get 49   dollars then send you a recpt for 51. "Nix funderstand"

  However I must of course call it 50 and rec[eip]t accordingly. I sent a note to Uncle Dr for one hundred dollars as he wished me to. You say had I looked after business I might have got 3 dollars for your pass to Leavenworth. Perhaps I might if I had had the 'pass' but I never saw any pass. Your fare was paid and that is the last I ever knew about it. When I read the letter George said that you said something to him about a pass, but <u>what</u>, he did not know and he said he had never thot of it since you told him, till I read something about it in the letter so I don't understand how you expect me to get 3 dollars for a pass that I never had or saw. Just so about Quindaro? What had I to do with your fare. I did not see the stage driver that you came with and don't know him now from Adam. If you will explain how I was to get the money I should like it.

148

Again you say I could "take the 1.75 that I paid <u>for the nag's from the 30$ and the $1.50 (or near that) for interest of the Dr note also</u> and then you would owe me 27"

Well really I cannot understand that or what I have to do with the interest on that note.   Why should I pay you any such thing, but if you will just write out and send me just such a recpt as you want me to sign, I will sign it and send it right back to you by return mail, sooner than I have sent this.

Sarah was going to answer your letter to her but she was awake a good deal last night and is so sleepy to-night that she cannot write and has gone to bed.   She will write in a few days so look out for it.

Is there any prospects of the Chicago Magazine being started again?   If so, send me one.

How is Woodard 2nd?   And the Adams' boys?   Gustavus wife especially.   Is Ed Loring in Chicago?

Your[s] Edward

Nov. 8, 1857

Dear Brother

I rec'd a letter from you day before yesterday dated the 28 ult and before this you have probably heard from me as at any rate I sent a long letter to you.

In reply to the question about the cash I must say that I cannot raise any.   It would be utterly impossible for me to raise 30$ without selling some property at a great sacrafice.   I have a share in Moneka that cost me 50$ that J.B. Wood, Treas. of the Com. considers worth 150 and it is, when money is easy, and now I am only offered 25$ for it by Mr. Wood but he don't want me to sell it even to him.   I am worth nothing except what is in land and that I cannot realize any thing from at present.   You might as well try to sell Father land (down East) as to sell at any decent prices now.

If it had not been for your kind loan in the spring I should have been troubled to finish my house and I have not had twenty dollars this summer except that I borrowed.

I am sorry that I cannot return you what you want now, but it seems impossible for me to do so.

149

You say I intend to find a place for John in the Com etc.   I read your letter to <u>John</u> and he says he is well enough off for this winter now.

He arrived here Thurs, the day before your letter, from Sumner, K.T. where he had been for a fortnight with the rest of the Hopkinton folks.   He intends to go back there in a day or two and expects to run a kind of shingle machine this winter or if he does not do that he will chop wood.   Wheeler & he are talking of putting up a shingle machine. Wheeler finds the money & John does the work.   I guess he will do pretty well there.   I talk some of going up to Sumner with him when he goes.   I don't know as I shall

Our Election has gone well enough considering we should have carried every county had it not been for fraud.   The ProSlavers, Not Dems, carried Leavenworth by stupendous frauds.   Parrot is elected and has got in _____.

There was a mass meeting at Lecompton to sustain Gov. Walker in his course in throwing out the fraudulent returns from Johnson & McGee counties.   And the Band was hired to go.   We had a first rate time and a first rate supper when we got back.   That was a week ago yesterday.

Sarah sends love.

Edward

Nov. 11, 1857

Dear Mother

Three of your children are sitting around [our] only table writing, some to you some not; John arrived here last Thursday P.M. walked right in onto me before I had time to think, so he has been here a week.   He had been at Sumner about two weeks before coming here and now is helping me dig potatoes and when I get them dug I am going back to Sumner with him.   I expect it will be almost like going to Hopkinton to go there.   There were so many Hopkintonians there.

I recd a letter from you a week ago tonight saying that Uncle Dr. was sick etc.   The letter is mislaid and cannot be found just now so I cannot answer in detail but I dont remember that there was a thing of very great importance that needed any particular answer.

I am glad to hear the news you speak of from Weymouth except Dr.'s sickness.   Where is Florinda now?   I am some what busy digging potatoes.   I shall have, I expect between 30 & 40 bush[els] that will keep me in eatery [for] some time.   We eat a great many, however, for we have nothing else to eat.   What is the reason that the boys dont write to me?   I dont know any thing that is going on at home any more than a dead man hardly.   They might write to me just as well as not but I dont have much time to write to them.   Tell George that I guess I can find him land enough on my claim to build his brick house on.

John will probably stay at Sumner this winter at any rate.   He has altered some since I last saw him (the day he was twenty one).   He is more manly but not very steady yet, but he has learned something of life in the West within the last year, much that he would not have learned in Hopkinton in a life time, but he cant tell how he is to get along or what he will do yet.   Father asked me a while ago, <u>now</u> I say buy a share in Sumner, and have it fixed for him to see to and let him keep it by staying there.   He thinks Sumner is "bound to shine."   I dont see but what it <u>may</u>.   He thinks some of getting a claim now somewhere around here.

We had a little snow here last Sunday & a little one yesterday & today and today it has rained so that we have not dug any potatoes.

I wrote to Mr Webster some time since, two months at least, about getting a letter from the Church there.   Is he the man to write to for that purpose?   Three of those four ministers have got here and the fourth Mr Cordley is expected to stop here when he comes.   Mr Parker, one of them, preached here last Sat.   I did not go to meeting it was so cold. There were but few out.

John tells me that Uncle William is dead, the first time I have heard of it.   Have you heard from Mr Savage?   If you have not I dont know how you can send that box as Mr Johnson is now at Sumner.   I dont know as I can tell you the precise time that you made me that promise that I spoke of, but I know you did and also promised me some other things, among which were a pair of Fire irons, which you afterward gave away to someone else and I reminded you of it at the time.   But it is rather strange that you do not hear from Mrs French for the things there were not hers but belonged to Sarah and she has no right to keep them back.

Tell the boys to write and I will try and write to them some of these long
evenings.
Yours
Edward P Fitch

151

Nov. 19, 1857

Dear Mother

    This sheet came out of the box you sent so you see that it has reached me or rather the things that were in it or a part of them for when Mr Savage got to Springfield he thought he could not fetch the box that you packed them in (though he could just as well as not if he had only been a mind to think so) so he took them out of that and re packed them in an old trunk.   In repacking he lost the first sheet that you wrote and the first that Elijah wrote too so that the beginning of both your letters is "honest".   He found also that two of the cans had begun to leak a little and so he gave them away to Mr Hood's folks so we have only one can and dont know what is in that.   We are going to open it for Thanksgiving next Thurs and have some puddings & pies made of the dried fruit you sent for our Thanksgiving dinner.

    We are ever so much obliged to you for the fruit and also for all the other   things you have sent.   I suppose there must be some history attached to some of them but what we cant know until you write again since the letter you wrote was left.   The boots are <u>very large</u> for me but <u>will do</u>.   Number 8 of <u>that</u> pattern would have answered.   I am very thankful for them and was very glad to get them.   The thin boots that I had made for me before I came first to K [Kansas] are almost worn out so these were just in time.   Where were they got and what did they cost? The great coat will answer very well.   Sarah thinks I look funny enough in it.   The other things Sarah may say what <u>she</u> pleases about.

    Now for some news.   Mr Savage arrived here last night but contrary to the expectation of us all he brot no wife with him.   It seems that he got all ready to be married; the day was set which was to be Mon. the 2nd of Nov.   He waited three weeks for her to get ready and then the Fri. before they were to be married she gave him the mitten so he is now no better off than if he had staid here.   We were all very much surprised at this as you may suppose & I should think he would feel cheap enough. I am provoked with him for not fetching the box just as you sent it.   I did not want him pulling over the things that you packed and I suppose the reason that he lost the letters was because he did not know what he was doing thinking of this false sweetheart.   Well it was the best thing for him probably for if she would do so she would not have been good for anything if he had got her.   Those who knew her, none of them spoke well of her, but all wondered at his choice of such a one.

I arrived at home last night too.   I left John at Sumner on Tuesday morning and came to Leavenworth on Tues and came from there yesterday.   The roads were so bad that it took me about twelve hours to ride from Leavenworth here.   That is a pretty long time to sit in the saddle.   I rode in company with or rather escorted Gen Lane from Leavenworth.   He made a speech there and had been threatened pretty severely but I dont suppose there was much actual danger from their threats.   Be that as it may we were not molested but we left L. at four Oclock in the morning two hours before daylight and I got home about four P.M.   Wheeler & Claflin came to Leavenworth with me on their way East.

John has bot out Luther Phipps in the lime business at Sumner & Wheeler & Barnard both think he has done well and will do well in that business.   His partner in the business is a Mr Bender who is spoken very highly of by Barnard & Wheeler both.   John will probably buy him out after a while and then he will have the whole swing.   They have given John a lot adjoining the one on which the lime kiln stands and he intends to build him a small house on it and board himself and partner.   I hope Father will be able to buy him those shares that he wants him to for it will be a great help to John and will I think tend to steady him down to have something there that he must attend to.   The property will be valuable too, I think.   I traded some property that I had off for a share in Sumner myself and I wish that I could get some money to pay Father toward what I owe him so that he could let John have it by paying for those shares but I dont see exactly how I can do so.   My Quindaro property is not going to be so profitable as I anticipated, I dont think, but I hope to get out of it whole footed as they say.   Whether I shall remains to be seen.   Sumner is more sure property I think now.   Wheeler Barnard & in fact all the men there think they have got something very nice there.   The townsite is somewhat rough but they are making it look better fast.   It is the farthest point in to the Territory on the Mo. River and is in such a position that it must draw <u>some trade</u>, not to say a <u>great deal</u>, from Leavenworth/ on account of the bad hilly roads that must always lead from Leavenworth, that they [Sumner] will not have.

Last night was the coldest night and today is the coldest day we have had this season.   It has been almost impossible to keep warm in the house today.   My upper lip is swelled up very much in consequence of a bad cold, much the same as it did a number of winters ago only it is now much more sore.   It is so bad that I have not been out of doors today at all hardly.

You ask me something about my cow and horse, hay etc. I cut some hay on the prairie for them and it all got spoiled and now I have no hay for them. I shall keep my cow at Mr Savages yard with his and she will fare the same as his. We have corn fodder to feed them on which will probably last them all winter. My pony I shall keep there part of the time and part of the time in one of the houses that I have on my claim, the one that Kitchenman lived in. It is quite a piece from the house but will do for the want of any thing better for this winter. I think the signs are in favor of an open winter such as we had three years ago here but it may not be.

My potatoes I did not get dug soon enough and I shall lose many of them by having them frosen.

We shall think of you on Thanksgiving day tho this will not reach you by that time probably, as I cannot send it before day after tomorrow's mail. I wish I could be with you but probably one more Thanksgiving after this must pass before I can spend that season with my much loved friends at old Hopkinton. Two years from this fall I hope that the whole family will be once more together. The last time we were together was more than three years ago but it does not seem very long to look back over it. We may never all meet again but I hope we shall have that privilege more than once more. I have filled a pretty large sheet and with much love I remain

Your Affectionate Son,
Edward

DEC. 23, 1857

Dear Parents

I have not heard a word from you since I rec'd that box by Mr Savage and I have written two or three times since. What is the matter.

I believe I have not written since Thanksgiving. I had a very good time as for the first Thanksgiving spent at my <u>own</u> home (that is if my debts were paid.) We opened that can of preserves and I found it to be grape or at least we call it so. I had Father W, George & Muzzy here to dinner Thanksgiving. We had baked beef and potatoes to eat and pie (to look at). We have had very pleasant and warm weather for a month now; a great deal of the time it has hardly frose any nights.

The 18th & 19th of Nov were very cold indeed, the thermometer fell below zero. I got back from Sumner on the 18th. John and I had dug and piled up and covered up about 60 bush[els] of potatoes and that night (17th) they all frose.   Out of the 60 bush there were only 5 bush that I saved that were not frosen.   My potatoes were all that I raised this year that I had to sell as I have only what corn I shall want to use myself so it has just spoilt my summer's work and I am poorer than ever.   They would have been worth at least 125.00$ I hope I shall be able to dig a cellar before next fall to put my potatoes in.   I have been   at the Land Office on business connected with land eight days this month.   This land business is a great bother and no mistake.

I believe I have not written about that Land Warrant of _____.   I tried to get a chance to locate it in Mo but there is no good land in Mo where I can locate it without going 150 miles from here to get to a land office and that would not pay for one warrant.   Why don't you see James Bowker and see if he won't let me have his in the same way.   Perhaps if I had two I might go to Springfield Mo and locate them.   I think now I shall locate this there on somebody's claim at the halves.   If it was only 160 acres I could do that and make a lot on it but 120 [acres] are not so good.

      I had something for supper tonight such as I have not had before, since I eat it at 'Elmwood' and that was brown bread and milk.   The bread was made of Graham flour and Indian [meal].   My cow is doing pretty well this winter; she gives between two and three quarts of milk a day.   It is very rich--we make a little butter.   I sold a pound and 1/2 for 40 cts per lb. the other day.   My hens lay a very few eggs now and they are worth 40 ct per doz.

Sarah has been quite unwell with a bad cold and a cough for some time. She is better now and will get over it.   I think I have a bad eye.   I don't know what is the matter.   It is swelled up considerably and very sore, has been so for three or four days.   Who is Representative from Hop[kinton]. Mr. Sen. Douglass is to be the next President, I guess I shall go for him. We are rather snarled up in political matters here now.   We are going to vote down the Lecompton Constitution on the 4th of Jan.   This week Mon was the time that they voted on Constitution with Slavery or Con without Sla.   The vote at Lecompton was 100 Con with Sla., 38 Con. without Sla, and one Slavery without the Constitution and in Leavenworth some voted, "To Hell with your Constitution."   There were no voting ballots at Lawrence.

155

Dec. 24, 1857

Dear Father

It is now 1/4 of twelve Oclock. We have just this minute shut up the store. We have all three been so busy since four Oclock PM. that we had no time to eat any supper so we have just been out and had some Oysters.

Our Sales yesterday Cash were $133.00 and today $78.00 for this week we have averaged 49$ per day cash sales. The best weeks work we have ever done. I sold yesterday one lot for cash for $102.00 that we made 40$ on. That is more than twice as large as any sale ever made by any of us ever before.

That 100 we shall send to you, I think on Mon or Tues and we shall want you, after taking the interest on the Bonds, to use the rest for us.

Keep the coupons till you hear from us. I will write more at length just as soon as I have any time to do so

Yours   Edward P Fitch

Jan. 9, 1858

Dear Parents

I have had absolutely no time to finish this before. The Band has met for practice almost every night since I began it except had one of which we gave a Concert and one we furnished the music for a Grand Party or Ball in honor of the First Legally Elected Legislature in Kansas. It was held on last Thursday night. There were Five Governors of Kansas present and we had a first rate time.

Last Monday was the Election for State officers under the Lecompton Constitution, a part of the Free State party went into that Election and voted for officers so as to get control of the State Government if we are admitted under it but I did not vote for them. I think it was folly. The result cannot be known yet. I voted against the Lecompton Constitution of course as all Free State men did and many who will not allow themselves to be called Free Stater. Since I began this we have recd a letter from you (Mother) which I will proceed to answer. That Mr Savage took anything from the box that you sent I don't want to believe and cant exactly but he lost the first part of your letter and part of Elijah's too. He took out the preserves because he says they were leaking and they must have been because we found the things   they had leaked on to.   I am glad that Uncle Dr. seems to feel any interest in me.   I have written to him twice or more and never recd any answer.   I knew before from your letter that Miss Parker was to be married to Dr Stimson but she is a stranger to me.   I should not know her if I should meet her in the street of Boston or Dedham.   I know that there was such a person at Aunt Clark's and always heard of her but never saw her to know her.   I am acquainted with Mr Nute now and dont think <u>overmuch of him.</u> However if you could get him to come to Hopkinton and deliver his lecture on Kansas and have him at your house I should like it and would go to see him when he returns to pay for it.

His lecture on Kansas or Rev Daniel Foster's would be first rate no doubt.   I did not get a chance to speak to Mr Foster when he was here and saw him only once.   I did not know that the paper was especially for Sarah but I have used considerable of it in writing to you and others.   My nose and eye have got well now, it was kind of boil on my eye.

I think that it is very likely that Father could easily find places for a company of boys here if he would come in the spring.   I am going to inquire around and see how many I can find in the neighborhood and let you know.   I have found two or three now and all say if he would bring a lot of girls he could find plenty of places for them.   I hope he will come. What would be the age of boys generally?   I want to tell folks here.   And what are the conditions that they are placed under when they are sent to places?   Please answer the questions as soon as you possibly can as it may materially assist me in finding places for some.   We had a very pleasant Thanksgiving; we had five kinds of pie and have not made pie since that time.   I thought of home on that day often.   We have had very pleasant weather all winter almost.   Today it has been raining but is getting cold.   I have not got all my corn husked yet and I don't know how soon I shall.   I plowed and harrowed in wheat the first day of this month. The Territorial Legislature meets at Lawrence now and State Legislature under the Topeka Constitution too.   My health is good now and so is Sarah's.   The Band expect to give another Concert this week, Thurs night, so I shall be busy.   You never said a word in your letter about what I wanted to know most that was what you had done about John & his Sumner property.   Please let me know.   I had a letter from him a short time ago.   He is well but whether he is doing well or not I don't know.

Yours in haste
Edward P Fitch

If you ever write to Senator Wilson of Mass I wish you would tell him that I should be very glad to receive from him speeches and such documents as members of Congress send over the country. E

Jan. 26, 1858

Dear Father

I recd yesterday a letter from Mother giving an account of the burning of your barn on the 10 inst.   I am very sorry that it has happened but I suppose that will not do much toward rebuilding it.   And I am not sure that it is best for you to try to rebuild it at all.   I have been planning all day for you and have thought out two or three things some one of which you may think feasible.   But at any rate I think you had better come to Kansas.   That is if Mother is willing to leave Mass.   I should like very very much to have you come out here and buy a farm next to me and go in farming here.   You will find by referring to that map or plan that I sent some time ago that the claim exactly south of mine and adjoining for half a mile is owned by Rev Mr Dennis, Presiding Elder of the Meth. Ch. in Kan Ter. and it is for sale.   He has preempted it so the title is perfect. Now if you could only come and buy that and live close to me we together could make something farming and no mistake.   There are two good things.   First, if you can afford to buy it you will not have to live on it to hold it, or even see it for that matter, for the title is perfect and it would be just the same as buying land in Mass.   2nd.   If you bought it and came here you could, by buying it in Appleton's name, go and preempt a 160 acre lot yourself and so own two claims.   The reason why you would have to buy in Appleton's or my name or someone elses, is that when you take the preemption Oath you have to say that you did not go from your own land in this Territory to preempt that, so that this farm would have to be owned by someone else till you had preempted and then be deeded over to you. so much.   Then the extra value both to you and me of having farms so near together would be considerable.   We could not fence it all in together, because there will probably be a road between my claim and that, it being on a section line.   That claim is a good claim for a farm.   It is all prairie, but it lays in a good place.   The improvements on the place are worth about 1000$.   They consist of 30 acres broke and fenced, a large hewed log house with an addition of framed strips covered with siding on weatherboards, good and tight, a small log stable, a good never failing well of good clear water.   The claim itself is high enough to live on

158

tho not quite as high as a part of mine, and low enough for good corn land.   In what estimates I give on this of the value of things I have not relied on my own judgement alone but have spoken to others today and got their opinions.   The price of this claim is 4,000.$ which is between 18 and 19 dollars per acre for land and no one here doubts that the land around here will in a very few years be worth from 25 to 100$ per acre. Every foot of the claim can be plowed.   There is no stone on it and no stock water.   (I have water on mine.)   4000 is just about the real value of the claim now.   In all probability it would sell for more than that in six months.   So much for the claim and its advantages.   Now for the other side, the terms of the sale are not as liberal as I wish they were.   I have been to see Mr Dennis today and he says that a man from Indiana was here last fall and wanted the claim and was willing to give the price he asked then and went after his money but since that he has been obliged to preempt and asks 500$ more and he expects this man back every day and if he comes up to the price he will get it but I have the refusal of it for five weeks unless this man comes in and then he is not to make any bargain with this man till he sees me.   I am afraid that you will not be able to come up to his terms but they may be made easier if there is any chance of trading.   They are one half (2000$) down, the rest in 3 mo and 1 year.   If he don't sell pretty soon he will rise 500$ on his price and get it too.   If he dont sell before spring he will not sell at all. The reason why he sells now is his wife is not well contented there as he is gone so much of the time and then there is no company near.   She wants to live in town or somewhere where she can have more society when he is away.   This is the only claim that I know of for sale any where about here now and probably the only one within a mile of me that will be for sale for a good many years.   The one north and west of me will not be sold as long as the present occupants live.   The one East I dont know much about.   Well even supposing that you made no effort to get this there are plenty of places in Kansas where you can go and put the price of your farm into a shape that it will double in one tenth part of the time that it would where it is and you might come and live with me on my claim and wait for a good opportunity to buy a farm somewhere near here or if that does not suit you I will give you 40 acres of my Claim if you will come out here and live for what I owe you.   That would keep you busy for a while and you could buy more land for E. & Calvin.   If you cant sell and buy Mr. Dennis farm you might all come out next spring or you, Father, could come in the spring, bring Calvin with you and let Elijah take care of Mother through the summer, (leave them a horse & cow) and then you could leave Calvin

159

here and go on after <u>them</u> (Mother, E & George) in the fall, as fall is rather the best time to come to this country.   If I only could get you here and satisfied I believe I should be happy.

Calvin could have a pony and ride to town to school every day if he wanted to.   There will be no doubt always be a good school there that is three miles off, almost too far to walk every day tho some do it.   Elijah could in a few years preempt some land for himself or some could be bought for him now that would be valuable to him when he got to be a <u>man.</u> (I dont know but what he is a man now.)   John, if he stays where he is would be within 60 miles of you and A. if he leaves Chicago, will be as likely to come here as to go any where.

Perhaps I have not written to you about our school here.   We have a Free School in Lawrence that is of as high a grade and character as the Hop. High School.   They have a good room and two hundred Scholars now.   All branches are studied from ABC to Greek & Latin. Appleton I have no doubt might be Principal of that School in a year only the salary would not be large enough for him at present.   We have now a very fine man for Principal from South Hampton Mass.   His name is C. L. Edwards.   He's a member of our Church and leader of our choir. Sarah says she is not able to write herself but if she was she would urge you to come out with all the eloquence she possessed.   The good points that seem to indicate that you had better come out here at this time are: A good farm for sale close to mine.   The fact that the family would be near together and that property here is rising very fast in value.   The only difficulties that I know of are hard times for money at the East and the fact that Mr Dennis terms are not as liberal as I should like.   You ought to come out here early in the spring and see the corn before you decide upon anything.

Now what I want you to do when you get this letter <u>is to write immediately to me</u> and tell me whether you think at all favorably of any of my plans especially about buying Mr. D's farm because if <u>that is out of the question</u> I want to tell him so that he can sell to someone else if he has a chance, but if there is any probability of your getting that wait ten days and then write again so that if you think that you can buy it I can tell Mr. Dennis and begin to make some definite arrangements with him.   If you wait ten days then by the time I shall get the letter the five weeks that he is going to wait for me will be out and if I don't hear something somewhat definite by that time he may sell and say nothing to me at all.

Write immediately whether favorable or not so I can act accordingly.

160

Feb. 7, 1858

Dear Parents

Last Tues night Wheeler spent with me.   He arrived in Lawrence the Fri before from Sumner.   John is well.   He says that he thinks that I made a very good offer to you Father of 40 acres of my claim and he thinks that this claim here, next to me, would be a good bargain at the price but he thinks that you would do better to go to Sumner and buy that claim that he spoke to you about there for 2500.00 and perhaps it would but we know that land here is worth a good price and always will be but we do not know how much of a town Sumner will make.   If Sumner makes a great city and I dont see any reasons why it may not, that would be the best trade but <u>Lawrence</u> is a fixed fact, let the wind blow as it will. The way that the Hopkinton folks are subscribing   to help you rebuild but I wish if you must stay there because they help you, that you could get along without their help and come here.   How much did you get in that way?

Day before yesterday I recd a letter from Mother dated Jan 25 but she don't say a word about whether you have progressed any in finding out the guilt of that boy.   <u>Can you prove the origin of the fire?</u>   Dr [Ida] sons ____ had some hard times and some interesting adventures in Nicaragua.   I know a man here who was with Gen Walker.   He had some hard times but says it is the best country he ever was in.   He is going back there in the spring.   Wheeler it is true has been elected Representative but it is under the Lecompton Constitution, an office that he does not think much of and that I would not <u>have</u>.   At any rate I would not vote for that Legislature of which he is a member.   I think very likely that he may be elected to the Council of the Territorial Legislature to fill a vacancy that has occurred in the county in which he lives.   You want to know if the Third Commandment is not broken here or something to that effect. Well I guess you would think it was if you was out here and heard some of the swearing that I have heard.   Gov Robinson once said that a man could not be a Christian without he swore in this country.

You speak of digging a cellar.   I intend to dig a cellar before next fall but I have not begun yet because I have not fully decided where to have my house.   I talk some of moving it about 80 rods south of where it is now -- don't know whether I shall or not.   I dont spend a great deal of time with the band except evenings now and I should not dig cellar much then at any rate.   Is there any prospect that you, Father, will come out with any boys from Westboro this next spring now?   I think that you could find places for a number here without much trouble.   We have had a splendid winter thus far till this last week.   It has stormed almost every day either rain or snow or both.   There has not been snow enough to any more than whiten the ground however.   Today it seems to be growing colder and feels as though we might have some ice to save.   Last year at this time I was at work putting up ice and hundreds of tons were put up here.   This year there has been none put up. Hoping to see you but won't very soon.   Sarah & the baby are very well.   We think some of calling the baby Julia Ann Sumner.   Wheeler says he will give her a lot in Sumner if we name her after the town.

I remain your aff son   Edward P. Fitch

I am going to ask a lot of questions and if Mother cannot get him to answer then I want Elijah or Calvin should as I want very much to know some particulars that I shall inquire about.

What man got to the barn first at the time of the fire? Where was William at that time?   How did he appear that day?   How much was burned when you, the folks got home?   How did Mother get home and the rest?   Did you all ride?   Did you have both horses at meeting?   If not, where was the other?   Was it sermon time or what time in meeting? How did it happen that the oxen were burnt?   And have you any oxen left?   Were both the little barns and the shed behind the barn burnt?   Do you suppose that he climbed up on to the scaffold and set it on fire or did he set it on the floor?   If he set it on the floor how did you make out to save anything in the cellar?   Was all the floor burnt through?   Was the big wheel of the cider mill burned, the horse power wheel?   Were the ox wagon, cart, hay rack, and such things burnt?   Were any of the horse wagons burnt?   How much hay was saved and in what part of the bay was it?   Could you tell which side of the barn was set fire to first?   How large are you building now?   And what shape is it, just like the other?   What kind of lumber are you using? and where did you get it and how did you get it on to the ground?   Who is doing the job of building?   Have you any Carpenter that I know?   Who lives in Father's old house?   Do the Ganons still live at the Mc place?   Who supplies the town with milk now?

Now Elijah or Calvin, as long as you have got to be Uncles, I think you can either one of you put on your dignity and answer all of these questions.   If you will I shall be thankful to you.

Edward

The four ministers that were to be ordained here in Oct have turned out this way. Mr Morse got ordained before he came and Mr [Richard] Cordley and Mr [S.D.] Storrs were ordained at Quindaro last week. They had two ordained ministers there & that was all to perform all the services, vis, Mr. Lum of Lawrence and Mr Bodwell of Topeka. Mr Cordley staid with me Fri. night. I like him very well. He is a fine singer. He is liked very well I believe by everyone. If he lives ten years he will make his mark on Kansas or somewhere else!

Feb. 23, 1858

Dear Parents

I have been looking for two or three days for a letter in answer to the one that I wrote about the claim but it does not appear to get here yet. I have been as well as usual. Sarah has got pretty well and the baby (six weeks old today) gets along finely except that tonight she seemed to be somewhat worrisome and we cant tell what does ail her.

I have been chopping wood in the woods today and quite a good deal of the time for a week or two. I take my gun with me to the wood and I have got within a week or two, a doz rabbits & some quails. I got six rabbits in one day. They have kept me in meat for quite awhile. We had splendid weather till Jan was out since which we have had a good deal of strong cold weather but not much snow yet and we shall not have much this winter probably.

I am thinking some of leaving my farm and going into the city to live and tend store but I dont know as I shall do any more than talk. But one thing is certain, I cant get along here another year as I have the year past. I have had to borrow money and then have nothing after all. If I go away from here it will be to stay for some years till I can earn money enough to get me a team and stock my farm and then come back on it. Father Wilmarth thinks that we might do quite a business in his store if we would go into it. He is doing quite well now. I can go in with him as a partner or as a clerk.

Feb. 27, 1858

We are all well still.   The baby grows finely!   I expect that Mr Cordley, the smartest of those four ministers that came from Andover last summer, is going to stop here.   We had a meeting a short time since and raised 500 for him from the persons that were there.   He is liked very much here.   I dont know of a single person that has heard him preach but what likes him as a minister.   He was here and staid over night with me two weeks ago.   He is a very pleasant man, loves to laugh and joke as well as Mr Webster and we call him here a very smart man indeed.   His sermons are short but to the point and are full of thot.   His health was poor but he has been gaining ever since he came out here and is some better than he has been for a long time.   He is a <u>very inferior looking</u> man as he has but one eye and is small. He dont look as you meet him in the street as tho he knew anything but hear him preach and you find <u>_a whole man_</u>.   If he lives in Kansas ten years he will make his mark where it will be seen.

Feb. 28, 1858

I have not been to meeting today.   Our meeting house is not finished and it is impossible to warm it such a day as it has been today -- a strong cold wind.   There was no meeting last Sunday for the same reason it was stormy.   There is some religious interest here among the Methodists.   They have meetings almost every evening.   There is room enough for quite a reformation here.   The Sabbath is not observed at all by many people here unless it is to go shooting or at the time the Legislature was in session here they did as much work on Sunday as any day except that they did not have sessions but the Committees did, I think.   There is plenty of drunkenness here now.   Two men have died of "delirium tremens" within a few weeks one of them a member of the Legislature and at one time acting Gov. under the Topeka Constitution.

The baby gets along nicely.   She is just the prettiest baby that ever was.   Sarah has not written a word since she was born yet but will write you a letter soon.

Love to all in which she joins.

Your aff son
Edward

164

March 16, 1858

Dear Parents

Hope deferred maketh the heart sick says Solomon and I find it to be as true now as it was then for I am sick at heart for want of some news from you.

I wrote a long letter to you Jan. 26th almost two months ago telling you about that claim that was for sale and also about your granddaughter-- either of which things I thought would bring an immediate answer, how much more both. Three weeks ago yesterday I began to look for a letter in answer and I have been to the office, or sent, every day but two or three since that time and no letter yet. Neither have I had any news from Appleton for a long long time, I believe not since Dec. The last news I had of him was in a letter from you and I am nearly heart sick waiting for letters.

I hoped before this time to have heard that Father would buy Mr Dennis claim and come out and live with/near me and now if you cannot buy that claim and come out this spring I want you to tell me if there is any probability that you will come next spring for Mr Nichols, my neighbor on the west asked me the other day if I did not want to buy his claim for you. He wishes you would come and buy Mr. D's but his wife is so homesick here that he says sometimes he thinks he shall sell and go back to New York state where he came from. His friends there all want him to come back and he and his wife are getting old. He was one of the prominent men where he came from especially in the Church. He was Class Leader and Church steward for a great many years till he came away. His farm lays right along side of mine and is a first rate one. There would not be quite so much land fenced on it and there is not now so good a house but he is going to build this spring and he is going to build right across the road from where I am going to build by & bye. I wish you would buy that farm and move out here next spring if not before and perhaps if you should buy and conclude to come out here next spring I may come on East this fall and so come out with you next spring. The price of this would be just about the same as the other but probably the terms of payment could be made easier.

That is considerable high to pay for a farm but land is getting valuable here fast. Mr Morgan, who owns (or did own) the claim in the extreme N.E. corner of this township (I believe it is on the map I sent to you) sold his claim a few days since for $10,000.00! And Mr Babcock whose claim lies East of his and directly South from town has sold half of his for $10,000.00 too.   A pretty good judge of the value of land told me a day or two since that my claim was worth between 4 & 5 thousand but I dont value quite so high as that.   Mr Nichols thinks it is worth some more than his because I have stock water all the time and he does not. You can preempt a qr. Sec. [section] yourself after you come out if you only buy in my name and have me own it nominally till you had preempted.

So much for land, now for weather.   We have had a very fine open winter and now have spring.   Folks have been ploughing and sowing for the last two weeks and more.   Last night and today we have had a fine rain and the grass and wheat look nice and green.   Things look now like an early spring.   The first few days of March were rough and cold, enough like a lion to warrant the belief that Apr. will come in like a lamb.   Sarah and the baby are quite well and so am I.   The baby grows nicely.   She is nine weeks old today and she laughs and plays very prettily.   I never knew little babys were half so pretty before.   Her forehead is like mine, her eyes like Father Wilmarth's, her nose like Sarah's and her mouth like George's so you can tell just how she looks.

How does the barn progress?   Have you got your stock home again?   Do the boys, either of them, go to school now?

Since I wrote before I have become 26 years of age.   I feel rather like an old man.   Just to think on my last birth day I was a single man. Now I am married and a Father!!   I can hardly realise that it is so but I suppose it is nevertheless.   How time slips away.   It does not seem but a short time since I was a boy.   (I mean a small boy for I suppose you will say that I am only a large boy now, men being children of a larger growth) and played in the hay at the old barn on the old place and how Father scolded at Appleton and I for sliding down the hay mow.   A short time since I was sent up to that same barn to turn out and clean out the oxen and I staid a long time and did not do it because I was afraid of a hen that was setting there and looked at me.   Those times look near to look back to them and I almost wish I was a boy again,, but I should "want my wife and baby."

I dont feel much like writing a letter tonight and in fact I have not got any thing in particular to write as I know of.

The Territorial Legislature that was called Free State was just about as much of a Border Ruffian one as the one which we call the "Bogus" Legislature.   They have saddled on to us most of the old laws and some new ones that are fully as bad.   They were a set of swindlers and managed to fill their own pockets and that was about all they did do.

They called a Constitutional Convention which meets next Mon. There has been a great strife over the Election of delegates to that Convention.   One part of the Free State party trying to elect men that would reenact the Topeka Constitution and another part trying to have an entirely new Constitution.   I believe the Maj. are in favor of the Topeka and I hope they will readopt it   and make Congress swallow it in spite of them.   That is, with some slight amendments that all seem to agree that it needs.

Mr. F. Conway is one of our delegates from here.   He is strong for Topeka.

Hope that before I write again I shall hear something or other from you.   Till then I remain

Your aff son Edward P Fitch

March 22, 1858

Written from Sumner, Kansas and on stationery with the letterhead of Secretary's Office of the Sumner Company. It listed the following individuals on the letterhead: C.F. Currier, President; John P. Wheeler, Secretary; Samuel Harsh, Treasurer; Arthur M. Claflin, Agent.

Dear Parents

I left Lawrence on Fri morning last for Sumner Leavenworth Delaware & Quindaro and arrived here Sat noon stopping at night at Leavenworth.   I find folks here all well.   But John I fear has Dear
not been doing as well as he should this winter.   He has not burnt another kiln of lime yet and he has not taken sufficient care of what he has burned and some of that has spoiled.   He thinks too much of fishing and hunting to attend closely to his   business.

I have heard nothing from you since the middle of Jan. just after the barn was burnt and I dont know what it means for sure   or to have thot you would have written -- about that business. That I wanted to know about right off.   I left Sarah and the baby very well.   Julia weighs 15 lbs 10 weeks old.   She seems to be very healthy indeed and cries and worries but little.

I leave here this morning expecting to get to Delaware tonight & Quindaro tomorrow and home the next day sometime.   I expect to get my deeds and the drawings of my lots up here this time but shall not be able to get the deed as the blanks have not arrived from Boston yet.

167

Wheeler said he would give Julia a lot here if I would name her Sumner but you need say nothing about it so that it will get back here. Fear he wont like it perhaps. When I get the deed for the lot then I am going to put Sumner into her name, not before.

Have you made any progress in fixing the guilt of setting the barn on fire on that boy William. Was he a mulatto?

The city Charter of Sumner was pocketed by the Gov. so that their city Govt will not go into operation til another spring. Probably then John will be city Surveyor.

Quindaro, Tues night. I arrived here this afternoon leaving Delaware this morning. I find quite an improvement in the looks of this place since I was here a year ago, much more than there is at Delaware. They have here quite a number of fine houses and warehouses, stores, & so on and are beginning to look quite citified. Property is low however and I could not sell my share for much if any more that I gave for it, perhaps not as much.

Baptist Mission, Wed eve. I left Quindaro this morning and went to Wyandotte and Kansas City. I have not seen those places before since 1855 and there has been a great deal of alteration in that time, I assure you. This mission is the best place to stop at that I know in the Territory. Everything is in order, and neat.

March 26, 1857

Here I am at home again. I arrived on Thurs afternoon having rode about 180 miles on horseback. Been a week about it and spending 3.75 that was just the cost of the trip (pretty cheap traveling). Muzzy went with me and that was what it cost apiece, 3.75. I found on my arrival home a letter from you that arrived the night before I did. The first I have had from you since just after the barn was burnt. I am glad William has got a steady home for awhile. But what surprised me most was that you make no allusion to that long letter that I wrote to you dated Jan 20 or thereabouts and telling you about that farm next south of me that was for sale and I asking you to buy it. You dont say a word about it and the only thing that makes me think that you even got the letter is the fact that you speak of its being easier for me to sell out and come to you than for you to come to me.. Perhaps it is easier but you could make more money by coming here than I could by going there.

I have written since about another.   The one lying west of me I suppose it can be bought for about 4000, perhaps a little less. I wish you would come and buy it and then we could do some great Farming.

I heard tonight that the President has issued his proclamation for the sale of Govt. lands here so that we shall have to pay for our land before the 5th of July or lose it.   Now how I am going to pay for mine within that time I am sure I dont know.   There will be a great many poor Free State men in the same fix   and that is what Buchanan wants for he thinks that the Free State men will lose their claims and then the rich southerners can come in and buy large farms and have their niggers.

It is a shame there are lands in Minnesota that have been settled much longer than this that the right of preemption has not run out on but just on this hard time Kansas settlers must pay for their land or lose it!! Buchanan ought to be shot-- to do that is too good.   He ought to be hung, drawn, & quartered.

I drew a Levee lot in Sumner; if you have a map you can find it. Lot 7, Block 13.   There is to be a three story brick building put up on the lower corner of that block this summer, which will tend to make mine valuable.

March 28, 1858

Dear Mother

I was not going to write any more but I was looking over your letter and see a little that I want to notice.   You pay Appleton quite a complement I think saying that he was the homeliest baby that you ever saw.   I suppose that it is what makes him so handsome now and also makes me so homely now seeing that I was so handsome then.   Sarah will have it tho that I am the best looking now, but she is prejudiced and therefore not a fit judge.   It is as you say a great responsibility to become a parent, and I hope we shall be enabled to train up our child in the way she should go and that she will be kept in that way.   I hope we shall not worship tho of course we think a great deal of it.

Tell Calvin I am very much obliged to him for the letter he wrote and especially for the answers to my questions.   I am glad that William has got a steady home but that will not build the barn again.   How much did Hopkinton folks raise to help Father rebuild?   Wheeler said that Lee Claflin headed a paper with 100$ I hope Father will sell and come and buy next to me.   That is if I am lucky enough to keep my claim which I shall not do unless I pay for it before the 5th of July next. Are you [willing] to come out here and live? and do you want me to come on and bring Sarah this fall and come out with you next spring?

Your affectionate son

Edward P Fitch

I wish you would tell me whether there is any prospect of your coming out here next spring or not. Mr Barnard thinks it would be a good move. He says if he buys a farm and settles down any where here it will be in the vicinity of Lawrence. The river towns will have some advantages over the towns in the interior for a few years but we will soon have Rail Roads and then we shall have as many as they do. That is one advantage of Lawrence. All the river towns are trying to build themselves up at the expense of all the rest but they all look to Lawrence. You go into any river town and they will prove beyond doubt that their town will be the largest and best town on the river. Why? Because we are going to have a Rail Road to Lawrence and so they all expect to build up Lawrence and have Lawrence build them up. So Lawrence is bound to be a place in spite of anything. We are to have a Court House built here this year which will help the town some. But if we have all got to pay for our land before the 5th of July it will be quite a pull back on us all for many will lose their claims because, on account of the troubles they have not the means to pay. John has taken a claim back in the county from Sumner and not in a first rate place I dont think. I think he had better have come here and get a claim about 20 miles S.W. from Lawrence where I think it would have been more valuable but it might not have been.

Your aff Son Edward

I have been trying the last week to get a team but have not made out yet. I found a team for sale pretty much what I wanted and I could get them for three hundred dollars and my pony. There were a span of chestnut collored horses pretty good sise--one nine & the other eight year old. They were almost exactly alike so near that when I rode one of them up to Mr. [Mallory] (who is the best judge of horse around here) and asked him his age and how much he was worth and then in about two hours rode the other one where he was and told him it was the match to him and I wanted his opinion of his age. He said it was the same horse I had before and would not be convinced that it was not the same horse until he looked in his mouth and found he was a year younger, so you can they must look alike. They were as well mated as any span I ever saw except

170

one thing.   The off horse did not walk nor trot <u>quite</u> as fast as the other making the draw uneven a little.   They could bring a load of 20 or 25 hundred from the river to Lawrence easy if I could have raised the money.   I should have traded for them but after spending two or three days trying to get the money I gave it up.   I never saw such a time before.   I could not borrow 200$ in town on good security and I never saw a time before that <u>I could not</u>, but I suppose it is all for the best, indeed I am rather glad that I did not get the money.   I know now where I can get just about as good a team, one that will do full as much work (the horses are <u>larger</u>) for 300$.   It is very cheap and if I could sell property so as to make it [true] I may get them yet.   They are not quite so fancy a team as the one I talked of buying before but the horses are younger some -- both eight, I believe, but I don't hardly know as it is best to buy a team this spring at all.   Money is so scarce and I have got my claim to preempt soon and I have not get the money yet to do it with.   Our land here is to be sold at public auction in July if not preempted before.   Do you suppose that Uncle Doctor would lend me 200$ at 6 per ct. so that I could use it to preempt with if I want it.   I may be able to do some other way yet. I will leave the rest for Sarah

Your af son Edward P   Fitch

I have fully made up my mind that it is not wise to get a team of horses this spring as I should have to buy corn to feed them on during the summer before I can raise any and besides teaming is going to be so cheap that I cannot make much at that.   I think more seriously than ever of going into town to live and go into the store with Father Wilmarth.   He is about to enlarge his business and will have to have some one with him at any rate and it is not going to be very profitable farming here just at present.   I dont think corn will not be over 25 or 30 cts per bush. next fall certain unless we have a very large emigration indeed. Father has a business established.   It will not be like trying the experiment of setting up in business but it will be stepping into a flourishing trade.   If it seems best for me to go over there I shall calculate to stay away from my farm for 5 years at least as meanwhile I shall let the farm if possible and have some one fencing some every year so that when I do come back I may make something off my farm and have a team etc.   I should build in town and then when I left there I could let that house and receive something from that.   If it is best for me to do this the way will be provided for me to do it -- if not, if the indications of Providence pointed to my staying here, I suppose I shall stay.   Father expects to move his store into the same building as the P.O. which will help him not a little.

Your aff. son Edward P. Fitch

Spring, 1858

Dear Mother

I must write some to you I suppose or you will think you are slighted sure but it is late and I have not much time to write.

Sarah recd a letter the other day that was intended to be a mystery to us and it would have been as great a mystery as you meant it should be if it had not been for George, for I should not have known that picture as little George at all if brother George had not told me that it was him, then I saw it in a minute.   I knew that velvet coat that Mr. Webster gave to Calvin and all about but who did you get to mail it up in Wisconsin and how did you get it there.

We are all pretty well now.   The baby is getting along finely.   We are having pretty good weather now the grass has begun to grow green and green grass is something that you have not got in Hopkinton now I'll bet.   I should like to step in some night and see how you all look down there at Elmwood.   Excuse blots.

But here I am tied to my wife and baby, cant go anywhere or do anything.   But by & bye the baby will be a little girl and can run alone and take care of herself somewhat.   Then perhaps if we are favored in business I shall come and see you all.   I hope I shall sometime.

I have no more time as the mail will be off so good bye
With much love from you aff son,
Edward P. Fitch

April 11, 1858

Dear Mother

I was very much pleased last night to receive a good long letter from you dated March 28th.   You say "I write saying we should have Carpenters - - should not be able to write and since that you have written two letters."   Well if you have we rec'd only one and that reached here the 27 of March, one day before you wrote this but one.   I did not blame you for not writing only that I wanted to hear whether you would come out here or not but Mr D's claim you cannot have now I suppose though I do wish you could come out here and buy Mr Nichols for the boys and I will give you ten acres off from mine for you to live on, if that is all you want, or sell it to you.

Did your first baby make you forget that there was anybody else in the world?   So that you think all young folks are just so?   To be sure we think every thing of it but we have not forgotten you yet.   I will hug and kiss her for you but I wish you could see her yourself.   I dont believe you ever saw any thing quite so pretty.   Your story about what assistance you have had in building the barn astonished me for Wheeler said that Lee Claflin headed a paper with 100.$ to help you re build and that others contributed something also.

Appleton writes but little you say.   He writes less to me for I have not had one line from him since last November some time.   I wish as you do that he had a <u>good wife</u> as good as mine but no matter.   I dont suppose I should know Elijah now but I should like to see him.   Tell him that I suppose he has given up all hopes of having Emma Claflin and Sarah has got a Lady picked out for him that will just suit him I think.

I am very glad of what I hear by the papers of the revivals in the different States East.   We have a very little of the same spirit here.   I attended a morning prayer meeting this morning before the regular church service commenced.   There have been some few converts here, two were immersed in the Kansas river last Sunday.

I sent a note to Uncle Dr. a long time ago for 100$ half of which you sent and the other half Appleton last June.

I found the first violets of the season last Fri.   Apr 9th.   I guess you dont have any in Mass now.   We have had rain almost every day now for a week and the storm does not seem to be gone yet.   I think that I write pretty often to you especially when I dont hear for such long times.   Do you sell milk now?   I asked you two or three times to send me the headings of that Family Expense book you once had and I wish you would if you could just cut off the top of a leaf or two and one of the monthly summary.

Mr Savage has gone East again to get him a wife as he failed before.   I hope he will have better luck this time.   The lady he has gone after is just about the age of my wife.   The Catholics have gained quite a foot hold in this Territory now.   They have a Mission among the Indians west of here and they have the largest church in Leavenworth I guess now. There are more Germans here than Irish and they are, as a general thing, a better class of citisens than the Irish.   They are mostly Free State men while the Irish are Democrats which is Pro Slavery to all intents and purposes.   We have four or five kinds of flowers now in blossom on the prairie and the grass is green and it looks splendid.   Have you any green grass there now?

173

April 19, 1858

Dear Parents,

I have waited a week or more since I wrote the other sheets of this letter for Sarah to write but she has been so busy that she has had no time until today and as I have not been to town since a week ago today, I have not sent mine yet.   I have been at work this past week for Mr [Joel] Grover, one of my neighbors carrying the hod.   He is building a large stone barn (not very large either, 30 x 40 feet).   I began to work for him Wed morning and that was the hardest day of work I had done for more than a year so it tired me a good deal and then I laid awake with the toothache during the night and the next night.   Later I could stand it no longer and I went to a Dentist and had the offending tooth pulled.   It was the wisdom tooth on the right side upper jaw.   I had the next tooth to it pulled a short time since by the same dentist and he says that the next tooth is now ulcerated and the nerves is dead but it will not probably ache because there has a kind of ulcer formed and burst on the outside of the jaw (inside of my mouth opening) & as long as that is there it will not Ache. Sat morning we got our gangway plank fixed to carry up the stone to the second story or rather onto the scaffold of the barn and in carrying up the second load of stone the plank gave way with Mr. Grover and my self on it. I was up the farthest and as Grover let go of the hand barrow it struck my foot and knocked me down but I jumped from the plank before it struck the ground and I struck on one foot and one knee hurting my knee some, no so much but that I worked all day. But yesterday it was difficult for me to walk much. I ti a little sore today. I have not go any of my ploughing done yet bu think I shall begin day after tomorrow if we don't have any more rain between now and then. It has rained eight days out of the last twelve and the ground is pretty wet.

I want you Father to see what Mr. Williard Morse is going to to about that Land Warrant and let me know immediately and if he does not want me to use it on my claim and pay him 100$. I want you to ask Uncle Doctor if we will lend me $200 at 6 percent and take security on my land if he will, please get it out of him and send it to me in a draft on the Suffolk Bank of Boston or the the Metropolitan Bank New York, if possible, as drafts on thos banks will be sell better her than any other Boston or N.Y. Banks & tho any one will do but those are the preferred. If he cannot lend it to me let me know just as soon as possible that I may contrive to get it in some othe way as I must preempt soon or the the rush of business at the and office may be so great that I may lose three or four days about and then if I should put it off too long and not get through before fifth of July it would be sold and I should lose it. I shall try and contrive som way to raise the money without asking you if he cannot let me have it. The reason that I ask for 200 is that I may have enough in case of any unforeseen occurrence preventing me getting a Land Warrant but if Uncle Dr. or you can buy a Warrant for 160 acres and send that it would be just as well. I fyou bought of a man that you knew to be responsible so that the Warrant was sure to be good for many fail in not being properly assigned or some other reason, and if you should send a warrant that proed to be worthless I should be badley off indeed and uless you were sure of this man being responsible you might fail to get your money back for it. It is a little safer buying here because tha are all warranted and if not good you can go and get the money right back. I ezpect to be able to buy here for 160$ or 165 at the most if I buy pretty soon. Let me know what can be done about it as soon as you possible can.

Your aff son E.P. Fitch

April 30, 1858

Dear Parents

   I suppose you will begin to think it is time to hear from me again by this time. It is just a year tonight since Sarah and I first came to this house. It was a [rainy] night very much such a night as tonight. I have been plowing for the last few days and have got done about all the ploughing that I intend to do this spring unless it is to break some more prairie. That I may and may not do. I have not got any thing planted yet but am going to plant tomorrow if I live till then. Mr Savage got home from the East three days since with his new wife. He was disappointed last fall you recollect. Well just before he left Springfield to come back he saw a young Scotch woman whom Mrs. Hood his sister introduced and recommended to him. He was pleased with her and has corresponded with her during the winter and [line crossed out] he left here the 2nd of Apr, was married the 14th and got back here the 27th. She appears to be a fine woman just a month older than Sarah and he is 35. 9 years difference in age, that is almost too much I think.

   We have morning prayer meeting here every day from 11 to 12 Oclock besides 4 or 6 other prayer meetings during the week. There is some considerable interest for such a place; here, the noon meetings are said to be very interesting. I have been to one and while in there I opened a letter from Whiteman in which he said that <u>Calvin</u> had spoken in meeting the night before and tho he said he did not know as he was rejoicing in hope yet he was in the faith that leads to life. I was so glad to hear that the letter fell from my hands and my feeling overcame me. Is it so? Has Calvin found the Savior precious? How does Elijah stand affected?   Is he at all anxious for his eternal welfare?   Do the morning prayer meetings continue?   Is the interest increasing or the reverse? Appleton wrote that the interest in Chicago seems to be rather on the decline.   I dont know of any more in particular that I want to write and I am so sleepy that I cant write any more at any rate so I shall not.

Your aff son E.P. Fitch

May 10, 1858

Edward gave up trying to support his family by farming in May, 1858, and went to work in his father-in-law's book and stationery store in Lawrence.

Dear Parents

I dont know why this sheet has not been sent before but it may be worth reading (or may not.)   We are very well except that the baby is a little worrisome this morning, more than usual, and she did not sleep quite well last night.   The religious interest still continues here.   Four were united with our Church by profession yesterday.   A week ago yesterday was so stormy that Communion was put off till yesterday.   I understood from Whittemore that Calvin was hoping that he had found the Savior.   Is it not so?   I hope it is and as you say I hope the work will not cease till all the world is brought to the knowledge of the Savior.

Yours in haste EP Fitch

Dear Father,

Your letter of the 29th ult. reached me day before yesterday and in reply I have to say that I can buy [120] acre Land Warrants here for 111$ Cash.   They are a little higher than they were when I wrote before about them but I should have to find the Cash to pay for it now which would not be convenient so I will take the Warrant and pay you 120$ for it if it proves to be right at the office.   I shall go to the Land Office this week sometime so you had better wait a few days before you tell Mr Morse you will take it -- for if the Land Office should refuse to receive it I could do nothing with it of course and should send it back.   I have just been looking it over and find that it is badly assigned but perhaps it will pass muster, if so all well.

I have no time for news as I have to go to town right off to see about hireing a house as I expect to let my house and land and go into town to live myself.   I intend to go into business with Father Wilmarth. I shall have a stated salary and a certain share of the profits of the business.   Appleton wrote to me some two weeks ago, was almost sick but hoped that he should recover this vacation.

E P Fitch

May 16, 1858

Dear Parents

I went to the Land Office last Wed to preempt my land but was unable to "prove up" because I had no witnesses to the fact of my first settlement on my claim.   I took the claim in Apr 1855 before I came East, and had three persons as my witness at the time.   One of them is dead, I believe one in California and the other I dont know where he is.   I thought that I might date from the time that I built this house but I cannot because I did not file within three months of that time so it is going to make me some trouble, tho when I told at the Office all the circumstances they told me how to evade or rather how to 'get round' the preemption Law and said that by making a new settlement in presence of witness and moving out of my house and then moving back I might preempt without building another house and that is what I have got to do now.   I took my claim over again on the 12 after abandoning it so that it might have been jumped if any one had known of it.

We are having a wet and cold spring after all.   It has rained more within the last two months here than it ever has before in four months since I have been   in Kansas.   We have got but little of our corn planted yet in this neighborhood.   It will be a good year for grass I think.

Perhaps before you get this Mr Muzzy will have been at Hopkinton to see you.   If not he will be there soon.   I think he promised to go down soon on his return and I expect that he got to Worcester last Wed or Thurs.   I think I have mentioned him in my letters to you.   He has been with me almost all the time since we came to Kansas, that is near me.   We lived together at Mr Stearns store all the winter of 55 & 6 except when we were both in our quarters during the war.   He was a member of the artilery and I of a rifle company.   Then we lived together at Mr Savages during the summer of 56 and fall and since I have kept house he has been here a great deal.   He seems like a brother almost, in some respects.   When he does come to see you have lots of puddings, for he is as great a hand for pudding as I am.   He comes here, or did come, almost every Sunday to get a piece of pudding and the last dinner he took before

177

he started he had here and had a pudding with some of those berries that you sent me in it.   By the way I dont know as we have acknowledged the last you sent, those you sent by young "Wheeler".   They came safe to us; we thank you a <u>thousand times</u>. I wanted to send you something by Muzzy but could get nothing curious that he could carry. I tried to have the baby ambrotype taken but she would not be still long enough to have it taken so we shall have to wait till the next one that goes from here to Hopkinton. The baby is very well and grows finely.   Sarah is not very well today and I am staying at home from meeting to take care of her.   Something she has eat does not agree with her.

My Cow is doing finely this season.   She calved the 24 inst and we have so much milk that we dont know what to do with it.   We use all we can and throw the rest away.   We have no pig because I thot I should sell my Cow and did not want any.   We churned yesterday for the first time --had between two and three pounds of butter and very nice butter too.   I have got one of the best cows to make butter from that you ever saw or that I ever saw.   I found a stray calf on the prairie last week and have been keeping that along with mine for four days so we dont have quite so much milk.   Both cows are <u>heifers</u>.

I had something to eat yesterday that I have not had, ("the likes of,) before since long before I left home and that was hulled corn and milk.   It was good, tasted like old times.   I think now that the Land sales will be put off but I dont know certain as they will.   They ought to be but I shall probably preempt mine <u>now</u> whether or no for if I move away it will be better to have it paid for.

Have I told you that Mr Savage has finally got him a new wife? and that she is only a month older that Sarah?   Muzzy will tell you about how and where he got her if you want to know.   How is the interest in religion there now?   There seems to be some here, tho not a very great deal.   How does Calvin feel now & Elijah.   How is George & where is his mother?   Give my respects to all who inquire for me.   Show Muzzy all that is to be seen.   Let Elijah or Calvin go with him to <u>Whittemores</u>.   He knows Muzzy['s] sisters in Worcester.

Write as soon and as often as possible to.
Your aff Son
Edward P Fitch.

May 20, 1858

Dear Father

Your letter written at Westboro has just come to hand but too late to save the Warrant.   I Preempted my claim yesterday using the Warrant and 60.$ of the 100. that Appleton sent me.   I could not have preempted at all without more than the warrant of course.   The Warrant paid for 120 acres.   50$ in cash paid for 40 acres and it takes 9.50 to get through the office that is for fees.   1.00 for certificate of filing, 5.00 for preemption proof, & .50 for locating warrant, total cost to me calling warrant 120. = 179.50.   Ten dollars more than it would have cost me if I could have had the money and bought a Warrant for 160 acres which I could have got for 160$ or perhaps I might have had to pay 165$.   So you see it would have been impossible for me to have sent back this warrant and preempted now and circumstances were such that it was important that I should preempt immediately.   So if I had bought a Warrant with the 100 sent by Appleton (which by the way was sent for another purpose), where would the 69.50 come from to pay up the rest?   To be sure the Land sales I suppose <u>now</u> are postponed till Oct. That will not make me any better off if I wait till then.   If it has been one year then it would have been of some benefit.

English's Bill or rather juggle has passed Congress.   Well, you say, if we accept we ought to be Slaves so I say but I am sometimes seriously afraid it will be accepted or at least so declared by the Gov.   And now I will give my reasons first stating some facts.   English Bill is worse than Lecompton-Walker for it gives us less land.   It is worse because it leaves the matter wholly undecided.   It settles nothing, ends nothing only keeps the matter open and leaves it in a worse shape than ever.   The Crittenden Bill finished the business but this Bill even the Fathers of it dont know whether it submits the Constitution or not.   But now for my reasons.

1st   Every thing that can will be brought to bear to make us accept the Prop. of Congress.   The original Lecomptons are for it.   They of course carry all that they can influence in the same way.   Then the Whole force of the influence of the Land Office will be brought to bear for it.   The Officers talk to every man that comes there from all over the Territory and tell them what a good thing it will be for us to get into the union right away.   Now that either the Land sales will be postponed or else that 5 per cent of the sales will come to the State Government.   Then they tell them that the only way to keep and secure <u>peace</u> is to be admitted, as a state. Many believe it and will vote For on that promise.

2nd   There are lots of men here who care more for getting a Rail Road than they do for Free State principles.   They vote "For" because it will build Rail Road and increase the value of the lands. They will influence all they can to vote for the proposition and be admitted right away.

3 There are those who pretend to be Free State who Because the Leavenworth Con. makes the negro a voter will turn a[nd] support the Lecompton Con. just out of spite to the other.

4 A Majority of the Boards that have this matter in hand are Democrats & Pro slavery. Gov Denver is no better than he should be. His Secy Walsh is a perfect tool and will do any thing and his Atty Genl is of 'the same stripe'. They then have the power according to the bill to do the whole work with out any chance of Babcock & Dietzler having any chance to do anything. They will receive, I have no doubt, all such returns as Gov. Walker and Secy Stanton refused to receive last October and then the Majority for the Proposition can be swelled to any amount without voters.

5th The Blue Lodges of Missouri were never in more successful operation than at present. They are making every calculation to send men all over the Territory quietly a little while before the Election and have them stay and vote after the manner of the 30th of March 1855 only more quietly and if that is done of course Gov D & the rest will ignore the fact and say it a fair election.

6 There will be renegade free State men enough that will think that the advantages of Rail Roads will overbalance the disadvantages of living under the Lecompton Con. for a while for they say that we can change the Constitution within 60 days and have a Free State Constitution. For they say Calhoun will give the Certificates to a majority of Free State members and they can do what they please.

These are some of the reasons why I think the proposition of Congress may be accepted tho I hope that it will not. As far as I am concerned if Congress had offered to give every man in Kansas his claim I should have been against just as firmly as now. The people, as a general thing, are right but these influences being brot to bear up on them may turn the vote in favor of the Proposition. However I think it more likely that it will be carried by imported votes from Missouri . It is their last chance and good for nothing at that for let us be admitted under that Constitution and we are just as sure to become free state as we live one year, mark my word. It is perfectly impossible to make Kansas a Slave State just as impossible as it would be to make Hell out of Heaven.

For my own part I should rather remain a territory for the next fifteen years than to come in under the "Lecom Cons" but I believe that the next Congress will be such a one as will admit us as a Free State if we reject this Constitution - the English Bill to the contrary not withstanding.

But as you say we ought to be slaves if we accept it, then you agree with me exactly. Yet for the reason stated I think it may be carried. You of the North have no idea of the state of things here and cannot see all the influence that will be brot to bear on the Free State men for the Constitution there for you will not sympathise much with us if we seem to accept it but if you were here you would see how it is.

I have let my Farm to a couple of families from <u>Indiana</u> who have come on here with their families. In the two families there are only 19 persons here, the rest having staid in Iowa. There are eight of them now in the house [while] I am writing. One family consists of Mr & Mrs Coon with four children, two grown up daughters (both good looking and educated for teachers), one daughter 9 and one son about 7 years old.

JUNE 5, 1858

Dear Parents

The last week, or rather the last part of it, has been one of the most exciting times that I have seen in Kansas not <u>just such</u> excitement as was prevalent during the time of the war but a deeper sterner feeling.

One man has been killed here in the city, his murderer wounded and another man belonging here has been killed in the neighborhood of Council Grove. Another man here shot his arm almost off at the wrist. These things with some claim difficulties of minor importance have made it quite exciting times.

The great tragedy of this week has been the killing of Mr [Ganius] Jenkins by Gen [James H.] Lane and the circumstances are as follows.

First however the parties: Mr Jenkins was one of the head men of the town. He owned 1/4 of the new Free State Hotel now being erected. He was one of the treason prisoners confined with Gov Robinson in the Summer of 56 at Lecompton. He had a wife and four children, the oldest a young lady about 18. Gen Lane you know something about. His wife, to whom he has recently been remarried, she having obtained a divorce two years ago, was living with him. They have I believe one child, a little boy.

Jenkins & Lane both lived on and claimed a qr Sec of Land lying partly within the city of Lawrence. They were contending for it at the Land office, but it being a School Section it was somewhat doubtful

181

whether either of them would get it as it was thought by many that it would be sold for the benefit of the School fund.   There has been considerable animosity growing out of this difficulty between Lane & Jenkins.   They both lived on the claim but in houses some 30 rods apart.   Each one had a lot fenced in around his house.   There was a well in Lane's yard from which both families had been in the habit of getting water.   But a short time ago Lane forbid Jenkins coming there after any more water, for if he did he would shoot him and for a few days he did not get any there, but on Thurs last (the 3d inst) Mr Jenkins said in town just before dinner that he was going to get some water out of Lane's well if he got shot.   He went home about noon and sent his man over to get a pail of water.   The man went but Lane would not let him get any and told him if he or Jenkins came again he would shoot them.   The man went back and told Jenkins.   Jenkins said "I will go and get some myself.   I guess there will be no trouble about it."   But he took his pail and took a rifle and an ax with him and then took other men with him armed with revolvers.   They went to Lane's gate.   <u>Meanwhile</u> Lane had nailed the gate up so that they could not get through.   One of the men with Jenkins took the ax to cut down the gate but Jenkins thot that he was not quick enough and so he set down his rifle and took the ax himself and chopped the gate down and then started for the well which was right between the gate and Lane's house.

As Jenkins advanced toward the well Lane came out to meet and told him not to come to the well.   He said "The relation between you and me are such that we had better have nothing to do with each other and I do not want you here and wont have you."   He was at this time unarmed.   What reply Jenkins made to this I do not know but Lane went on to say "Jenkins, if you come up to this well or advance any further I will shoot you."   Jenkins still came on and Lane then steped into the house and took out his gun and fired at Jenkins.   He threw up his arms and said O!! and fell Dead! on his tracks.   At the same moment almost one of the other men with Jenkins fired at Lane the first time wounding him pretty severely in the leg and the second time the ball going through his hair close to his ear.   The reports were so near together that men at work close by could hardly tell whether there were <u>three</u> or <u>more</u> or <u>less</u> reports.   Some said that they fired first at Lane but he said he fired first. He said he knew that if he did not kill Jenkins, Jenkins would kill him, but I am not sure that it is so.   Jenkins had been drinking pretty freely that day and was under the influence of liquor at the time no doubt, while Lane is now and has been for some time a member of the Temperance

Society of Good Templars.   It seems that they had both sort of made up their minds that that day was to decide about the well trouble, for Lane bought some caps that forenoon and said "I don't know but I shall have to kill a man before night", while Jenkins said that day that he was going to have some water out of Lane's well if he shot him.   One of the men that was with Jenkins has since said that if his first cap had not refused to go Lane would not have shot Jenkins, which would just prove that he was intending to shoot Lane and that he only acted in self defense, but I do not believe that Jenkins would have shot Lane myself.   The stories are so various in regards to it that it is impossible to say with any accuracy what were the facts.

We are fast tending here to the same State of affairs here that made the Vigilance Committee needed in California.   You have no idea I think of the state of things here at all.   Imagine what a stir it would make in Hopkinton to have Aug Phipps or Col Wood or Lee Claflin shot down in daylight because he came to another man's well to get water, but there is no such stand here.   To be sure there was quite an excitement that day but it soon subsided and now (Wed 9th) it is almost gone.   Lane has had no examination and I don't believe he will have, just because he is <u>Jim Lane</u>.   Horse stealing is getting to be common here again, something as it was in Indiana in the first settlement of the state.

Mr Jenkins funeral was attended at the Congl Church on Sunday afternoon.   Mr Cordley preached the funeral sermon, said to be very good.   I did not go but staid at home so that Sarah might go.   He was followed to the grave by the largest procession that I ever saw here.   He was <u>pretty much respected</u>   as we say here.

I hope that from this time Lane will be a vagabond in the Earth till he shall exclaim like Cain, my punishment is greater than I can bear.
Edward P. Fitch

June 9, 1858

Dear Parent

I have taken so much time and space on Gen Lane that I have not much for any thing else.   I have got family moved into the city and have been in the store a week and a half.   We have got the store moved into our new place and are doing quite a good business for the hard times. Sarah is as well as usual and so is the baby.   I am in hopes that this move is going to be for the best.

The business is going to be Large.   I have just been putting up an order the bill amts to about 50 dollar and last Sat we took in 40. just from one days trade.   I dont expect to make a fortune in a minute or a year but I think I can save some thing in a year or two that will help me on my claim, but if we should happen to fail, then I should have my claim to fall back upon.

Your aff son
E.P. Fitch

June 10, 1858

This morning it was found that all the prisoners confined in our jail, some 6 or more, had broken jail and gone.   Horse thieves & all.   We shall have to have a Vigilance Com. here before long and hang a few of them.   E. P. F.

July 13, 1858

My Own Dear Mother

Your letter of June 25th has just reached us tonight.   There has been considerable delay in the mails lately which accounts for its delay.   I cannot tell you how glad I was to see it.   It seems so very long since we have heard from home.   But I feel, too, somewhat sad since reading it.   I fear from its tone you are not well.   Oh, how I wish we were near you, that if possible I might cheer your drooping spirits and aid by those many little things which only a <u>daughter can</u> do.   Gladly indeed would I do it were it in my power.   But situated as we are I see no way at present but to speak to you through the imperfect [medicine] of a letter.   I have written but very few letters for a long time.   I hardly dare look back & think how few for I do think my friends have good reason to accuse me of negligence. But it is not <u>intentional</u>.   My days are fully occupied and the weeks slip by <u>so quickly</u>.   I suppose you know long before this of our removal to town etc.   <u>I</u> enjoy it much & as Edward appears to I was <u>happy</u> on the claim. But I must confess that always having been accustomed to near neighbors & friends I did <u>sometimes</u> feel a <u>little lonely</u>.   I am so glad to have my Father & brother in once more <u>at home</u> with us & they enjoy it so much.

184

I would love to show you our home.   It is very pleasant.   We have two rooms below with a small chamber.   Our sitting room is a very pleasant room.   Large, airy, comfortable.   The kitchen, tho I suppose you would scarcely term it a very <u>nice</u> room, answers all necessary purposes very well.   We have very pleasant neighbors.   By the way, Mr. & Mrs. Savage (the <u>old</u> people) are among my nearest neighbors.   They are such <u>good</u> old people.   We always call them ["Grandsir] & Grandma" and I do enjoy running in there & they are here very often.   It seems homelike to me for I was always accustomed to having a "Grandpa's house" to go to at the East and my old Grandfather -- dear good old man -- is yet living -- oh, how I long to see him once more!   But I almost fear I never shall he is so very feeble.   Oh, if I could only bring <u>all</u> my friends here to Kansas!   but still I suppose they wouldn't all want to come.   It sees to me sometimes as tho I <u>must</u> come & lay our baby, our precious little Julia in your arms. You would love her I know for she is a very <u>lovable</u> little thing -- always so pleasant & good -- always a smile for every one who comes in.   You would be pleased to see her when Edward comes home.   All play things are dropped and the little hands outstretched to go to him -- and the little mouth open for the kiss that is always sure to come.   Whenever E or Father or George come home the first word is for "the baby".   She was six months old yesterday.   Does it [seem] possible?   I have shortened her dresses and she <u>sits alone.   Isn't she smart!</u>   I sit her on the floor with her playthings & she will amuse herself nearly all the forenoon as happy as can be.   I wish you could see her.   She is quite fleshy a "real fat baby" people say -- very white, clean skin -- eyes a very deep blue -- so deep that sometimes you would think them almost black -- a good deal of hair now comes two or three inches in length of a light brown.   People call her (you needn't have it all on <u>my</u> "say-so") a very pretty baby -- and of course I agree with them.   Isn't it perfectly natural Edward has just come home and the first thing he is reading the sheet I have just completed.   Isn't he a saucy fellow?   I don't wonder you love him for he <u>is</u> just the best -- but I won't say any more.   You will certainly think me a very [foolish] woman to talk so about my husband & baby but I only wish you could see them both -- and <u>me</u> too.   There is a lady here in town -- Mrs Fuller -- who E. says looks very much like you & I love to look at her -- and wish it only was yourself.   The first Sabbath in July we had baby baptized -- by the name Julia Sumner.   The day previous was observed as the 4th and a very pleasant celebration we had.   A picnic, with oration, Dinner etc was the order of the day.   The "Good Templars" -- a Temperance Order -- had the management of affairs and all went off nicely.   A beautiful place was

185

selected on the bend of the river opposite the city.   An Oration was delivered by J.C. Vaughn, Editor of Leavenworth Times.   Music from the Band --- singing by Lawrence Glee Club etc.   Every one seemed to enjoy themselves -- it was a lovely day -- and we had as pleasant a time "away out here in Kansas" as one could wish.   One thing would have looked strange to you Eastern people -- and that was a group of Indians in their gayest dresses looking on with curious interest -- enjoying with the rest. I would love to describe some of the fanciful dresses of the women but could hardly do it upon paper.   But they seem fond of the brightest possible colors and one could almost see the tints of the rainbow on any one of them.   I am sure the boys would be amused and interested in watching our dusky neighbors.   By the way, you say nothing of little Georgie.   Is he still with you? & well?   Dear Mother you must not work so hard as to get so exhausted.   If you are sick how I shall long to be with you, but I trust you will not be.   Write often to us.   A few lines even are welcome.   I will try to write you more frequently if that will have any effect to amuse or interest you.   I will leave the rest for E. to fill up.   Love to Father.   I was sorry to read that he was unwell.   Hope he is quite will by this time.   Remember me to my brothers.   Have they [never] a word for their sister -- as I long to be indeed as well as in name.   We could get somewhat acquainted by a few words occasionally.   Much love to yourself and ever think of me as your
Affectionate Daughter

Dear Parents
      Sarah has said all that there is to be said I believe only that about this Land Warrant.   I will try and pay something toward it at any rate by Nov. but I dont know.   Business now is and times are very dull indeed and I am afraid I shall not get much of a crop from my farm this year.   I have just been having ten or twelve acres of corn plowed up and am going to have Buck Wheat <u>sowed</u> in place of it.   My potatoes look well.   My neighbors ____ some of them are not going to cut their wheat at all it is so <u>poor rusted and shrunk up</u>.
      I've got the prettiest baby in the world.   I don't care who say not, I never knew what it was to <u>love</u> a child before but she is <u>so lovely</u>.   I dont know but I shall almost make an idol of her.   You know as well as I do that I cannot write letters so I will not. I am   sorry that you are so unwell.
Your aff Son E.P. Fitch

186

Nov. 7, 1858

Dear Parents

You will see by the date of this letter that I am still away from my home at Sumner. I have been here now three weeks and shall remain three or four days longer so as to help Edward about moving, i e take care of the baby.

I did not intend to be gone from S. (Sumner) more than a week when I left there, but I got caught down here by the rain which raised the streams so high that it was useless to attempt to go back and so I am waiting for it to clear off. I have not been entirely well but a small part of the time for the last two months; but have my usual health now.

Dear Parents

I suppose you are wondering what has become of those children that they dont write to us. Well the fact is we waited about three months for a letter from you and then one came and the reason that we did not answer it was that we expected to be there in Elmwood ourselves by this time to answer verbally anything that might come up but it seems to me that I am in Lawrence now and not in Hopkinton so I must write if I want you to hear from me.

John is here with us having come down from Sumner to see us before we started East. He arrived here two or three weeks ago and it has been so stormy that he could not get back at all. It has stormed almost incessantly for two weeks now. We have had only one fair day in that time and today it is snowing. Today is supposed to be Sunday out here. Father has gone out of town to see a friend & George has gone down to a funeral. There has been but one meeting in town today and that one the Baptist. All the other churches are being fixed and have had no meetings. We have not had any at our Church for five or six weeks.

There was a young man that belonged to the same Lodge of Good Templars that George does that was married a week ago last Thursday and on Wed last he went to carry his wife to her mothers about nine miles from here and in returning he was drowned with both the horses that he was driving. He is to be buried this P.M. She was sixteen. He was about 21.

John has been quite sick this fall before he came down here and has not got entirely well yet. George has been sick about two weeks with Fever & Ague but has got over it now pretty much. Sarah & I have been pretty well and so has the baby. She grows prettier every day. She stands up by a chair and amuses her self a great deal.   She tries to talk and says <u>Mamma</u> as plain as I can write.   She tries to say "Kitty" but does not make out quite as well.   She will be <u>ten months</u> old this week sometime.   She has not got any teeth yet nor any signs of any.

It is growing cold today very fast and I am afraid that my potatoes on my claim will be frosen before they get dug.   They would all have been dug I suppose before this time if it had been weather fit to dig them but for more than two weeks it has been too wet to dig potatoes anyhow.   I shall have a little Buckwheat if it dont get spoilt in this storm.   Corn I   shall not have a very large quantity, not more than 100 bush I dont think and that wont bring much this fall as it is now selling for about 25 to 30 ct per bush.   Still my place will have been improved some this season and that is about all the profit I shall get from it.

We expect to move from the house we now occupy this week so you see we have a job before us and a bad one too.   Every time I move I wish I had not half so many things.   I have given away some of my things now to some poor folks and think I shall give away more.   I have many clothes that I shall not wear while in the store that I think I shall give to some poor person.

I suppose you will wonder why we did not come East as we intended but the story is too long for me.   When we get moved Sarah will write again and perhaps tell you all about it.   Our business is not very good now but we hope it will be better sometime.   We have had quite an excitement about kidnapping here within a few days.   The paper will tell you that I suppose so I wont.
Yours in haste, E.P. Fitch

I hope you will write once in a while.   E.P.F.

Nov. 21, 1858

Dear Parents
　　　I dont know hardly what you will think that you have heard nothing from us for so long but you will see by the parts of the letter that you will receive with this that we have thot of you sometimes at least.

John began this letter and wrote so much and left.   He went away from here on Friday a little more than a week ago today.   I have not heard from him since so I dont know how he got home.   We have been very busy getting in new goods and not selling many lately.   We had the baby's picture taken this last week and have got one of the best if not the very best picture that I ever saw of a child.   We have now a superior artist here and I think I may perhaps send you some pictures after awhile.

Sarah has just come home from meeting.   She has been there forenoon leaving the baby with me as I am the only one that can take care of here when she is gone.   We have a little girl staying with us now that the baby takes quite a liking to but she was not very well today and we could not leave her with her.   We expect to get into our Church again (it has been closed to be plastered and finished) next Sunday and we hope that we shall be able to go together then.   We have not been to meeting together for some time.   John helped us move before he went away.   We now live only about 1/2 as far from the store as we did before.   We have a nice little house with three rooms on the ground floor and an attic, small to be sure but quite comfortable.   We have to pay a fairly good rent but it is a good tenement.   We expected to build a house ourselves this fall but we could not make it come right and now I dont know when we shall live in a house of our own again but I hope some time.

Nov. 28, 1858

Another week has passed and this letter is not sent yet.   Well it will perhaps be good when it gets to you.   I have been to meeting once today to a "Swedenborgian meeting".   We had no meeting of our own today but expect to have next Sunday.   The Church I believe is done but was not dry enough today.   We had a real old fashioned Thanksgiving on Thurs. I thot of you at home a great deal.   We had a very pleasant time in the evening.   Our Minister Mr Cordley, Mr T.D.Thatcher, the Editor of the Lawrence Republican and one or two other gentlemen and their ladies spent the evening here and we had a glorious sing and a very pleasant time.   Mr. T is a very nice man and very sociable.   He has been married and has lost his wife.   Mr C. is unmarried and as full of fun as Mr Webster.   They are both excellent singers.   We have got a very pleasant room here to sit in and a first rate one to sing in too.   It is almost square and quite high so that singing sounds first rate in it.

If this letter is not in enough pieces so that each one of the family can have a piece to read and all read at once it will be no fault of mine if Sarah should write as much on as many pieces as I have.

I dont know as I [shall] say much that you will care any thing about hearing for some how whenever I sit down to write all my ideas vanish into thin air and I are gone.   I have been talking with you today. I say you I mean the folks that I think the most of, that I have Daguerreotypes of them, viz. Father. Mother. Appleton, Whitteman & Mary Baker and I now have got the pictures all setting on the table in front of me to see if I cant draw some inspiration from them.   I sat very nearly an hour today and did nothing but just look at them and I could conjure up all kinds of times and places where I saw I could make you frown or smile just according to when I wanted to see you.   Father would occasionally draw down his eyebrows and say "Edward!" just as he has many a time for some caper that I had been cutting up, and [first] I would know he would smile and almost laugh aloud as he used to when you told some of those ministerial stories that you are so fond of telling.   Then I would [turn] to Mother to see her just smiling at this same story and just that minute Georgy would be up to some mischief and she would compress her lips and say "George" as stern as possible and then the expression of face would again change and she would look anxious as if she were saying "why dont Mr Fitch get home.   Here it is ten Oclock and he was only going to be gone a little while."   Hark "Those are our bells", no they go by, what can be keeping him".   But the prettiest picture of all is little <u>Julia Sumner</u> Fitch as she sits looking straight at me with those little bright eyes.   So cunning!   I send you a copy which is almost but not quite as good as the one I have left.   At any rate you can tell by something how she looks.   She is now asleep the little darling as pretty as a little Angel.   O how I should love to see you all and have you see my Baby!   if you did not say she was the prettiest thing you ever saw I should think you were poor judges of beauty.

But now to come down from the sublime to the real.   I want to know whose sewing machine that is that you have got: How much it cost?   and How large it is and how it works now?   And where in Boston you got it?   I think I shall have one by & by, how soon I cant tell.   We all are very well now.   John I have heard nothing from since he left here. Business is not very brisk but we keep busy part of the time.   Money is scarce & times are hard.   We hope for better times in the spring if not before.   I hope we shall hear from you sometime before a great while.   I believe we have not heard from you since the last of Aug or first of Sept

Your affect son E.P. Fitch

Jan. 7, 1859

Dear Mother

Father's letter saying that he had got that 16$ at Boston came a few days since and before this you have no doubt recd the draft to pay the interest on those Bonds.   Tell Father he may send the coupons that were due the 1st inst. [the present month] to me now.   I am obliged to you for the offer to keep those cakes till I come but as I do not expect to be in Hopkinton again until the middle or last part of June I am afraid that they may be spoiled before I come.

I want you to send me that <u>Poem</u> on <u>Hope</u>.   I will return it to you in a good condition as it is now.   I want to copy it.   I should have done so when I was there if I had had time and the right kind of paper.   Please send it immediately and you will oblige me very much.

We have got some more business that we would like to have Father do for us in Boston pretty soon.   Send on the coupons. All well.

Your aff Son
Edward P. Fitch

Jan. 9, 1859

I think it is about time that this letter was finished and sent off and I guess it will be before this year is out.   I have been so busy for the last two month that I absolutely have no time to write.   I am so busy at the store that I have almost become a stranger to my wife and baby.   Our business for the last month or more has been pretty good and we have been getting in a lot of stuff for the winter that keeps us pretty busy.

The Legislature have adjourned to Lawrence and we hope that will help us some more.   If as long time ever elapses again between times that I write to you it will be strange but in a letter that I recd a short time since you say "In some of the many letters we have written since we heard."   I have recd just two letters from you since I wrote.   One came in the first of Oct and I did not answer it because I then expected to be at Hopkinton within six weeks.   Then I recd one from you in Dec. and that is all I have recd from you since June last or perhaps July.

Jan. 19, 1859

Dear Parents

Your letters of Jan 1st reached here last evening.   I am sorry that we have not written more but we will not let so much time pass again without writing.   The Daguerreotype that Sarah speaks of you will not find as this letter was so heavy.   We will send it soon.   I intend to answer both your letters in detail very soon.

The notorious Capt. Montgomery speaks in our Church this eve. Geo. has gone over to hear him.   Father has gone to prayer meeting and so I am alone in the store.   Business is not very good just now.

The Legislature is in session here but they dont seem to do much yet.   We sell considerable amt to the Legislature if we only get our pay. Last year Father furnished them paper and Stationery to the amt of between 3 and 4 hundred dollars and the Gov just paid all but about 100.$ and that has not been paid yet, but the Sec of the Terr. says he will pay it soon.   We are now furnishing them with a lot of stuff which we shall do well on if we only get our pay in good season as we hope we shall.

I wish you would write & tell me the news from Hopkinton, the every day news.   Who is married, who is dead etc.
My Respect to all Friends
E P Fitch

N B   In some of my letters I shall send some Kansas Gold.   Be very careful when you find a small packet in a letter.   Open it carefully so as not to waste the Gold.   E

March 1, 1859

Dear Father

I suppose you think that it is about time that your letter of Jan 4th was answered.   Well I suppose it is and I will try now that I have a little time to answer it.   None of the reasons that you speak of would be altogether the true reason why I have not written more.   My time has been pretty much occupied in the store so much that <u>time enough</u> to <u>write</u> at once never comes.   I am thankful for your offer of sympathy and I hope that I shall ever have that sympathy, and always in prosperity.

I am not engaged in Speculation much because I have nothing to speculate with and my efforts in that line have turned out so badly heretofore that I dont think much of the business.   I am as sorry as you are that I ever went in that Quindaro operation.   It is a little singular that so many of our best and shrewdest business men got 'bit' in the same way in that matter.   The time may come when we may work out of it but it will be a long time first I fear.   There is a project on foot now that if it works will make that something of a place after a while but like property in niggers, as the darkey himself said, it is might uncertain.

The state of Religious Society here is not what I wish it was.   We are in a cold state spiritually.   We have got a very good minister Rev. Mr. Cordley (see his lecture in the Republican of last week); if he has the strength of body that he has of mind he would yet be a bright light in this part of the country and will.   As it is I think he gave us one of the best sermons that I ever heard last Sunday on Parental Responsibility.

I shall send you the prospectus of a weekly paper that is to be started here this spring if you can try and get some subscribers for it among our church members.   Mr. Cordley will be one of the Editors.

Give my best respects to Mr. Webster and his family.   I am glad he had such a good Donation party.   I wish I had been there.

I suppose you are having cold weather there now but we are having fine spring like weather tho today is cloudy.   Folks are plowing some and things begin to look like spring.

I wish you could come out here and see us.   We should be so glad to see you.   You came very near seeing us in Hopkinton last fall but just missed of it.   It seems that you yet supply Hopkinton with milk.   Does the business pay as well as it used to?

I wish you could come out here and buy the farm that lies next to mine on the west.   It could be bought cheap this spring and it is a good farm but I suppose you <u>cannot so it is of no use to think of it</u>.   I hope that I shall be able to send you some money before long but I dont know.   It is pretty hard to get any money except <u>just enough to live on</u>.

I have thot some of going to Pikes Peak this spring but I think now it is very doubtful about my going.   George, Sarah's brother, may go. We think of establishing a branch of our business there but cant tell yet exactly what we may do on the premises.

193

One week from today I shall be 27 I expect!?   Such an old man I am getting to be with a wife and family to take care of.   It seems queer to think of it.   My sheet is getting about full and time is precious.   Our City Election comes off next Monday.   If I am elected Mayor I will let you know.

Yours filially
Edward P. Fitch

Dear Mother

     I have just finished a sheetful in answer to Fathers letter and now I am going to do the same by you if I can get time enough today.   I have to run and wait on somebody every minute or two so that I am not at writing half the time.

     I have got the Rheumatism in my right shoulder today and cant use it very easy.   Father has gone out on to his claim today and George and I are here alone.   George has been sick with the chills for some time, that is he shakes every other day but is able to be about the day that he does not shake.   He shook yesterday.

     Now for your letter.   I thank you for your wish on the New Year and wish you many of them and will assure you that we have not forgotten old Hopkinton nor our Mother that lives there tho we may have neglected her apparently.   It has not been intentionally.

     I am sorry that you felt so about us and much more sorry that we ever gave you occasion to feel so.   I hope we shall not again soon do so again.

     I should like to see little George.   Has he forgotten me?   Tell him I have not forgotten him yet.   How large is he, how much has he grown?   Is Elijah bigger than I am?   If he is not, I suppose he will be. Alexis Ide went to study for the ministry just about the time I came to Kansas, I think.   I should like to see him.   How are Ides folks?   Do you ever see or hear of them?

     Give my best respect to them if you have a chance; also to Mr. Marshall's family.   I have had a very severe cough this winter a while but have got over it now.   I have a little cold in my head now but otherwise I am very well.

     You say that you dreamed (wide awake) that we should drop in upon you at Thanksgiving.   Well, that dream came very near being fulfilled.   I fully expected to start for the East at a certain time for some weeks but did not start on account of not being able to sell my horse and cow and raise the money.   I thot too that perhaps you would say that I

194

had better use the two hundred dollars that it would cost me to come and see you to pay what I owe to Father and I thot that I could not pay you and come and see you too.   I hope someday however to be able to do both but I dont know how soon it will be.   I wish I could see you all and the old places that were once so familliar to me.

"How dear to my heart are the scenes of my childhood
When fond recollection presents them to view"

I wish Calvin would write his _____ or to me or somebody else for a letter.   I cant get any of the news from Hopkinton somehow or other. That little package that you sent last Sept. came to hand on New Years Eve and was a very acceptable New Year present.

I am sorry to hear such bad new from Lewiston.   I have not heard from them for a long time, only once since Uncle William died.

I have not heard from John for some time.   He talks quite strongly of going to the Gold Mines this spring.   I rather think he will go. As I said I almost was going but think I shall not now.

Appleton I have not heard from for some time.   He was well I believe when I heard from him.   I can write no more today.   So Goodbye.   Have no fear that I shall ever forget such a good Mother as I have.

Your aff son
Edward.

March 18, 1859

Dear Father

We recd a few days since a letter from you on the same day that I had sent one to you.   The letter is not now at hand so I can not answer it in detail but I have a matter of business that I want to hear from you in regard to immediately.   We have in our business here furnished a great many things to the County and have taken their Script in pay and now we have just been about to get all our Script into County Bonds.   They are Bonds of the County of Douglas bearing ten percent interest payable semi annually at the Metropolitan Bank New York the principal being payable March 1st. 1861.   5$ dollars on each 100$ will be paid at the band on the first of Sept 59.   5$ on the First of Mar 1860.   5$ Sept 1st 61, and also the principal.   The Bonds are for 100$ each.   Now what I want to know is: First, Will Mr Morse take one of these 100$ Bonds for that 100$ that I owe him on that warrant or will the man of whom you may have borrowed the money to pay him. He would be getting ten percent on his money then.

Second I want to know if I could sell any of those Bonds to any body that you know of around Hopkinton or any town round there. Lee Claflin, Wm Claflin, Robt. Wood, Aug. Phipps or any of these men. That is, in case Father Wilmarth should visit you during the spring, could you help him to sell any of them to any of these men or any one else.

Third could you get the Hopkinton Bank to buy them if we would take their bills and bring them out here. If we should bring their bills out here and put them in circulation, half of them would never get back to the Bank so they would make something in that way. These three things I want to know and I want very much that you should make some inquiries (if you don't know without). Especially of the Bank officers and see whether anything of that kind could be done.

If you would see what could be done about it and let me know immediately we should be very much obliged to you indeed for we have got considerable money in the Bonds and if we could get the money on them it would help us amazingly in our business.

Also I would like the same questions answered in regard to Territorial Bonds payable in New York. The same way only the principal is not due till 1865, for we have some of these bonds that we want to raise the money on too. I should think some of the rich farmers that you know of would be glad to get such things for they will be sure of ten percent on their money and no possibility of loss at any rate or in any way.

Now what I want is for you to find out what you can about this matter -- And write to me right straight off. Father W. has been writing to some of his friends today to see if he can raise some among them. We shall have, I expect, more that 1000$ of these Bonds and if we could get 1000$ in money it would give us a start in business that would help us much.

If there is any prospect that we could dispose of any of them, then Father will come there if he goes East with them to get the money. So I want you to let me know right off immediately. I ought to hear from this letter in three week[s] time..; that will be the 15th of April or there-abouts.

And I hope your answer may be favorable.

Yours truly
Edward P. Fitch

April 20, 1859

Dear Parents

Three Cheers!!!!! Hurrah! <u>Julia Sumner Fitch</u> can walk alone!!! Two years ago yesterday I was married, they have been two happy years. Today the baby walked alone several feet right along!!

An't that a strange coincidence. Oh! I'm so glad! She has walked all around with just the least help that ever was for some time. Yesterday a Mrs Waters who has a little child just about the size but three months older that Julia came to stay a few days with us. Her little one walks alone and the baby after watching her a while today she thot she might as well walk herself so today she took a start and walked. She did not take up her bed but I suppose that will be the next thing.

Julia has been very sick with inflamation of the Bronchial Tubes. She was taken the first day of April, and was sick for almost two weeks. She was very sick for several days. On Sunday the third she was so sick that we did not know as she would live but God has graciously spared her to us and we I trust are thankful. She has not yet got so strong as she was before she was sick. Had she not been sick she would no doubt have walked before this time.

We have had rather a backward spring thus far tho it is fair and warm now. We are all as well as usual except the baby. She has not got quite strong yet.

I am sort of unwell with this headache today.

Your aff son
Edward

This letter was written after I came from dinner. At night when I went to supper she came all the way across the room to meet me. Now she walks all over the house. E.P.F.

We are all well except for Father who is afflicted with a bad boil.

April 20, 1859

In this letter Edward is concerned about his father's response to this request to try to sell some Douglas County and Kansas Territorial bonds for cash. See Edward's letter of March 18, 1859

Dear Father

Your letter in regard to those bonds arrived here four or five days since. I am sorry that you could not give me a little more encouragement about them but I hope you will be able yet to find 8 or 10 hundred dollars that wants to be invested in a safe place at a good rate of interest for such I consider these Bonds to be. We have not yet recd our Territorial Bonds but we are expecting them very soon now. They will be first rate stock for those men who have money to invest in for they are just as sure as anything can be and at good interest. The County Bonds will be just as good for there is no possibility of their not being good. They are well secured for there are but a few hundred dollars of Bonds issued and the County is worth a hundred of thousands and I dont know but three times that. I want you to do all you can to find some chance for us to get some money on them. When we get the Bonds we shall think of starting after the money. If I had any of these Bonds myself I would give you some of them, as Mother spoke of, but they dont belong to me so I can not well do that. I shall try hard to get some money for you this spring but I dont know whether I shall make out much or not. I would like to let you have thee or four hundred if it was possible to do it. Please do all you can for us in the matter of the Bonds and you will much oblige Yours truly

E.P. Fitch

Nov. 25, 1859

Dear Father,

I enclose some Documents which I wish you to make the following use of. I want you to go to Boston and call at No 31 State St and see Mr Place. Give him the enclosed letter. Let him read it and then see what he will do about it. If he pays you the $16.00 give him the ticket and it is all right. If he will not do it find out why. See exactly what the reason is so as to tell me as then I shall try another plan to get the money back. Tell him that he agreed that these tickets should be good and, as they were not, of course he ought to make them good. Show him the tickets and the Envelopes that came with them but dont give either of them to him unless he pays you back for I shall probably want to send them all to Mr Houpt at Philadelphia. If Mr Place says he must take them and send to Philadelphia himself to get them paid back (which I dont believe is necessary at all) make him give you a receipt that shall bind him to either return you 16$ or the same two tickets and then if he should return the tickets be sure that they are the same ones with the

State St Office Stamp Oct 22 on them.   Make him pay you if it is possible. If he will not do it readily at first after coaxing awhile try a little threatening & see what affect that will have.   Tell him that I have access to the news paper and may be able to do him more harm that it would to pay the 16$.   Dont threaten too much because I should not [want] to make him very mad as I have some hope of getting it out of Houpt if I dont out of him.   Tell him that he knew this ticket would not be good for the "Union Line" has not been running for a year.   But the "Pacific Union Line" has and that is the ticket he should have given me.   Tell him this only if you have occasion to threaten him.   I saw the conductor and the Business Agent of the Pacific Rail Road and they would neither of them take the ticket and no Boat on the River would take it either.

Dont give up the Tickets unless you get the money for them unless it is to leave them for him to get the money, and then take a recpt so that if he does not get the money he will give you back the tickets.   I send you one of the Circulars that they give out there that you can see and show him that you have got the regular advertised rates to the two places. Dont give this up but keep it for I want that sent back to me with the Tickets if nothing can be done so that I can try again.

I want you to attend to this as quick as you can conveniently.   If you will be going to Boston in a week or two,   that will do but see to it soon.   If you have to go on purpose to see to this I will pay your fare.   If you get the money keep it till you hear from me again on the subject.

Do the best you can for me.

Yours truly
Edward P Fitch

How is your hand.   I will write more soon and tell you of our journey home etc. EP

Dec. 26, 1859

Dear Father

I enclose to you a Draft for $46.69 which I believe is the interest due on those Bonds the first of next Month.   Keep the coupons till you hear from me again.   If it cost anything to get the Draft into Cash there we will pay you if you will let us know how much it is.

199

Last week on Monday was the smallest sales we ever had any day and Fri. the largest. The week together was the largest cash recd we ever had. Today is dull enough.

I want you to go to Worcester and get some things for me if you will. We will pay your fare and expenses so as to have you see that the things that we sent for are right. Go to Hartshorn & Trumbulls Envelope Manufactory, Worcester. It is near the Washington Square Depot. -- That is the Lower Boston Depot, or Western Depot. Uncle Charles or Harvey can tell you the place -- and buy of him 4 thousand Envelopes, No. on the Box 5640 - 9. They are exactly _like_ in size & quality the one in which this will be sent. Then I want 8 M. [thousand] of the size of the enclosed envelope, at any rate not any shorter than that and if they should be a _little_ longer it would be no matter. If the enclosed Draft 30$ will not pay the Bill, if you will pay the rest we will send it to you. Get the Bill of the envelopes and send it to us by mail. Have them put them in a Box and send them off to us just as fast as they can. We are in a great hurry for them.

Have the Box Directed

O. Wilmarth Lawrence   Kansas

Care of N. McCracken   Leavenworth

by Hannibal & St Joseph R.R.

Via "Great Western Despatch"

Tell them to get the company to agree to put them through in the quickest time possible. I got some Envelopes of them thru Uncle Charles and we want more. When you pay the Bill make them take off 5 pct for Cash. The Draft will be the same as Cash to them but if you should be in Boston you can get it cheaper for Cash at Par there. And if when that much is put up there should be room in the Box, not filled up, have him put in enough to fill up of either kind so as to leave no waste room. I want these to be on their way immediately. I sent to you because we have not dealt much with them directly and [line cut off].

So if you will see to it immediately I will see that you are paid for it. It will cost you 1.00 to go to Worcester if you go to Cordsville with the horse and you only need to be there two or three hours for that business.

Yours

Edward P Fitch

Jan. 28, 1860

Dear Parents

We recd your letter of the 11th inst yesterday. We have got two as big "Boobies" in our Post Office as ever were made any where. One of them asked me yesterday what my name was and when I told him E.F. he went and took out <u>five</u> letters out of the F box in the general delivery that were directed to me that they had neglected to put in our box. Some of them had been lying there more than a week. I expect by the dates yours had just come. Then when I saw what you said about the letter that the P.M. [Postmaster] wrote about I went and asked about that and there was the letter in one of our envelopes with our card upon it--Directed to John A Fitch and there is no other Fitch in town but me and the folks did not know enough to come and see if I knew any thing about the letter, but wrote to you. The letter is of no consequence now. It was only a half doz lines written just before I sent the Drafts saying that I would send them in two days more.

Dont worry about those Bonds but send me the numbers of them. They will be paid and you shall have your money quick enough to meet your note at the Bank at any rate. I dont know yet whether they will be paid in New York or not but shall know soon. I shall probably send you a Draft within a few days that I shall want you to go to Boston and pay out for us and take up two more Bonds that are due the first of March. We send it to you because we had rather pay you for going to see to it than run the risk of having any "Sculduggery" played upon us by Stedman, who holds the Bonds. You remember my speaking of him how he would not let me have them again when I wanted them to let you have. So if you are thinking of going to Boston for any thing just wait till you get the Draft if you can. Any way the recpt that we have for the Bonds only keeps them from selling till the fifteenth of Feb. so we want them paid before that time.

I have been sick abed all day today -- only got up at five Oclock this P.M. so as to rest better when I should go to bed again. I have had I suppose a touch of the Quincy. My throat has been very bad but it is much better tonight. I had also the sick headache and shall bring it on again if I write much more so I must stop. My eyes begin to ache now.

Jan. 31, 1860

I have had no time till now to finish. Yesterday I recd your letter enclosing the Coupons for the 7 Territorial Bonds and the Bill of Envelopes from Worcester. I am sorry that the bill could not have been

201

filled sooner for they may now be too late for the Legislature and that is what I wanted them for. We shall send you, as I said, a Draft for you to pay in Boston and then I wish you would make out your bill so that we can see how we stand. You recd 16$ at Boston, 30$ in Draft to pay for envelopes & you have been to Boston once or more and to Worcester twice. Please send a statement of this, of course putting in you going to Boston to pay Stedman etc and please send it immediately after you go to see Stedman.

I did not suffer from the Cherry Rum that I was going to have but suffered so much for want of it that I had to buy some wine at Pittsburg that is not all gone yet.

That Gold Dust I left up in the closet in the dining room with the little phial to put it in. You can keep that till I come at any rate.

Sarah is pretty well and I have got well again. I think my throat is not sore now. Business is mildly lively. The Legislature is at work now and the Gov. is here with them. I expect to hear tonight that Congress has organised today. I shall be sorry that they have to give up Sherman but it may be all right.

Your aff. Son
Edward

,

Feb. 1, 1860

Dear Father

I send you with this a Draft for 150$ which I wish to have you take to Boston and settle up Father W [Wilmarth] acct with D.B. Stedman & Co. You will find them at No. 80 Broad St upstairs. The acct is on this wise. In Oct 1858 we bot a bill of goods of them amounting to 250$ or more. We made two payments as you will see by the enclosed statements but the balance of the acct was over due when I was there last summer. But Oct 3d /59 I went there and made this arrangement with them.

I gave them two Bonds of this (Douglas) County to hold as Collateral security for the payment of the bill by the middle of the present month and they were to wait until that time for the pay, they giving me the recpt for the Bonds which is enclosed with this. Now I wish you to go to them and settle up the acct with them. Take a recpt in full for all demands against O. Wilmarth up to the present time. Give them their Recpt back and take the Bonds and send them on to us immediately, or rather you may keep them till you hear from me again.

202

The reason of our sending to you to have you attend to this acct is they have acted in such a way that we thought they might take advantage of us if we paid them before we took the Bonds from their possession. They tried to make me allow 10 perct interest on the note but I would not. They will likely enough try to make you allow ten p. ct. Fight them on it and make them settle at 6 pct if possible, but if they stick for 10 pay them that and settle it rather than leave it without a settlement. They have not treated us very well and we wish to get our of their power. Then we shall probably tell them pretty much what we think of them and their actions

The Statement of Acct you will see is dated Boston Oct 3d, the time I was there to see them.

We have credited them with the whole amt of our note to them due   Apr 1st   1859$254.90   and the interest on it to Oct 3d 7.73 and charged them with what we sent them in March which they credited to us on the 14th$ 65.00 and the interest on that till Oct 3d   2.11 cash pd them in Apr they credit on the 14th $47.52 Inst on that till Oct 3d 1.35 making the Balance Due there on Oct 3d$146.65 which we credit them with.   Then we reckoned inst [interest] on that from Oct 3d to Feb 15th which we make 3.22   which added to it make $149.87, the amt now due with inst at 6 pct.   If they demand 10 pct that makes it $5.00 more according to our calculations and if you cant settle any other way pay them that.

Yours
Edward P. Fitch

You will please to attend to the settlement of the within acct. immediately and charge to O Wilmarth your expense to Boston, time etc and please make out a statement of what we are owing you for this and other business that you have transacted for us and any money you have recd or paid for us and we will straighten the balance immediately.   Inquire a little in Boston to see that Exchange on New York is at par and, if so be, that it is not allowing Stedman the difference.   We cannot get Drafts on Boston here at any rate as none of our Bankers keep any funds there.   Let us know of the result of this business just as soon as possible and you will much oblige.

Yours etc.
E.P. Fitch

You will find with the Recpt the statement made out by Stedman himself when I was in Boston.

Be sure and get a Recpt in full of all demands to the present time.

April 6, 1860

Dear Father

I was just commencing to write to you this morning when George came in from the P.O. with a letter from you.   The Bonds came safely and I intended to acknowledge the Recpt of them immediately but I suppose I did not from your letter.   They came soon after the first of April and we got the interest on them but the principal has not been paid yet and will not be probably for some months.   Father is out of town now and will be for some days.   When he returns I will send a note for two hundred and ten dollars, the amt due you from us on the Bonds which you had.   The other two hundred we will try and send soon as the note is due and I have forgot when that was.   Let us know immediately.

Business is tremendous dull and times are awful hard.   The Legislature, or rather Walsh, has not yet paid for what the Legislature had this last winter and the Bill for a year ago is not paid yet either.   We have got to have some money from somewhere pretty soon or we shall be in a bad fix.   I was thinking of coming East again this summer so as to try and get some more money on <u>some bonds</u>   of some kind but if your credit is impaired by my connection with you it will not be of much use for me to try that.   I may come East however as I can save something in buying myself.   I wish you knew as well just what we want as I do on   that.   I could write and tell what I want as well as I can tell myself.   If I could do so I could give you a good deal to do that we could well afford to pay you for doing and save something ourselves by the operation.

But the trouble is you nor any one else out of the business can not understand all the [turns] of the market and so we have to send directly to Dealers and let them make what I could save if I was there myself.

In regard to that Quindaro Share, I will transfer it if you think it best, but I had better not do it until I get the Deeds for the lots, I think. A Rail Road to Parkville (opposite Quindaro) is to be finished this fall and that will make that stock more valuable, but not worth what was paid for them.   As to those Certif. of Sumner Stock that you say John wants, he had ought to <u>want</u>.   I have written to him six or seven times to have him come down here but I have only heard once from him direct   and then he was coming down.   I have been keeping them till he came down.   Also the things I brot for him I have told him of them three or four times and I think he ought to write some thing definite to me if he is not at Sumner only once in a while.   I dont want to send the Certif. there to have them lost.   The only thing he has written to me was saying he was well and Mrs. F. also and that all the whites had left or were leaving Sumner, leaving it for (Pukes) (Missourians) and Dutch.   I shall write to him again if I get a safe way to send there.   I will send them not without for things are safer here.

Yr aff Son
Edward

SPRING 1860

Edward and Sarah visited New England during the summer of 1859, added a boy to their family in the spring of 1860 and, with Mr. Wilmarth, built a house in Lawrence.   Edward attempted to alleviate the suffering caused by the severe drought of 1859 and 1860 in Kansas by distributing clothing and money supplied by family and friends in Massachusetts.

Dear Mother

I have answered Father's letter -- and as you say, have said enough perhaps, but I must write a letter to you.   I have been very busy lately tho we have done nothing in the store much.   We are now about starting a Branch establishment at Topeka.   George is going up there to attend to it.   We are in hopes that we may get off some of our old stock by that means as well as sell some new. We are building a house, have got a good cellar & well all finished and most of the lumber on the ground and we expect the house to be put up next week and if we have good luck we hope to move into it by the first of May, but we may not be able to do so.

I have most certainly forgotten saying any thing about having a girl from Lancaster and I think now that what I said must have been in fun, but now that I have thot of it I dont know but some such thing would be well enough, for Sarah will need some one to help her.   I am afraid, or rather I know, she will and perhaps I would take some one if I was sure of getting a good girl.   I am glad you like your 'Katy' so well, hope she will not disappoint your expectation.

I dont remember the circumstance you mention about 'Freddy Stimpson'.   You must want to make me out to be an old man and when you spoke of Mr.S.' death I did not know whether it was the Providence or Dedham man.   If Appleton sends for that letter that you speak of we will send it to him if we can find it.   I dont know as we shall be able to do so until we move, as we are so much mixed up that it would be hard finding any thing.   We have preserved all your letters but they are not all where we can put our hand on them at any time.   That letter is valued and I dont know but Sarah has it laid away some where, where she knows where it is.   Thus far I believe I have answered your two letters and now the next thing will be some thing else.

You spoke in a former letter of a 'time' they were to have in the vestry and you said the knowing ones knew what it was for.   What was it? And did you entertain Mr Steeper, Miss Morse and others from Westboro as you expected to?

Perhaps you will notice in the paper that your hopeful son has been elected to an Office in the city worth $000.04 per year.   I feel highly 'tickled'.   The Election was about as hotly contested as the Connecticut election has been but came out right --as that has.   "We", that is the Anti-Lane Republicans, met at the Court House to nominate a City Ticket. The 'Lane' men came into our Caucus and tried all they could to control it and when they found they could not do that they bolted and got up a ticket and headed "Regular Republican nomination."   They worked hard but we beat them and the Democrats together by ninety majority.   The Democrats nominated their ticket on purpose to help them elect Fuller Mayor but they could not come it.   We elected every man on our ticket except one.   There was a Citizen Ticket got up with my name left off but I beat that.   The contest was about as hard on Marshall as any thing. There were three Regular and one Independent candidates.   I send two or three tickets so you can see how they mixed up the things.   There were no less than a Doz diff. kinds of mixed tickets.

We had an Election the week before for Delegates to the State Convention to elect delegates to Chicago and the Lane party beat because we did not work.   They bragged over that all the time and told what they were going to do at the City election but we rather dried them up.

Your aff Edward

April 18, 1860

Dear Father

I have (yesterday) recd another letter from you about those Bonds.   Before this time you will have heard that the Bonds came all straight enough and with this you will receive a note for the amt of the Bonds and Interest.   We shall not get our pay on the Bonds till Fall and if you could manage so as to let us keep it till then before we pay you the Note (which however we will make on demand and try to pay when you want it) it would be quite an advantage to us.   We have never been quite so hard up as at present, and it is in a great measure owing to the way we have been served by the Government Officials.

Sec Walsh [is] refusing to pay the Bill of the Legislatures that have been bought of us. The bill that he bought himself this winter (1860) amt to some $150. he refuses to pay or rather says he has not the money to pay it with. The fact is I suppose he has used the money himself and has not got it to pay over.

And the Bill of last winter 1859 they now refuse to even give us script for. We are about to sue the Government for it. And I am in hopes we may get it. We put it into a Lawyer's hands and he is to have ten per cent for collecting if he gets it. If not he is to have nothing. If we can get along till Fall we shall get through I think.

You said you had extended your note at the Bank or had got the money again but you did not tell for how long. I hope you can make arrangements & let us have it till fall. We will send a note bearing interest at 1 per cent a month and as you can probably get it at half that rate it will leave a little to pay you for your trouble in getting it.

There was a man went up to Sumner from here a day or two ago and I sent those Cert. to John to be given to him if he was there. The man has not yet returned so I dont know whether he found John or not. I may see him before this letter goes.

We are all pretty well.

Yours
Edward P Fitch

We could not get a Draft today so we will send tomorrow or as soon as we can get one. E.

April 20, 1860

Dear Father

Enclosed you have a Draft on Boston for 200$ [to] liquidate that Note of Mr Lincoln's. The interest I will speak of before I get through. Apr 21st. We shall now send you the money for the interest on the Lincoln note and enough more with the balance that you have in your hands to pay the interest on the Bond up to the first of March. Then we send you a note drawing interest from the first of March for the 200. two hundred. We will also send you a statement of acct. today or tomorrow

207

so you can see that that will just make us square.   If you have to pay any Exchange on the Draft charge it to us.   We will pay it but being on Boston I think there should be no Exchange on it.

We have just found that we shall be too late for this morning mail so we shall send all tomorrow.   I hope it will be in time so that Lincoln will not be in trouble for the money.

You will very likely hear by the paper that a United States Marshall has been killed while in discharge of his duties at Topeka.   It is so.   The facts are these, as near as I can ascertain this morning.   Last night just before night Dep Marshall Arms went to the house of Mr [John] Ritchie in Topeka and told him he had a warrant for him.   Mr R. said he could not arrest him on it as it was for some Political Offence in [18]56. Mr. Arms said he should do his duty.   Here some say he, R., shot Arms dead in his tracks and some say they both went into the house and both drew Revolvers, but at any rate Arms is dead -- shot thru the throat.   He was the same man that undertook a month or two ago to kidnap a Negro woman from a house in this city but was driven off without getting her. It is a very unfortunate affair at any rate to say the least.

Arms was not much thot of in the community except by his relatives and his Democratic friends.   He was in about as good business as those men from Boston that undertook to arrest Sanbourn at Concord a short time since.

There is nothing more of news that I know of today.

We are all well but hard up for money.

Your a[ff]

Edward P Fitch

May 3, 1860

Dear Mother

I have this moment (nine O'clock AM) rec'd your letter dated Apr 25 in which you say that you have heard nothing from me about that money.   I wrote two letters to you about it before the money went and one with the money, which went from here the 20th of April containing a draft for 200$.   Another went the 23 containing $11.92 to ballance acts [accounts] with Father, that is Father Wilmarth's acct's, all except two

<u>hundred</u> which we sent a note for. That shall be paid when it is wanted if you will only let us know how soon it must be paid.

I am very sorry to hear of that Daniel Eames transaction. How much was the note that he signed, you did <u>not say</u>. We are in a bad fix about money matters but I hope we shall get out some time. We should have been all right, had it not been for the rascality of some of the Government officers out here. They have made us a great deal of trouble but if we can make out to keep afloat till fall we shall get thro I think, but if things should concentrate and come down on us before that time we may go up Salt River all together, but I hope we shall weather the storm.

You ask what I meant about Mrs. F. and John. You have it just as I had it from him and I don't know any thing about it only I know now that he is not married now. He was down here last week and stayed two days. I could get nothing out of him about what he is doing hardly at all. He tried to give the impression that he was to be married soon but I don't really think it is so. He is building a house he says at Centralia and said he was going to write to have Father come out there. He <u>will go of course</u>. John has got in to some trouble and does not dare have those Sumner shares stand in his name and so is going to have them still made out to Father. Wheeler cheated him out of considerable but he has got Wheeler's instruments and he says he means to have them attached and sold for debt and buy them in so as to get them in to his hands in such a way that Wheeler cannot get them away from him. I don't know what to think of John; he perhaps will come out better for you than I have. He will not drag Father down with him as you seem to fear I shall. I hope I shall not but I have probably called on him too much. I have tried to keep my own stand good at the expense of running the risk of hurting him. I hope he will not in the end suffer by it.

I hope before this time you have recd the money and so are out of your immediate trouble about my affair and I hope I shall not get you any deeper.

All well

Yours
E P Fitch

Nov. 1, 1860

Dear Parents

I suppose you are wondering what has become of us that you have not heard from us before this time. Well it is too bad that we have not written more but I can tell you I dont have much time to write, neither does Sarah. You know we are all together in the store, Father, Brother George, and myself. Well, tho, we did not do a great lot of business there was always something for all of us to do all the time. Last spring we began to build this house and I had the whole management and direction of it and it kept me out of the store a great deal. The most of the work was done in April & May. Then we started a branch of our business in Topeka and Brother George went up there to attend to that, leaving Father and I to do what we had always had three to do before for they had one other and part of the time two others with them when I was East, so we have had more than our share of work to do this summer, but now business is dull and we do not have much of any thing to do. There having been no crops in the Territory in many places, trade of all kind is dull and ours feels it full as soon as any kind of business.

I am spending the first evening at home that I have spent except Sunday evening for a long time, the reason of it being that I was at home just at night and there came up a storm so that I thot I would not go up so that I would write a word or two to you. Did you know that Mr. Edwards was married? It was in our paper here and I did not know but he might send a paper from Springfield with the announcement in. He was married the 6 inst I believe. I have heard once from Calhoun since he went to Hannover and had a paper also. John I have not heard a word from since he was here in the spring. He told Sarah he was coming down here again in Oct. but he has not come yet. Appleton I have heard once from this summer. And I guess I have had two letters from you in six months. I had lost all track of Hopkinton matters till your last letter gave me some of the news. Who goes Representative this year? Have you much excitement about the Election there? Do you feel very much alarmed about the prospects of the secession of the South after Lincoln's election? The papers just now before election are full of what they will do but when the time comes they will wait.

You told me in your last about a girl that was here from the Lancaster School. Why did you not tell me who it was and who she lives with? Little Charlie will be five months old the day Lincoln is elected President. He is a fine little fellow and he laughs and grows fat fast. He is very strong of his age I think. He stands very firm on his feet. O I wish you could see him, you would be delighted with him I know. Julie remembers you, both of you. She gets your picture (Mother) very often and kisses it and says "I love my Grandmother way down to Hopkinton" and then she says "poor Grandpa got a sore hand "'<u>too bad</u>'".   She says the boys Elijah & Calvin have "gone to school now".   She is mighty pleased tonight because I have brot her home a little bedstead that I have been getting made for her - a crib so that she cant roll out.

There is going to be and there <u>is now</u> a great deal of suffering in Kansas this fall and winter.   You have no doubt seen the accounts in the papers of cases of extreme suffering.   Some of them may be overstated but in the main part they are true.   Thru a great portion of the Territory there has not been anything like as much raised as was planted.   In fact take the whole territory together, leaving out three or four counties, and that is the case in all of them.   Three or four counties on the river have had middling good crops.   I could tell you of many cases of real suffering if I could afford time and could write out all the particulars.   I will tell you one or two.   There is a family here that I am acquainted with that consists of a man & wife with two children.   They are honest people and temperate but very proud.   They have not got clothes to keep them warm and within two weeks they were without any thing to eat in the house, the man sick so as to be confined to his room and much of the time to his bed. The youngest child sick so that it was not hardly expected to live.   The woman came up [the] street and some benevolent person went thru the town and got a little money for her and got her some things to eat.   When that is gone she must look, I dont know where except to God, for more.

I know of a family where there are eleven children and a woman died near them leaving one little child without a Father and they took that into their family making 12 children and now coming on cold.   All the clothes that these children had was some made by the mother from an old wagon cover and all they had to eat was a little corn meal and what nuts & roots they could find in the woods.

I know of another place where there is quite a little settlement that are living entirely on nuts and herb tea.   In the south part of the Territory there are very many who have not clothing enough to keep themselves warm in only moderately cool weather.   What they will do in the winter I dont know.   All of these cases I <u>know either by personal observation</u> or <u>from men whom I know to be the most reliable sort of men who have been eye witnesses of all these things</u>.

These are the poorest class.   There are thousands who have left the Territory to winter in Iowa or Missouri or Illinois, most of those who had teams and could by any possibility get away have gone.   A <u>great many</u> in the counties along next to Missouri have gone in there to winter.

Folks from Illinois have been here and bought up all the hogs they could get and took them off. The farmers sell their hogs very low for they have nothing to keep them on and so they sell them very cheap.

The whole that I got from my farm this year for my 1/3 of the crop was $2.50 and my taxes this year were about 12.$. So much for the suffering at present. Then there was no wheat raised this year so there is none for seed next year. That is a great difficulty. The Merchants of Lawrence sent a man to Illinois to get some wheat for the farmers in this county. They got 7 or 8 hund[red] bushels given to them and they have furnished it to the farmers here at the cost of transportation so that there has been some sowed this fall but not one tenth part of what would have been had there been wheat raised here this year. So much for wheat. Now there is a large portion of our population who have farms and who can live if they can get thru this winter but on account of failure of crops they have nothing to live on this winter. They do not like to receive aid as a gift but if they could have money lent to them from the East they could repay it in one year without interest and get along. There is a movement on foot now or trying to start to get money in the East for that purpose -- to have the money sent here and the persons to whom it is lent to give a mortgage on their farm for the amt with no interest. I believe this will be a great benefit to some of our folks if they get such help.

Take it together we are a great deal worse off than we were in /56. Then there was some money in the county. Now there is none. Then there was good crops where the Missourians did not destroy them, now there are no crops at all. Mr Thadeus Hyatt with Arny and Genl Pomeroy have been traveling over the Territory pretty extensively and they give a sad picture of the state of things as they found it. Mr Hyatt intended to give 10,000$ for the needy in Kansas himself but when he found that that would not more than relieve one county he thot he must secure some cooperation from other rich men. He has bought and sent into some of the most destitute portion of the country some thousands of dollars worth of provisions & clothing. Now there has been a kind of scheme got up to make folks think they were helping Kansas and at the same time build a Rail Road that probably to one who knew nothing about the matter would look very favorable, but it is one grand nonsense. Dont you for pity sake give one cent to any such object. In several places when meetings have been held it has been deemed advisable to say by resolution or otherwise that it was best for folks at the East to send money, clothing and any thing else they had to spare direct to their own friends in the Territory and let them dispose of it so that it would not be misapplied as a good deal of

212

what was sent to the committee in '56 was for we know that much of what was contributed at that time for Kansas got into the hands of designing men and was appropriated to their own ends and use.

Now after all this prelude I have got this to say that if you will send out some clothing or any money to me I will put it where it will be doing some good to the poor in this Territory.   I am poor myself, poorer than I was <u>last fall</u> but I have now given away more than once or twice to those that were much poorer than myself.   If you could among your acquaintance around gather up some clothing such as you sent me before you would be doing the cause of humanity good service and if you should try and get any thing of that kind you ought at the same time collect money enough to pay the freight on it and send it on to pay it with, for it is better to have it paid at this end of the route, but there is no one here to pay it or advance the money.   And another thing there is much more need of money now than in '56 for now food must be purchased and at a higher cost than then.   In Illinois they are contributing flour and wheat and sending it on here to be given out.

You are at liberty to make what use of this letter you see fit and if you should see fit to do any thing toward sending out money or anything else for the poor of Kansas I will take charge of it, make the most of it I can and report to you what is done with it.   This letter is written in a hurry and I have no time to read it over.   The ground is now quite whitened with snow and it is quite cold. God help the Poor is the prayer of your Edward P. Fitch

I was when I commenced going to write about my own affairs but I got on to Poor of Kansas and there I stuck.   I cant write but I could talk if I was there.   E

Nov. 18th, 1860

My Dear Dear Mother

How I wish you could just look in upon us this evening and see how cosy we look and how happy we are.   We have got a noce 'cosy' <u>little</u> room as you ever saw.   I'll try and descrobe it and its fixtures to you.   I wish I had the power of writing description but as I have not you must take the will for the deed.

Our house fronts the East and the front or sitting room extends across the width of the house except the width of the stairs which go up on the North side.   The house is 16 1/2 feet wide, that is I expect a little wider than your dining room is in the widest place.   The outside door is on the North side of the fron or at the N.E. corner of the house.   It opens into a little entry at the foot of the stairs just the width of the stairs which go straight up to within three steps of the top when they turn to the left so that you would not run your head against the roof in going up.   The space at the bottom of the stair is about 3 x 6 ft, a little larger than your south entry.   A door to the left as you come in opens into this room where I now write.   This room goes back 11 1/2 ft and is 12 feet wide clear.   You can measure the size of it on your Dining room so you can see just the size. Suppose you take the Dining room the South end of it and I will make this room of it.   Remember to set this room in there would just turn it round completely East would be West and North South, that is the East side of the Dining room would be the West side of this.   We will call your dining room 11 1/2 feet from the South entry door to the Kitchen Door and take twelve feet the other way.   That makes the size of this room.   Now start from our front entry that would be just outside of your house to come into this room, you come south thru the door that would be coming in at your South West window.   At your righthand as you enter the room hanging on the North wall of the room in the center is our large glass just as yours hangs on the right of that window under it just where your table stands, stands our Melodean or rather Seraphim.   It belongs to Mr. Wilmarth and is a very fine instrument, a large Piano cased one - 5 octaves.   Then as you turn the corner just in the same position of your kitchen door is our door to the dining room only ours is clear to the corner then comes the stove just in the same place with relation to the door that your stove is only nearer to it.   Our door opens in to this room while yours opens out. Then on the other side of the stove is a door into a closet with shelves for a china closet just like yours where you keep the cider, (I wish I had a bottle) only mine is not as deep as that being only 16 inches just the width of the chimney, but our stove we have got just the cutest little stove you every saw.   It is very small and looks something like this in front (drawing).   There are two doors that slide to-gether in the top part and they can be slid back so as to leave all that part that is dotted open if you choose.   The oval place at the bottom, that has the register in, can all be taken out so that it is almost as open as a Franklin stove if you want it. So we often have it all open when we have a good fire and it is almost as good as the Old Fashioned fire place.   We burn coal in it tho it is a wood stove.   We have a different kind of coal from what you do, much softer.

          After you pass the stove & closet door then comes the table at which I am writing.   It stands clear in the corner the end toward the stove.   There is just room for the door between the stove and the end of the table.   Over the table hangs the Bookcase containg many of the Books that I brot with me [and] <u>some more</u>.   Then you turn the corner and on the south side of this room, which would be represented by the partition across your dining room, in the middle of that side is our South window. From under the window to the other side of the room extends the Lounge. Just at this time it is occupied by little "Charlie" the prettiest smartest liveliest & best little Baby that you ever saw or heard of.   He was just five months old the day that Lincoln was elected Presdient.   I wish you could see him, the little rogue.   He is fat and chubby.   He laughs and crows and plays like anything.   He is very fond of music and as quick as anyone sits down at the instrument to play he wants to be right there.   He will put his little hands on and play away and seems to enjoy it hugely.   He has been a little unwell for two or three days now and has been rather restless so that Sarah's sleep has been disturbed and she has laid down with him on the lounge and both are sound asleep.

Over the lounge side of the window hangs a picture of Sarah's own <u>Mother</u>.   It was drawn by a Spirit artist in Columbus, Ohio and sent to Father by mail. It is a pencil drawing and a <u>very good picture</u> (of some person).   I can see in it a resemblance to the rest of her sisters that I have seen.   And Father thinks he sees quite a resemblance to his wife for whom it is intended.   There is something curious about it any how whether spirits or <u>not</u> had anything to do with it I can't say.   Then as you turn the corner the front side of the room has a window in the center and on either side a picture of Father and Brother George such a one as I left with you, only they are nicely framed.   This with the chairs and a new carpet that we have just put down this last week complete the furniture of our room and tho it is small we are very comfortable in it.

There is one more fixture however.   My oldest daughter sits by the Melodean reading.   She is a young lady of sixteen.   We call her Anna. She is neice to M.F. Conway, Member of Congress Elect, under our state government.   That is in this way: her mother was a widow and married Judge Conway's Brother.   She is a very nice girl, a member of the Baptist church.   We intend to keep her till she gets married, perhaps if Elijah come out here there may be a chance for him tho he had better not build too high hopes on it for a week ago tonight and two weeks before that she had a young gentleman here to see her, or at any rate I don't think he came to see me and he staid midling late.   He is the Probate Judge of thes County Elect under the State Gov. and a pretty good lawyer for a young man so if we keep her till she marries we cannot tell how long it may be.

She will make a most excellent wife for some person at any <u>rate</u> she is one of the best girls of her age I ever saw.   There is only one fault in her that I know of.   She is slow but everything has to be done nice and in order. She is very patient with the children and little Charlie will cry for her just about as quick as he will for his mother.   I think myself very fortunate in finding so good a girl to help Sarah and my best wish for Elijah is that he may get as good a wife for himself as she will make for the one that gets her.   She is large, a little taller than Sarah and about as heavy.   I wish John was here and would fall in love with her and she with him.

By the way I have not seen John since last May.   He has gone to Pikes Peak.   He went about <u>six weeks</u> or <u>two months</u> ago so I heard last week.

I think of my old home when I sit down of Sunday evenings after dark before we light a lamp.   Sarah and I often, as we did tonight, sit and sing.   It makes me think of Sabbath evening at Home when I was young (for I feel quite like an old man now, especially when I get my two children on my knee) when we used to sing "When I can read", 'Jerusalem' and those old tunes and then I think just how you and Father used to look as you sat in the old "Middleroom" or laterly in the Dining room where you now are and sometimes a feeling of sadness comes over me, "Can you tell me why Mother?"

My bass viol I do not use now at all.   It is lent to Mr. Kimball who plays at our Musical Association that meets every week.   Father can play on it first rate but he dont have much time and what time he has he uses the Melodean which he can play pretty well.   In fact he can play almost anything.   His favorite, or more properly speaking the instrument on which he is the most at home is the Clarionett.   He is the perfect master of that.   He plays it at the Glee Club.   They have an orchestra that plays after they have done singing that consists of 4 violins, 1 Bass Viol, 1 Double Bass, two Brass horns, a clarionett and a piano and they make some excellent music.

You spoke in one of your letters like this "Take care of your first wife for you dont know how a second one might train you".   I think I am taking good care of my wife in the way that I <u>suppose</u> you meant.   I had some body to help her from about the first of May till the middle of July that could do all the work and since she went I have had Anna all the time. She finds her hands pretty full with two children to attend to.   I expect so she dont get much time to write letters.   The baby & Lulie are both pretty good most of the time.   Lulie remembers you and Father and knows your picture just as well as I do.   She says thats my Grandma and that poor Grandpa got a sore hand.   She remembers all about it.

By the way how is that hand this winter and how is your health Mother?   How many cows horses & oxen have you got?   How was the hay crop this year?   Did you have the cider mill fixed up this year?   Why did you not elect Father to the Legislature instead of Milton Claflin?   Is there any chestnuts?   Or shell bark hickory nuts?   Are there any cranberries?   Is it cold weather there yet?   I am thankful that we have not yet had much cold weather for what thousands in this territory will do if we have very cold weather I dont know.   Are you doing anything there for "Starving Kansas" not "Bleeding Kansas" this time?   I shall send with this letter some papers, one N.Y. Tribune and Springfield Republican. Note the marked passages especially that letter of Hyatts in the Tribune. Also take particular notice of the articles in last week and this weeks Lawrence Republican.   The suggestions are all worth reading especially about giving to irresponsible persons.   There was a convention held here last week that framed a plan for the distribution of Relief thru the Territory.   They have the general and Local committees all over the Territory and I think probable that they will do as well as can be done. There are however some men now at the East who are trying to speculate out of the wants of Kansas, getting money and putting it in their own pockets.

Those are good suggestions about send[ing] things from the East old garments unless they are pretty good do not pay to bring but cloth fit for garments _____ or Ready made good serviceable garments are what is wanted.   The East ought to furnish the money to pay the Freight and the Western states will give all or nearly all the provisions we shall need if the East will send money to pay the freight and pay for sacks for flour, wheat & potatoes.   If you do anything about sending anything out and send it to me.   Do not send in Barrels as you did before but go to the Stores and get them to give you a Dry Goods Box.   Tell them what it is for and make them give it to you.   I have been applied to now to know if I had not some of the things left that I had sent before by those who I helped then who do not live here now.   If you should do anything about sending anything to me send it in a box if you send clothing.   I will see that it is given where it is needed or I will give it to the Committee as you say but if you send direct the Box as I will hereinafter direct   If you should send of Box of anything and nobody there wants to contribute money to pay the freight on it I will pay the freight on it for what you may send me in it for you said I believe that you had been drying apples and berries for your Kansas children so if you send me a lot of Dried Apples Dried Berries Nuts & a few Cranberries if things were put in a small box inside would come safe.   If you I say send me enough of such things I can pay the freight myself but there would have to be considerable for me to worth all the freight.   If you could get anyone there to pay some toward the freight and send me the money that would be better still.   I say send me the money for it is much better to have freight paid at this end of the route than that.   It comes thru safer when the freight is not paid.   If you have any notion of sending anything to me let me know immediately that I may be on the Look out for it.   If you send anything put it in a Box and Hoop the Box and direct it thus

O. Wilmarth   Lawrence Kansas
care of R. McCracken Leavenworth
via Hannibal & St Joseph Rail Road
"By Great Western Despatch"

The reason of having it directed to O. Wilmarth is so that there would be no delay at Leavenworth.   They send our goods over immediately when they arrive there.   If you dont send in this way and you have any apples or berries to send to me, let me know and I will contrive some other way to have them sent.   We shall be having some goods from Boston sometime so that we can get anything that you may want to send thru this fall.

I see by the papers that you made a grand wide awake Demonstration a little before the Election there in Hopkinton.   I should like to hear some particulars.   Who was there?   How many torches you had?   Where the speaking was?   How many Hands were there?   If you cant tell me I should think Elijah might do that.   We had a demonstration here the Thurs. night after Election over the Victory.   We got out about 150 torches.   We formed our club the night before so that we did not have much time to prepare and so did not make very much of a show but we showed our good will to do if we had had the oportunity.   Then we felt to[o] poor to make much parade and fuss.

How do you get along in the church?   I have not heard of Mr. Webster being dismissed yet.   How did that sermon on Standing in Prayer time affect the People?   Do they sound now any better than they did?   How do you like the new organ?

Are you going to have any Lectures this winter there?   You will see in one of the papers I send that Rev. Mr. Nute is going to Lecture on Kansas.   I think he would give a pretty good Lecture and it would not be a Bad idea to get him to lecture to you.   If he should come out there have

218

him stay with you if possible.   He knew me well when he was here.   But more than this if Mr. A.D. Richardson goes East to lecture, Dont you fail to have him come and stay with you too.   He is well acquainted with John and me too, more with John than with me for he lived at Sumner quite a while.   He is now in Utah but I think he is going to lecture this winter at the East.

What is the prospect of Wm. Claflin's being Collector of Boston now?   And what of you (Father) getting an office under him?   I hope he will be elected Pres. of the Senate this winter.   There seems to be some considerable Bluster at the South about Secession but I guess it will all end in smoke.   I don't imagine the Union is in <u>much</u> danger but like Gov. Hanks I say "Let the Union Slide" if South Carolina wants to leave let her go she is no account anyway.

Times have changed.   Birney in 1840 got about 7,000 votes, in 1844 he got about 17,000, in [18]48 Van Buren got several hundred thousand, in 1852 John P. Hale got a lot, in 1856 John C. Fremont carried most of the Free States.   In 1860 Abe Lincoln recd all the votes he wanted to make him the next president.   What year was it that you cast one of the 11 Liberty Party votes the first that was cast in Hopkinton?   Hurrah for Lincoln!   You are one of the Old Guard!   I enclose one of the tickets we voted here on the 6th inst.   We wasn't going to be cheated out of voting for president again at any rate.   Who did you vote for Pres. in 1836?   I dont perfectly remember all about that canvass.   My recolection seems to be dim on that point but I do well remember the Campaign of 1840; the Log Cabin & hard cider and the whipping I got for running away from school to see the log cabin.   I was a great Whig then.   I had a little flag and stuck [it] on the old front yard fence.   I went to Boston   [Letter incomplete]

Dec. 10, 1860

Mother

We have at last got our mail thro.   We had about 800 papers come for us today so I will send this on.   Sarah feels slighted that you did not answer her letter that she wrote to you just after I started East last summer.   Please write <u>her</u> a good long letter.   I am writing this at the store.   She probably would not let me put it in if she knew it but it is all right.

Business has been rather good for two or three days past, better than usual these war times.   Tell Father I will try and get that Interest

money on by the 1st Jan. but I may not be able to do that but will very soon after.   Does he have to pay the ten pct to Wood?   or did he make his take less as he got so well secured?   I will be as prompt as possible. Please write soon and as often as you can to you ever aff. Son
                                        Edward.

What do you think of the President's message?   I dont like it very well!

Dec. 23, 1860

Dear Parents
        I think I shall "Secede" pretty soon if I don't hear from you.   I have written at least three long letters home within two months, two of them very long indeed but I have heard nothing from you for three months at least and I think longer, not even a letter at Thanksgiving from any member of the family but Appleton.   How are you all?
        I am very busy indeed in the store tho we are doing very little business compared to what we were last year at this time.   There is nothing talked or thot of here but Secession and its effect on business. Business in Cincinnati & St Louis is allmost Suspended.   Exchange in the East is worth from five to 10 percent and that will smash any kind of business.
        Secession is playing the deuce with all kinds of business.   If we had any body but an old Granny in Petticoats for President we might get along.
        We have got a smart government.   They can hang any quantity of Methodist ministers in Texas and other Southern States but when we in Kansas hang two or three horse thieves and murderers the Army must be sent right down to wipe out Montgomery.   John Brown with seventeen men & a Cow can take Virginia and the whole power of the government must be brot down on him.   Kansas would not submit to Lecompton Constitution etc. and the Government must come down on us and force us to submit but South Carolina can secede and the Old Public Functionary say[s] the Government has no power to coerce her into Submission.

        O What a Great Country

Dec. 27, 1860

What are you all doing? I see that Wm Claflin is Pres of the Senate.   I am glad of that.   Why did not you go down and get some of the subordinate offices at the State House?   Our Legislature meets tomorrow at Lecompton.   I expect to go up and see what is going on there.   We expect they will adjourn to Lawrence in a few days at the furthest.   I am not a candidate for any office but go up to look after our interests generally.   Charlie is 7 months old today and he is a nice baby.   I wish you could see him.   He sits on the floor some alone but more generally sits in the high chair at the table or in the clothes basket.   Julie will be three years old next Sat.   She is a great girl now.   The girl that is living with us commenced to go to school last week so that Sarah is alone with the two children during school hours.

We gave a Donation Party to our minister Mr Cordley two weeks ago.   We had a fine time and as the proceeds he recd 88$ in money and almost 100$ worth of valuable articles, about 1/2 of which he said he should have had to bought this winter.   At any rate it was a perfect success in all its parts.   Every body that had any thing to do with it was well pleased.

I do wish you would write to me and tell me some thing what you are doing and what is being done in Hopkinton.   I do not have any letter from any body there now and I might about as well be in South Africa as any where else for all that I know about things there.   Do please write to me and let me know something about your [prospects] and troubles etc
Your aff Son
Edward

Do you hear anything of John.   Perhaps Sarah will write some time. How about send me any thing for the destitute.

Jan. 6, 1861

I wrote so much two weeks ago tonight and have not had time to finish it before.   "What under the canopy" as Mother used to say is the matter with you all that I have heard nothing from you. I have not heard one word from you for three or four months.   What is the Matter.   I have written several long letters in that time and asked a lot of questions that I wanted answered or else I should not have asked them.   I should like to have them answered very much.   I suppose you are thinking some by this time about the money due on those <u>coupons</u> of the Territorial Bonds, or have you sent them to New York and got them paid?   Do you want us to pay them.   I dont know how we are to do it but I suppose we shall have to raise the money if you want it.   Write us what you have done or want done about it.   Also that two hundred dollars that you have Mr Wilmarth's note for, when is the interest due? and when must it be paid? Make the pay day as far off as you can for money is scarce in these parts now.   Political troubles and smashing our money matters at the west considerable.

        We are considerable excited here over the news from South Carolina. We fired 32 Guns for Maj Anderson one night last week.   He has got the true grit.   We live in troublous times but I think the Government will come out right if The Old Pub. Func. dont spoil it entirely before Old Abe gets a chance to try his hand at it.

Jan. 25, 1861

Dear Parents
        I have tonight been made glad by the reception of a letter from you, the first word I have heard from you since sometime in Sept.   I think it may have been Oct. but I think more likely it was Aug.

        I have written three long letters and one that was not particularly long to you in that time.   You say Appleton complains that he does not hear from me.   I have heard from him once since last spring and I have written to him three times since I recd that letter from him.   Your letter was dated the 10 inst and you had just recd mine of the 6 of Jan.   I have written to you once since that and told you of John, what I had heard. Albert Barber is here.   He left the mines on the 20th of Nov. and John had been there about ten days when he started back.   John went out with an Ox team and arrived out about the 10th of Nov.   This is all that I have heard direct from John or any way from him since he was here in Apr last. I dont expect he will ever come back here till he has been to California and perhaps South America.   He told Sarah when he was here that he was going to rove around till he was 35 and then settle down.

        You speak of Mr Richardson.   Is that A.D. R.?   I suppose so. That girl that you want to know about, I know she lives about a mile and 1/2 from town.   She used to come to our Sabbath School but the folks with whom she lives are the strongest kind of Unitarian and they took her from our S.S. when they started one at their church.   She did not want to go at all.   She had a great deal rather stay at our school.   I will find out all I can about her as soon as I can and let you know.   We are having the best kind of sleighing here now, have had for about two weeks.   The weather is very cold.

We are all pretty well now.   Both the children had a little sick turn, the effect of a cold, but they are better now.   The rest of us are well and have been.

We did not find out about the coupons till about two weeks ago ourselves.   I will write more about them in a day or two.

Edward

MARCH 8, 1861

Dear Parents

On my birthday I thot I would write a word to you.   I have been so immersed in politics this week that I have done nothing else.   You will see by the paper that I was not reelected for which I thank my friends, for it is a post of some importance to keep illegal votes out.   I get more kicks than any other kind of pay and yet have the work to do.

I have neglected to send to you about that money because I have been waiting to send it.   We have been disappointed by the Gov. about the amt of our bill in the Legislature.   He now promises to pay it in a day or two and we will send the money as soon as we can get it.   I can not write any more tonight.   When I get so that I can write I will write more. I have been quite unwell for two or three weeks but am better now.   The same old difficulty that I had when I was East.

Yrs   Edward P. Fitch

How about your March meeting?

MARCH 16, 1861

Dear Father

Enclosed you will find a draft on Spencer Villa & Co of Boston for seventy two (72) dollars for which you will please send on those coupons that you hold that were to be paid the first of last year.   They amt to 70, the 2$ will I expect pay you the interest on that from that time to this and pay any trouble you have had in borrowing the money.   The reasons why this has not been sent before are briefly these: When they were due Jan.

1st we had been trying to find out whether they would be paid in N.Y. or not and at one time almost wrote to you to have you send them to our agents in N.Y. and have them present them for payment and if paid send for the money, but we could not find that they would be paid until the last of Jan and then we found out for a certainty that they would not be paid at all this year.

Then we were in another trouble. Ten boxes of goods that we had ordered from St Louis and N.Y. in Nov & the early part of Dec. with the expectation that they would get here before Christmas & New Years and which contained all our gift books etc for the Hollidays, also a lot of stationery that we hoped to be able to sell to the Legislature, beside our written stock of school books -- all these boxes, had not any of them arrived the last of Jan. (They finally all came the middle of Feb after costing us some fifty dollars extra charges beside the delay). This had put us to the extra expense of ordering what we must have by Express, thus costing more than ordinary and at the same time we did not have on hand what we ought to, to sell. The possitive loss from the delay on these boxes was not less than 200. to us. Then the Legislature, instead of buying their supplies of us as we rather expected, they would import most of what they wanted from the East. But they bot a small Bill from us, some 45. which they paid today and that money we send to you. Thus, if you can read and make sense out of what I have written thus far, you will see what troubles we have had to encounter from various causes this last winter. I have not read this over and I dont know whether it is sense or not.

I am not in a condition to write but shall not be any better off probably in the next week so I write now at a venture. Thus much for our private difficulty, now for the Bonds & their Repudiation. The Legislature of 59 passed a law for the funding of the Public Debt of the Ter. It probably was not contemplated in that act to include in the Debt the amts claimed by the loans in the trouble of 56 etc, but after the Bill became law, just before I came East in 59 and after we had put in our Territorial Script to get the Bonds, some of those who had large claims of that kind got them allowed and used up the whole amt that the law made provision for Bonding, viz 100,000$ so that there was only some 3,000$ of the real indebtedness of the Territory put into Bonds and the other 97000$ was based on these claims. Now then some of the men who had large amts of these claims and failed to get Bonds, Jim Lane for instance, went to work to try and prevent the Territory from paying these Bonds at all. The Bond Swindle as it was called was made an issue in all the

224

Election when it could be brought in any how and the Legislature of 1860 was <u>only just</u> prevented from repudiating those Bonds by the determined efforts of the Bondholders in the election of this last fall.   In many places the Bond Swindle was made the issue and when the Legislature met they elected a Speaker who was pledged to do all in his power to <u>rip up</u> those Bonds.   They just succeeded in so doing and as far as a Legislature enactment could do it, they made the Bonds invalid, but the question of their validity has yet to be determined by the Courts.   So that really they are just as good now as they were before and even if they make them out to be worthly, those which you hold will be good as they were for the honest debt of the Ter. and not for claims at all.

I dont suppose you will think this is much of an elucidation of the Bond question, but I cant write it out.   If [I] could see you I could explain it to you.   You are just as safe now as you were before unless we have another dry year, which seems hardly possible.   In that case my farm would not be worth half the amt that you have it mortgaged for.   We will try and pay up the interest more promptly next time.

All Hands

I have fitted one sheet exclusively on business and now I will try and answer in detail all that I can of the only two letters that I have had from home for 9 months.   First, the girl from Lancaster.   I went up to the school house and saw her two or three weeks ago.   She is as I told you, I think, living in a very good family (except that they are Unitarians) and she likes them very well.   She says she is well taken care of, goes to school and is well contented she says, and I should think she was.

I will find some way I think for you to send me those dried fruits that you speak of.   You, Mother, in a letter long ago said something about Father losing something by Dan. Eames and in a letter now before Jan 15 you say "Eames failed and paid nothing and Father's hand is now out of the lion's mouth & I think he will keep it out".   I wish you would explain it to me.   Tell me how it was, what it was, and all about it.   Or don't you suppose I care anything about Father's affairs because I am so dilatory in paying myself.   I have just been rereading your letter of Feb 17 and I cordially reciprocate the last sentence about Lincoln.   We have a Government now, I hope it will be a permanent one.   Lincoln is all right if he does abandon <u>Sumpter</u>.   I'll bet a hat he never would have abandoned it if he had taken his seat the first of Dec. instead of Mar.   We had his Inaugural here in print on Tuesday the 5th at 3 OClock P.M. That is pretty quick you see.   You got it a little earlier I suppose.

I see by the paper that John Q Goodrich is Collector of Boston, so your hope of Office under Wm Claflin are gone up. Cant you scrape acquaintance politically with the Hon. Lieut. and secure a fat berth in the Custom House or some other Fed. Office. Who is to be Post Master at Hopkinton this time. Is there any talk of electing one. Who wants it? Did you get any office at March meeting. Who are the School Com. Who is Town Clerk & c. How is the boot business now there? How did Milton Claflin get along in the Legislature? & lots more questions. Please answer them all. George I suppose will go East this summer. Whether he will think it worth his while to come to Hopkinton or not I do not know. He is at Topeka, has a store there. The Legislature meets there the 26th of this month. He intends to go East as soon as possible after they adjourn. They may adjourn in a few weeks and may stay there is session two months.

You ask whether Sarah has seceeded or not. She has not yet but I dont know but she will. We are all pretty well now. Julie is a great girl and Charley is a great boy. He sits on the floor and plays a good deal. He gets around considerable tho he does not really creep. He wants to stand on his feet all the time and with a little help he will stand for quite awhile. Julie helps considerable about taking care of him, but she is rather too rough and hurts him sometimes. We have a girl of 15 who lives with us and goes to school. She is a first rate girl and we expect that she will probably stay with us till she is 18 but she may not. The baby has two teeth and a good prospect of two more soon, but he does not talk yet. He is just about the nicest baby you ever saw or heard of. Here I had to leave to take the baby a minute and Sarah came along and read it all. She says she would like to know what I mean by her See Seeding and she would thank me to scratch that out, but I have not done it. If you think best you can scratch it out to suit. You almost find fault with me for not writing about John. I have not heard a word from him directly since he was here a year ago till this week. I recd a letter from him dated Central City Colorado Terr. He seems to be well and in good spirits. He is surveying yet, or rather he has got thru and the map is soon to be published. The man who is making it has now gone to Philadelphia to get the engraving done and have it printed immediately. John says we are to have some for sale as soon as they are published. There are many of my friends from Lawrence where John is. He has found out some of them he says. I am just writing to him today and now I hope I shall hear from him occasionally. If I do I will keep you posted if he does not.

I should like to finish up this sheet but I have no more time now.

I wish you would all of you write to me and tell me the news from Hopkinton.

Yours   Edward

March 20, 1861

Dear Parents

I enclose a Programme of a concert that we gave last night here (to celebrate the anniversary of your wedding of course).   The Lawrence Musical Associ. has been in existence since the fall of 1855.   I was one of the original members and so was Sarah.   We both sang last night.   I enclose a little pamphlet which may throw some light on the Bond Question that I wrote about the other day.

We are as well as usual except that I got cold in my head last night and it is not doing me any good in particular.

I wrote all the news the other day so I have nothing more to write.

Edward

The Bond Pamphlet would not go in my letter so I will enclose it in a Newspaper and send it.

If it should happen that it should be lost write me and I will send another.

April 14, 1861

Dear Mother

First, I am very busy preparing to go to St Louis and have not much time to write letters, for I have more business than I can do as it ought to be done.   I expect, if nothing happens to prevent, to go to St Louis on Wed of this week.   I wish I could come on and see you.   I shall then be within 3 days of you, but about 75$ off reckoning cost of going. The time I could spend better than the money.   Your letter of March 8th, 15 etc is before me.   You say firstly that you do not hear much from me and when you do it is not like the newspaper letter writer.   I wish I could write more and better but I <u>do not</u> have time to write letters but very little. We have been pretty busy for some time on account of the Legislature at Topeka & c.   We have also been sending quite a lot of stuff to the Mines in Colorado Ter. where your third son is sojourning for the time being.   I have not written hardly any letters.   I dont know as I have one except business and what I write to you, so you are more favored than any one else.   That ought to be something.   Then you say that I have the news

227

about you & until I got this last letter I hardly knew anything that had taken place in Hopkinton for a long time.   I am very sorry to hear that you have been so unwell.   I hope you are well before this time.   You seem to have all been sick except Father.   How is he?

The Coupons were all correct but I hoped to hear something from Father about how he got on about paying up etc.   Was there enough money to make the money transaction good?   I am anxious to get that family letter.   I thot the thing was a failure and Sarah and I proposed starting one from here a short time ago.   I hope it will get here soon. Who started it finally?   We had Julie['s] picture taken yesterday, the first time we have tried since we were East.   We got a first rate picture and we will send you one when George goes East, also Charlie if we can get a good one of him.   We intend to try tomorrow if it is a good day.

When I am at St Louis I may go up and see Appleton.   We had a letter from him a little while since he is keeping house.   I dont know certain as I can go up there but think perhaps soon.

You almost seem to be displeased because I asked about how Father got in to trouble about Eames.   You had never told me any thing except that he came near losing some by him.   It almost seems as tho you thot I did not care any thing about Father or his business.   You have, I believe, answered all my questions as well as I can expect and I am very glad for I like to be posted on your affairs.   Who is that Mr Sanford of Medway that you speak of having found a wife etc.   We have not suffered for any thing unless it is the want of business this winter.   You write as tho you thot we were in actual need, which I am glad to say is not the case. We have got the best teacher of writing here that I ever saw.   He has been teaching Writing School here for two evenings a week for some time. You can judge whether or not I have attended.   Tell Elijah that I am obliged to him for his letter and I wish he would write often.   I will send that piece of poetry that he wants if I can find it soon.   I have it somewhere but I dont know where it is.   I will look for it and if I find, will send it to him.   How is the farming coming on this spring?

Sarah has been writing so I suppose she has written all the news we are having or hear, had pretty stormy times here in politics electing Senators etc.   They have finally elected Lane & Pomeroy, neither of them were my choice but they did not mind what I said, but went and did just as they chose.   I hope now that they are elected they will do us all the good they can.   We are to have a new Post Master here.   Who it will be we cant tell.   That may make a great difference with our business.   It may do us a vast deal of injury and may do us good.   We shall know soon as I suppose he will be appointed before very long now.

I have made out to about fill my sheet and that will have to answer for this time I think.

I will write more when I have more time, but when that will be I dont know I am sure.

Your aff Son
Edward

I wish you would tell Sarah Fitch and all the rest to write to me.   E.

Part III
War . . . Where it will End God Only Knows

April 15, 1861

We have got the news of the Great fight at Sumpter and its fall. It may make some difference with my going East, tho I think I shall go. Civil War! I did not think that I should ever live to see that. Where will it end. God only knows.

April 24, 1861

The Civil War became real to Lawrence residents when local men were casualties in the Battle of Wilson's Creek. While Edward served only in local defense forces, two of his brothers joined the Union army. Fortunately the family was unaware that Edward, himself, was destined to become a casualty of the conflict.

My Dear Mother

George starts for the East tomorrow, & will come to see you. I must prepare a little note to send you. I suppose you have received the letter I wrote a little while ago. You must ask George all the questions you can think about us. We have all been very well with the exception of colds. Charlie has had the worst & last night had a severe attack of croup -- which occasioned much alarm & anxiety, but today he is much better & I hope now he will recover without further trouble.

If you have any thing, as you mentioned in one of your letters, to send us George will willingly bring it. There is one think I must ask you for that I intended to get when I came away but forgot, that was a <u>pattern</u> for <u>pants</u>, so I can make E. some this summer. If it will not be too much trouble.

How is your health now? & Elijah and all of you? I believe in my letter I told you E. was expecting to start for St. Louis in a day or two. The news of the <u>war</u> that was received decided him to defer it for a time & now it is uncertain when he will go. The news makes business very dull. I wonder when it is all to end. Has Elijah enlisted? We see from the papers that the whole North is alive with excitement.

I feel as tho <u>I</u> could fight when I read of the outrageous conduct of the South. The men here are forming companies for home protection & we hope we shall not have much trouble even if our Missourian neighbors do persist in "seceding." They had better let Kansas alone I think or they will get into trouble. I must close in haste for I have a number of things yet to do for G. and must hurry.

Yours as ever
S.A. Fitch

April 28, 1861

Dear Parents,

It seems like a very long time since I heard any thing from you. I dont know how long it is but we live in such times that a short time seems long. Important events crowd so fast upon each other that we live years in a few weeks. I believe it is two weeks since I wrote to you last. Then I was making preparation to go to St Louis. Now all is changed. I did not go partly because we have a war on hand. Only think, did you think that you would ever live to see it-- a Civil War, the most horrible of all wars. But the reality is upon us and there is no use talking. We here dont know what we may have to do. We may have to fight our way to the Mississippi through the state of Missouri to get our eatables, but if Mo. does not secede we shall let her alone. If she does we shall be in a bad fix if she pitches in, for there are no arms and ammunition here at all hardly. All the arms in Kansas have been drained off by the Pikes Peak folks. There are lots of arms at Fort Leavenworth and we expect to get them after a while but the Officers there have had no orders to give them out yet. The Military are organising in large numbers here. Here in Lawrence we have 5 Companies, four of them newly organised and without arms as yet. The other is the famous Stubbs with their Sharps Rifles. One company is Cavalry, and one Artillery, that I belong to. We are in hopes to get our cannon and small arms within two or three weeks. At any rate the companies drill every night at their armories.

I am very anxious to hear from Hopkinton to know who have volunteered from there. I suppose the old Hopkinton Company is defunct but there ought to be fifty volunteers from there. I suppose Elijah cant go because he must take care of the farm as Father cannot. We may have some trouble with the Indians on our South & West Border. The troops have been taken away, so many of them there has been a little trouble. Now the Cherokees & Choctaws will fight with and for the South when it comes to general war and they have no special love for us here. The Delaware and Pottawatomies will fight for us but there are but few of them, but a great many Cherokees.

George started from here to the East last Thurs. morning. I suppose about this time he is in Cincinnati. He is going right thru to Attleboro except a stop of a few days in New York. He will only stay there a short time, that is a few weeks. I want you to write to him and tell him what time in May, if any time, Calvin will be at home because he would come up to Hopkinton to see you when Calvin was there if he was going to be there any time while he was East. You had better wait three or four days after you get this and then if you dont hear from him, write to him and find out if he has any time in view to come and see you and arrange it with him when he will come. His address will be Geo. O. Wilmarth, East Attleboro, Mass. He expects to come back in June early. Any things that you may have to send me he will contrive to get here I suppose. If he can bring a grape vine I would like to have you send one or two but I dont know whether he will or not be able to. Dried apple he can (you tell him) take to New York or even send it from there by Express and have it packed in some of our boxes.

     Charlie sits here on the floor beside me crowing and laughing away. He is a fat nice baby (Geo. has his picture for you), almost eleven months old. He can almost stand alone. He has been quite sick this last week with croup but he has got over it now, I believe, entirely. He was just sick for two nights. We had to be up with him considerable. Julia is a great girl. Her picture that Geo. has for you is a good picture only she was a little afraid when it was taken. It was the first one that was taken and she did not know what to make of it. We are all pretty well, as usual. Father is at Topeka taking Geo's place and so I am pretty much alone. I have a boy with me to stay at the store while I am away for my meals but I have to be there early and late and all the time. I have just been out looking at my garden. I find that I have a good chance for two bunches of currants and two or three of gooseberries this year. I have got six or seven apple trees and four peach trees, 3 of them are alive at any rate. We have got several locust and mulberry trees set out this spring but they dont seem to grow much yet. I have not any grape vines yet, all those that I brot with me from Hopkinton died. I have a lot of rhubarb growing finely, not big enough to use yet, tho we had a pie of that kind last week.

     I wish I could get some news from Hopkinton in some shape or other. I cant hear any thing from any one there I might as well have never known where the place was. Write soon please.

Your aff son

Edward

If you have got any Hubbard Squash seeds or can get any I want you to send me a few by George. Don't forget it.

May 5, 1861

Dear Parents

What is the matter that I do not get any word from home now for a long time?   With all the excitement about war when I want to know what Hopkinton is doing.   I have not heard a word in a long time.

How are all the folks at home, Mother especially?   She was not well the last I heard.   We are all pretty well here now.   Charlie has had a little sick spell with croup etc. but is well now I think.   He will be eleven months old tomorrow.   He can get up onto his feet by my clothes or his mother's now and walks along a very little by the chair & lounge etc.   He is quite strong of his age I think.   If you want to know how he looks, all the folks that see him say that he looks just like me exactly.

I may direct some money to be sent to you from Worcester to be paid to Geo.   If I do and it comes, please pay it over to George when he is there or if it should not get there till he has been there send it to him if he says so.   If not keep it subject to my order.   It will be from Mussy of Worcester if it comes.

Who has gone to the war from Hopkinton that I know or that I dont know?   How is the feeling there?   Are there any that sympathise with the South now?   If so, who?   What is the prospect of a crop this year etc.?   Who is helping on the farm?   Who manages the work department?   Elijah?   I hope he is able to do it and do it well.   Has he grown any bigger than he was when I was there?

Do please some of you write to me a little oftener as long as we can get letters thru.   I dont know how much longer that may be if Mo. should secede.   She may stop the mail.   If she does we shall have to fight.   We have several military companies now formed here that will give good acct. of themselves if called upon.   Was the old Hopkinton Military all dead or is it on a war party now or on the way South?   I hope the South wont back down now that we have had a chance to whip them once at any rate.

Whipping them once in a good fair battle will I think show them that the Yankees can fight some when they get roused up to it.   It takes considerable to rouse them but when they do begin   I hope they will not stop as long as there is a Slave in the country.   War is terrible but sometimes it is necessary for the good of the whole world as a whole.

Please write to me and tell me the news from old Hopkinton.   I am very anxious to hear.   We have heard from George as far East as

235

Cincinnati and suppose by this time he is in Massachusetts. Hope you will see him before long there at Hopkinton.

I am alone here in the store. Father is at Topeka to take Geo.'s place so I have just about as much to attend to as I can get along with anyway. It is pretty hard getting [along] alone any way. We have just about as much as two good hands can do, that is those that are used to the business, so I dont have much time to write letters that is sure. Last night I did not get thru so as to shut up the store till eleven O'clock.

Your aff Son
Edward P. Fitch

How are Uncle Dr's folks? I have not heard anything from John for a long time.

May 12, 1861

Dear Parents

It seems like a long time since I heard from you and if as, "Lowell" I think it is, says "We live in Events, not years, in thoughts, not moments" is true, it is years surely since I heard from you. Not a word have I heard since Mar. 8th or rather a letter commenced then and finished a couple of weeks later. I have written to you several times since that time. Yesterday P.M. just before night some one came in to the store and said How are you? I looked up and behold John stood looming up. He said he rained down and I could easily believe that, for the night before I was on guard and it rained most tremendous hard. He left Central City in the Mountains on the 11th of Apr just one month ago. He looks pretty hearty and is as black as any Indian. He never was noted for being extra white. I dont know how long he may stay here. He never tells any of his plans, as you know. He intends to go back to the Mountains pretty soon, I believe. He came in with one of Artemas Johnson's boys. We are now prepared to fight here, having just recd last Thurs 1000 stand of arms & 50,000 rounds of ammunition from Fort Leavenworth and 100 kegs of Powder. Before that we were almost destitute of any arms, all the arms here having been sent to the mountains.

We are all in our usual health. Charlie is creeping around the floor. He climbs up by the lounge and by my knees and walks around by the chair a little. He has now cut one upper tooth making three teeth and has another almost through. He will walk I guess by the time he is a year old or soon after.   Julie gets along finely, is now sitting in Uncle John lap & telling him all the news and singing Dixie for him.   It rained tremendous hard all last night as well as night before and today it has rained almost all day.   There is no danger of a drought this year, but in some places the wet will destroy the crop.

We have not heard any thing from George since he was at Cincinnati but we suppose he is somewhere in Mass. and think perhaps you will see him before you do this letter.   I have all I can attend to and some more to take care of the store alone.   Father W. was down from Topeka this last week Tuesday, staid one day.   It is so dark I can not hardly see but I will finish without a light.   I wish you would write to me once in a while.   At any rate I should like to know something of what is going on in Hopkinton.

Your aff Son
E.P. Fitch

May 19, 1861

Dear Parents

What is the matter that I do not hear anything from you?   Have you all gone to the War?   I did not know but I should hear that Elijah or Calvin had gone.   The Company that I belong to has been accepted as one to make up the regiment called out from Kansas but I cannot go at present for to do that I should have to shut up the store, which would not do at all of course.   Have you seen George yet.   I have not heard from him since he arrived East yet and so don't know where he is.

We are all as well as usual.   Charlie grows fast, almost walks but not quite.   How does the work get on this Spring?   Who is doing it?   That is who has charge, Elijah or do you hire a man that knows?

I have not much news to write as I know of today.   We had a sermon on the Times and a first rate one it was too.   The choir sang America and the audience joined in.   It was very fine.   We are having splendid weather here now and every thing looks fine for crops now. We have lettuce, onions, radish plenty and peas almost big enough to shell. Shall have green peas in two weeks if not in one.   No fear of a famine this year unless it is by our supplies being cut off from the East within a few weeks and in that case we shall march an Army into Mo and fight our way thru to where there is stuff to be had, but I dont aprehend that we shall have to do that at all.

Sarah & I send Love, Julie sends a   kiss to Grandpa & Grandma
Your aff Son
Edward P. Fitch

May 28, 1861

Dear Parents

I have just this moment finished reading your letters of the 19 &
20 inst, the first word I have heard from you since some time in March.
My heart is full but I cant write it out.   You know it is difficult for me to
write letters.   I am thankful for your kind wishes but I am not making
much and we are not likely to make much more than our expenses this
year.   The war is going to make business dull except the Newspaper
business that will pay well, what there is of it.   I thot after I sent that
money that I ought to send some on that other note but I waited hoping
times would mend a little but they seem to be getting worse instead of
better.   I will, if it is the range of <u>possibility</u>, help you to pay something
on that loss about the horse etc.   At any rate the interest on that Note
shall be paid and we will try and pay part at least of the principal.

As I write the music of the fife and Drum (or not much music)
keeps up a continued racket.   The town is full of soldiers or men that
want to be. The Regiment that was ord. [ordered] out for 3 months have
been collecting here for a week or so.   They are ord. out to elect
Regimental Officer on Fri and have a Regimental Drill.   This Reg. is not
to be called out after all, I expect.   There are two companies here that are
going in for 3 years.   They march for Fort Leavenworth Thursday.   A
detachment of U.S. Soldiers are expected to pass thru here tomorrow on
their way to Leavenworth.   They are from Fort Arbuckle, etc. Arkansas
and the Choctaw Nation.

I dont know of much news to tell you.   It is too bad that you
could not have got up a company in town to go to the War.   That would
have taken up many that now are out of work.

You say you have just commenced planting.   We have
strawberries here and radish, lettuce and all such kind of thing.   I had
strawberry & milk for my supper on last Sunday.   They were first rate.
We shall have green peas in a week or two, perhaps this week.   I hope you
will [not] be disapointed and have good crops this year.   The prospect is
good here for crops now.

The Soldiers are having a regular spree tonight. All hands will be tight. They are going around with all the Drums and Fifes playing and drinking at every whiskey shop and there are about 20 such shops in town.

I had heard nothing from Appleton of the kind that you seem to indicate. I expect likely it is so. Dont see why it should not be. He cant get ahead of me tho. Let him do his best. I have the honor to be the Father of your oldest Grandson & Granddaughter too.

I shall write to him about it.

Your aff Son
E. P. Fitch

June 30, 1861

Dear Parents

I suppose you are wondering by this time what keeps us from writing to you, as I believe I have not written for some time now. I had a letter from   you some time since in which you said something about the good news from Peoria etc. I had not then heard of it from them but a week ago we had a letter from Appleton and Lizzie telling us all the story about the Boy! Well! it is all right. They have neither got the first child nor the first boy. I have beat them in both ways so it is no matter. Appleton must have a vivid recolection of how I looked when I was a baby for he says that Charlie looks like me when I was his age, that is 10 months. I sent him a picture like yours. What do you say about it? I am glad if he does, for you said I was pretty. That is the reason I am so homely now. But now I can tell you some as good news from here as you have from Peoria. I have got a boy and he is just the nicest baby you ever saw for a little fellow, bright as a dollar.

All is well as usual now. Has Geo been to Hopkinton? I suppose of course he has but I dont see why I have not heard of it from you before this time for according to what I heard from him he ought to have been there long enough ago to have us hear of it by this time. We are looking for him home every day now but he does not seem to arrive yet.

How does your garden get on this year? We have had peas & string beans (tho not from our garden) for some time. We have beets in our garden as big as my fist or bigger and we have small onions & lettuce & we have tomatoes that are half the size of my fist. Our garden is getting along nicely.   We shall have lots of cabbage and beets & carrots for winter.   We have some potatoes & onions & turnips also but not a very large lot of them.   We have had new potatoes to eat twice this summer now.   We have had tremendous rains within a few days, 5 inches of rain have fallen since Thursday noon.   There has been no such rain but once since I was in Kansas but that was in July 1858.   I have a cistern that holds about 100 bbls and this rain finished the filling of it so we have plenty of rain water all the time.

Charlie is getting to be a great boy.   He stands alone and gets right up in the middle of the floor alone but does not walk yet.   We have not named him yet.   Sarah does not like Jones; so give us another hint for a name.   I have been sick with boils for three weeks or more but have now about got over them.   Please write often.   Tell us about the haying, who is doing it etc.   Julie and the baby are well & all the rest.

Your aff Son
Edward P. Fitch

July 7, 1861

Dear Parents

We have been looking every day for a week now for George to come and that he would bring us some late news from you, but he has not come yet and we dont hear any thing from you either.   How do you get along with the Haying this year?   Who is helping beside Elijah and that man that you took off Mary Kenedy?   How does the milk pay?   Can you get the bills paid!

I wish you would some of you write often for I am anxious to know how you get along.   We are all well.   Julie grows.   She is out picking flowers now and Charly is out in his wagon.   Sarah is getting supper.   Charlie took three or four steps <u>alone</u> two or three times today. He will walk in a short time.

As George has not come I am alone yet in the store and have all I can attend to and more too.

We have not named the baby yet.   Cant really decide on what beside Charles will sound and look well.   <u>Jones</u> Sarah does not like exactly and Wilmarth will not do well because that would be C.W., same as Calvin.   I rather think we shall name him Charles Otis for his Granpa for I think it will please him very much.   We shall probably decide upon something pretty soon so as to have him baptised.

We had cucumber & Squashes from our own garden today, is yours as far ahead as that?   We had green beans, Apples (new), cabbage, beets, new potatoes and onions for our Fourth of July dinner.   Orchard apples I guess you have not had yet.   I cannot stop to write any more now but I hope to hear from you before long.

Your aff Son
Edward

Father how is your hand now?

JULY 8, 1861

Dear Father

I enclose to you 10$ which you will apply toward the interest on that note of 200.$ of Mr. Wilmarth.   I expected that Muzzy would perhaps have sent it to you but I have heard from him and he is going to send to me.   I was going to send only 5 but will send ten.   It is hard to spare it now but I think perhaps it will do you good from your letter.

We are having very hard times indeed and no signs of better till fall at any rate.

E.P.F.

AUG. 26, 1861

Dear Mother

I sent you a paper containing an account of being shot at on the Cars and I wrote to you from Chicago, so you may be anxious to know how I got home.   I left Brother A. last Tuesday night at nine Oclock and arrived safe at home on Friday night at nine.   I was tired and have been about sick since I got home, nothing serious however.   I found the folks at home all well and very glad to see me.   Julie has not stopped yet saying every few minutes when I am at home "O I'm so glad you have come." Charlie celebrated the event by commencing to walk.   He walked all over the house yesterday and today he still creeps some because he can get along so much faster, but he seems to be very much pleased with the idea that he can walk.   He is now this minute running round with Julie and they together are making noise enough to make a body crazy almost. Julie is awful noisy.   She says I must not tell you she is a naughty girl for she says she ant a naughty girl.

241

Appleton & Lizzie seem to be getting along pretty well.   Lizzie I found sick.   I got there Fri night and staid till Tues eve.   She has not been really well I dont think since the baby was born.   The Baby is a little thing, that is, it is poor.   If it was as fat as mine are it would be taller & bigger than Charley was at his age, I think.   He will make quite a tall boy, I think, if he lives, of which there is some doubt of course as there is with all children.   He seems to be gaining now, had gained a pound in a few days when I was there.   Lizzie says if he was fat & plump she should be proud of him, but as it is she is not much.   Lizzie has been pretty sick but when I left was much better.

O, I do wish you could see the two children.   They make noise enough to carry a sawmill.   Charlie is trying to dance as Julie does and is jumping up and down till he falls.   Then he gets up and goes at it again.   Then he will walk a little way, then tumble down, get up and run along.   It is more than one can do to keep them both straight.   Half of the time they tear round like little catamounts.

I was very sorry to hear such an act from Calvin as was in our letter and the one A. recd while I was there.   He talked the matter over some and I have come to the conclusion in which all of us, Lizzie, Sarah & all, agree that to us it seems best that he should leave College.   You can say with Truth that owing to the war and other troubles you could not keep him there longer and there will be no disgrace in that.   Poverty is no crime tho very inconvenient I find.   I am sorry C. would not do better for he certainly could, but so many absences from Recitation & Prayers there was no earthly need of.   What will become of him if he continues on that way I dont see.   I am very sorry to hear that Elijah is sick.   I hope he is well by this time.   I am inclined to think E. is one of the best of this family of boys, if not the Best.   When he feels his responsibility a little more he will do better yet.   Does he still think he shall stick to the old Farm.   I wish Father had taken the money that he paid for that Farm and bought land in Chicago with it.   He might have been better off and he might not, for some have lost what they gained, same as I did here.   I made enough clear to buy a share in Sumner and if I had only kept it then I should have hit it, but I ventured once too much and lost all.

By the way I met John P. Wheeler in St Louis.   He avoided me and did not intend I should see him.   He looked sheepish enough.   I tried to see him again but could not.   It was the last night I was in St Louis.   He was to meet me at Richardson's room but he dodged the issue. A.D. Richardson I met at St Louis.   He was at the Hotel where I stopped at first.   He is Special Correspondent of the Tribune now in the West.

242

He wished to be remembered to you and Father and promised to call on you when he was in Mass. again which he expected wont be this fall. He is in good health and spirits, plenty of excitement and enough to write about nowadays. I was reading today in a letter of his where he spoke of my being fired at on the Cars in Mo. He spoke of his visit to Hop. and seemed to recollect it with pleasure, only he said he had a stormy night to lecture.

John I cannot hear any thing of since I heard he was sick in the North part of the state. He did not state that he was very sick or how he was but said he was in good hands and I need not worry about him, but I do some. I have written to him twice within a month or two but can get no answer from him and I cant imagine what has become of him. I am going to write again and see if I can find out anything of him. If I do I will let you know. You said you think it would have been better to let all of us take care of ourselves after we were twenty one. I think probably it would have been better, tho I dont know where I should have been in that case. I hope I shall be able to pay back some of what I have cost you but this war will knock our business so bad that I dont know as I shall ever see thro. I find that business is all dogged [but] not by near as much as I expected to when I started from here, business was so bad.

I sent a lot of papers to Appleton telling all about the battle in Mo and told him to send them to you so I suppose you will get some extended accounts of it. It [the Battle of Wilson's Creek] was a hard fight but our Kansas troops sustained their reputation for fighting pretty well. They get lots of praise all around. There were several of my friends killed in that battle and a great many that I know killed & wounded in the Kansas Regiments. It seems like bringing war close to home. I have seen many of the wounded who have got home, some that are going back and some that are not. One that came over with me in the Cars the other day had one finger and part of another shot off, one Ball thru his arm and one in his side. Lieut Jones who was killed was a friend of mine. He was killed before he had been under Infantry fire three minutes and he had three balls in him, the last thru his Heart. He was trying to get up to execute or give an order when the ball struck his breast and he spoke no more. Sergt Lewis Litchfield, a friend of mine and Cousin of Muzzy's was shot thro the lungs and only said Good Bye Boys & died. He leaves a wife and one child to mourn his loss. Jones leaves a wife but no children. Lieut Pratt was one of the few who lived in Lawrence and came here before I did, for there are but few now. He was our County & City Clerk, a young man not married. He had a brother in the Regt but he was sick and not

243

in the Battle.   The other Pratt killed was no relation.   This is bring[ing] war close by.   Col Deitzler who was wounded is a   friend of mine and a farmer, also   Col Mitchell.   There are others but I cannot enumerate. Where will all this end.   Our trust is in God, only it seems as tho Truth and right must prevail.   I have no more time or space to write so I must stop.

Your aff Son
Edward

Are you better of your sickness?   Did you go to Weymouth?   If I had had 50. to spend when at Chicago I should have come to see you.

Oct. 20, 1861

Dear Parents

      Are we never to hear from you again or what is the matter?   I wrote to you about the first of Aug and then Sarah wrote a letter just after the family letter arrived here, which was the day before I left for the East and I wrote to you from Chicago and also since I came back but not one word from you have I heard since that Fam. Let. was sent.   Julie has been sick with the chills almost but she is better now.   Charlie has been unwell for a few weeks, something like a light fever but has not been very bad. We had the Dr. to him once.   Now Sarah is almost sick.   I am a little afraid she will have the chills but she says she will not and I hope she wont.   I am pretty well and the rest of the family enjoy their usual health.

      I dont know that I have much news to write but I should like to hear some from home.   How are you all getting along.   The last I heard Elijah was very sick.   That I heard in Chicago in your letter to A.   Calvin also you said was at home and you did not know what to do with him.   I wrote my ideas on the subject, also what A. & I talked of and I should like to know what was done about it.   How does Mr Webster and his folks do? Also Uncle Dr.   How is he?   The family letter has not gone from here yet. I have been waiting to get it to John but he will not see it now unless he should happen to come here, which is not probable now.   The last time I wrote to you I did not, I believe, know where John was but the very day that I sent that letter to you I recd one from him.   He has been sick twice with fever & Ague and Billious Fever.   He was pretty sick according to what I hear from him but he was well when he wrote to me last Sept 29th. He did not know whether he should winter here in Kansas or in the mines.   Said he would let me know when he found out.

I understand that there is no fruit in Mass this fall.   Is that so?
How are you getting along.   Is the harvesting done or are you making
cider?   Have you got your mill fixed?   How many horses have you now
and is that one steady that runned away so?   Tell Elijah that I wish he
would write to me about the farm, where the corn etc is and how much
you have got, how many Bush potatoes etc, all of which I should like to
know.   Is Aunt Mary Ann at our house yet?   How is Father's hand now?
How are Eames folks.   John Q Adams & wife were in Mass when I was in
Chicago so I did not see them.   Did they call on you.   Appleton has met
with difficulties I think.   I can feel for him.   I know how I think I should
feel if one of my children should be taken away.   I am so glad that I went
there.   I am afraid Lizzie will not get strong again for a long time.

I wish you would write to me for I should like to hear from you
once in a while at any rate.

Your aff. Son
E. P. Fitch

Dec. 8, 1861

Dear Mother

About two weeks ago I was rejoiced by receiving a letter direct in
your well known hand writing the first specimen of it I had seen for
months.   You say if I have not recd a letter from you since the family
letter, "There is a fault somewhere and I ought to investigate it."   That I
think is so and the cause is clear why I have had none.   That is because
there were none written to me.   You dodge the question very nicely but
the dodge is very apparent to me.   I was glad you may believe to hear
once more from you and now I cant answer the letter as I would like to
because the letter is lost or mislaid and I cant get it hunted up.   You told
me considerable news but not half what I want to know.   I have been
hoping I should get another every day written at Thanksgiving time but as
we have not had any mail for a whole week, that may be the cause; or it
may be that none was written.   We are all enjoying our usual health.
Julie has been running out of doors and playing with the dog.   She is
almost 4 and she romps around 'lots."   Charlie is now at the box to get
himself a cookie and he gets one for his Mamma also.   There was a plate
in the box and he took that and put two cakes on it and brought the plate
along for me to take one and then took the other to Mother.   Then as
Julie came in just at that moment he ran and got her one too.   He is such

a good little boy I wish you could see him.   It is a beautiful day.   We have not had any fire since the fire with which we got breakfast went out and it is not 1/2 past 4.   We have had a very pleasant winter thus far.   One week ago today was quite cold and on Monday we had two or three inches of snow but that has all gone and it is warm and pleasant now.

We had a very good time Thanksgiving.   Do you remember that once a number of years ago you had a turkey at Thanksgiving?   The only turkey that I ever knew you to have and do you remember that we did not like it and voted that turkey was not half as good as chicken?   Well I have had a predudice against turkey ever since and thot I should not like it but this year I conquered my predudice and bought a turkey for dinner.   We had it baked and it was <u>first rate</u>.   Our family of that day consisted of Father W. Brother George, and a young friend he brot with him from Topeka, Mr & Mrs Hanscom (It was the first Thanksgiving dinner <u>she</u> ever ate, she being a New Yorker and always having kept Christmas), Sarah, our three children and last but not least a young man whom you may have known at some former period of life -- named Edward Payson. We did up the dinner after the most approved style, said dinner consisting of turkey with stuffing, sweet and Irish potatoes, onions, & cranberry sauce, mince, grape, squash, & Whortleberry pies of Sarah's best make. You can imagine they were good when I tell you that the day before Thanksgiving she had 35 pies and Sunday after there were but 4 left -- so we think she is a pretty good cook.

[the writing changes to Sarah's]

You may accept that as one of Edward's stories -- in the first place I only baked <u>25</u> and instead of 4 left there were 10 & 5 of those that disappeared were taken away whole -- so you see we were not such enormous eaters as one might infer from E's statements.   Mine you may depend upon as fact.   I wish you had all been here to enjoy our dinner with us -- we would have all been willing to sit close -- and keep our elbows down -- to make room for four more plates -- poor little Georgie -- I said <u>four</u> more plates -- Georgie should had an extra one in the very first place with an extra share of plums in his pudding.

[writing is again Edward's]

Sarah has been trying to make out that I have been telling a yarn but when I tell you that George and his friend stayed till Sat. noon and that George is as great a hand for pie as I am (you used to know something about that when you always had to hide the pies away from me) and when I tell you that every time we were in the house we were eating pie you will take her statement with some grains of allowance or at least think she may have made a mistake when she tried to write the number of pies we had, for the other is what she told me or I understood. In the evening we had a social time singing and playing chess & chequers eating cream & jelly cakes, apples & nuts (that were not eat) and drinking wine, real good grape wine, of our own make and I think about equal to that currant wine that you bragged so much on when we were East. And if we had only had two or three bottles of your cider we would have discussed the question whether (John A Fitch) (Ethan Griffons) cider was not fully equal to wine, which question might have been decided the way the liquor was strongest. But as we were all able to walk straight after a nights sleep I think the wine was pretty good.

So much for what we eat on Thanksgiving and as eating seems to be the great thing on that day we must have had a good Thanksgiving.

We had a meeting at our Church in the forenoon. Mr Cordley preached. I did not go. There was not Patriotism or feeling enough in our Merchants here to shut up their stores so most of the stores were open all day except a few shut up at meeting time and kept shut an hour.

We have had no mail for a week and I dont know as this will get thru to you. There seems to be some trouble somewhere but where it is we cannot tell as yet. There is a good deal of fear among some of our folks here that we will have a hard time this winter -- that we are in more danger than ever before etc but I dont really think yet that we are to be overrun here but there is no knowing what may take place. They have a chance to do us a great deal of damage this winter if they go at it and they may be led to do it in retaliation for what Lane has done in Mo. By the way I see by Telegraph that Lane has been making a speech in Boston? How did it take? He is a great blow tho he has done some good things, but his course in Missouri has not been just right. In fact it has been all wrong. He has stolen any amt of money and goods of all kinds and taken them without any authority. By his being a member of the senate he will be able to make it come out all right perhaps.

You want to know what I think of the removal of Fremont. Well, I think just this, that it was the most stupid thing that has been done. The whole campaign on the west or in Mo. has been a farce and the removal of Fremont right in the face of an enemy was one of the greatest of outrages on the American people. When I heard of it I did not care how quick I heard Lincoln was dead and let Hamlin take hold and see if he could not do something someway as it ought to be. He at least would not have a traitor wife to be telling the plans of the Government to the Rebels. I hope that the people will rise in their might and make

247

Fremont the next President. There is nothing I would rather see than that. He has been grossly abused by men in high places because they thought he was getting to be more popular than they themselves were. It is in the bounds of possibilities that he may be as incompetent as he was said to be but it will take some time to make me believe it. Every time he got ready to strike some blow he had to send his best men off to protect Washington. I think if the Eastern and middle states cant keep Washington safe without calling upon the states west of Ohio they had better let Jeff Davis have it and done with it. The <u>West</u> will take the job by contract to defend Washington and clean out the whole South only give them the arms and the money but instead of that they take the arms that Fremont bought for his army and keep them at Washington and then prosecute him because he paid high prices for arms which he must have or lose Missouri. It is ridiculous. I almost wish that the Rebels had, after Bull Run advanced and taken Washington and then see whether there was any spunk in the East or not. But <u>Wilkes</u> will suit me and if they will hang Frasier & Slidell that will do better yet. I hope they have shot Kerrigan before this time and will keep on shooting all traitors as fast as they find them. If they have to shoot some members of the Cabinet for there are some of them that are not any better than they should be. Depend upon it, if Jackson had been there instead of Lincoln he would have kicked Seward & Blair both out before he would have removed Fremont, and that is what Lincoln ought to have done.

Your aff Son
Edward

Do write often.

Dec. 27, 1861

Dear Parents

I finished and sent off a letter to you last night and this morning I recd one from you dated at various times from Dec. 13 to 17th. Sarah says she thinks Father must have been blue when he wrote it for it has made her blue all day to read it. She says she is very much obliged to you for the answer to her letter that she never got but she did think it was almost too bad that you did not take notice of it. I find that you feel just about as I do about the Administration, the course it is taking and has taken I think if Douglas had been in the place of Lincoln we should have seen something different entirely, but perhaps it will be all right in the end.   But Lane's speech in the Senate suits me pretty well.   I want to see the thing put thru.

I was very glad to get your letter.   I had heard nothing before of Uncle Nat buying the Old Place.   What will he do with his own where he is, keep it or sell that and go up to the other house.   I am sorry to hear such news from Aunt Mary Ann.   I heard from Sarah Fitch that she was very unwell with a cancer as she said, but I hope to hear that she is better next time I hear from her.   Let me know about it.

I wrote to you last night that we should not send the money for the Coupons at present but we have concluded to send it on immediately and let something else wait, so I enclose Drafts on N.Y. to the amt of 100.$ vis

$43.50   Park Bank Draft
 26.50   Ocean Bank Draft   amt 100$
 30.00   Ocean Bank Draft
We calculated thus
 Amt due on Coupo $70.00
 Interest on note from Mar 1860   to Mar 1st 1861 20.00
 Interest for Mar 1st 61 to Jan 1st 62   10 months 16.66
   "   "   on 10$ up to July 8, the time it was paid   .33
   "   "   on 10   "   " June 1, 62, .80   107.59

I have made this morning a calculation to see how much money to get to send you and that 100$ would pay the interest up to this time, but I find I made a mistake and that 100$ will pay the Coupons and pay the interest on the Note up to March 1st 62.   What do you say to that.   Please calculate the amt and let me know so that we can fix the acct to suit your acct.

Let us know immediately on recpt of this money as we shall be anxious to hear from it for fear of loss.

Has Calvin grown any since I was at home?   If he has not I should think he would make a poor show as a School Master.   How does he succeed?   John I have not heard from since Oct last.   I dont know where he is or what he is doing.   I wish I could hear from him and know what he is up to.

Send on you statement of acct so we may know how to settle up all the whole affair.

E.P. Fitch

Jan. 9, 1862

I am now going to commence numbering my letters as I used to do so that you may know whether you get them or not for either you have been very remiss in answering or you have not got one in three that I have written.   I sent you a letter the 26th or 7 along there some where with 100$ in Drafts in it.   That letter would make some difference if it should happen to be lost.   I am awaiting with some anxiety to hear of its safe arrival there.   I want to know if it gets there and I want to know if it dont. If you dont get that Letter nor this one I want you to let me know immediately if not sooner, so that I may see if I can stop payment on the Drafts.

Have you got the Duplicate for My Land.   I just happened to look up an old letter of yours in which you want me to send it so that you would have some evidence of my indebtedness to you and you said you would send me a recpt so that I also might have some thing to show for my side but that I have never seen so that now I have nothing to show for the title to my land.

You complain of high taxes.   We think we have to pay pretty high tax out here.   My tax on my Land this year was a little over 25$ beside the Highway tax of between 4.50 & 5.00 and my Ministers tax, or rather what I pay to support the minister is 20$ per year making 50$ on the Little property that I have got to pay on and taxes are going to be much higher here next year on acct of the Domicil tax   etc. Taxes will almost eat Land up in this country but I suppose we have got to stand it till this war is over and if it does cost us high taxes for a few years and slavery is put out of the way it will be a good thing.   But we have got to have different policy from what we have had yet or we shall never come out right.   Emancipation is the word now.   It ought to be done and must be before we should do any thing that will amt to   a hill of beans.   Lincoln is no account.   Seward is worse and Bates nobody.   I wish Douglas had lived and been President!

We are having quite an excitement here just now over the question -- who shall be our next Governor -- Robinson claiming to hold over and Crawford claiming to have been Elected this fall.   There is quite a clash between the two but it will all come out right in the end I suppose. I think Robinson ought to hold over but I dont know but the court will Decide different.

Lane is doing every thing he can to that end and has been all the time.   He worked against us for the Capital and gave it to Topeka by that means just to spite Robinson & his friends for Lane has more property here than any where else in Kansas.

Next week I suppose will tell the tale in regard to the Gov. contest. It looks almost as tho we might have another Dorr War but I hope not.

We are all of us as well as usual, tho I have had a bad cold in my head for a few days.   I have got mostly over it now however.   It is getting late & I am so sleepy that I shall have to put off writing any more till next time.

"So no meor at prisint"
"from your Intirely"
Edward

Let me hear from you as often as possible <u>Please</u>. How is Aunt Mary Ann?

Jan. 15,1862

Dear Father

Your Letter dated Jan 7 enclosing coupon and Rect for interest for 30.$ I was glad enough to hear that the money arrived safely.   I was getting anxious to hear about it.   I am glad that it came at a time which would do you good.

You say you have sp[oken] after the mortgage once.   What do you mean by that.   Is it out of Robt Woods hands?   If it is or if it is not can you not get it in some way so that you get the money for 6 per cent and so you make the 4 pct for your troubles?   Or have you done so before this time?

If the mortgage is out of Woods hands who holds it?   You was to send me some kind of recpt for that Duplicate on my farm but I have never seen it yet.

I have not heard anything from John since Oct and I did not know where he was.   I should like to hear from him but dont know when I shall.   How long is Florinda going to stay or how long did she stay.   I wish she would come and live with you. If she is there give her my love. Who is Representative for Hopkinton & Ashton this year? That is something I have never found out yet!

It is pretty hard for us to have to pay the interest on those Bonds and get nothing for them and it will be harder yet if we have to pay principal and all but that I dont think we shall have to do.   Still there is no knowing how it will turn out.   That and the 400$ that the U. S. owes us and wont pay and 200$ or so that the Territory owes us and the State has not assumed yet make it hard for us to keep our heads above water, but I am in hopes we shall weather the storm yet.

If this horrible War was over I think we might have better times but there is no knowing how it will end. At the rate it is going on now it will end by the Gov. being bankrupt so that it cant carry it on and that soon too. I wish we had a <u>man</u> for <u>President</u>. One who was worth something. This lazy stile [style] of waiting till no one knows when before they do aught is ruining the Govt and every thing else. This spending 2000000 a Day doing nothing dont pay at all. Trying to make war and not touch Slavery is like trying to put out fire without water. I wish they would do something, whip somebody or be whipped, one or the other.

We are having splendid sleighing here today. There was about six inches of snow fell yesterday and it is first rate sleighing now. It seems like old Massachusetts.

The children are both quite unwell. I think they are going to have the measles as they are very prevalent aroung now.

It is almost too cold for them to be sick now. It will be so much worse to take care of them. Measles are very plenty around here. Almost every body is sick with them. Except that, we are all pretty well and that is nothing serious I <u>hope</u>. It is late and I have nothing more to write so Good night.

Edward P Fitch

April 27, 1862

Although Edward drilled with a military company organized for local defense, we have no evidence that he ever belonged to the Kansas militia or took part in any military campaign.

Dear Mother

I am almost beginning to think that you too are forgetful of your Kansas children. I say you too because I have not heard a word from Father for I dont know how many months, and it is a long time since I have heard from you so long I dont know when it was, that is, that the letter was written. A week ago last Fri night I got thru at the store at 2 Oclock in the morning of Sat. I rec'd a letter that PM (that is Fri,) from Appleton & Lizzie enclosing one that you wrote for us here and then sent to them. I had a good time reading it. I assure you all the folks went to bed of course long before I came home so I was all alone and some what sleepy but that kept me awake.   We have been very busy indeed for the last four or five weeks.   I hardly ever get home from the store before 11 Oclock and the greater part of the time it is 12 & 1 Oclock in the morning. I am pretty near worn out.   George being East, too Father has to be at Topeka some of the time and it leaves me the whole responsibility here on my shoulders.

There have been some Regiments of Soldiers paid off here at Lawrence and they made trade pretty lively.   I had two extra hands in the store for 4 weeks and it kept us all moving pretty lively all the time.   Our sales ran up pretty well for the stock we had; if we had only known before hand that they would be here we might have had on hand and sold 1000$ worth more of stuff but as we did not have it we could not sell it.   I am beginning to be anxious to hear what you and Calvin and all think about his coming out here.   It seems as tho I ought to have had some answer to the letter I wrote about that before this time.   We have got a young man with us now that is very good help having been in a book store considerable but we dont know how long he will stay with us.   He is a Bookbinder by trade and we may start a Bindery in connection with our store.   If we do we hope it will enlarge our business and help us along in that way but it will take considerable extra Capital to start it which we dont want to spare really just now but still we may do it, in the end it will no doubt be of much advantage to us.

We are all as well as usual excepting being tired out.   The Spring is very backward this year - more so than any year since I have been [here] possibly with the exception of 57.   We have just got a few things planted in our garden; nothing up yet.   Grass has got pretty well started and it is pretty warm now, tho it has been cold all this spring till within a few days.

I have not got news to write to you as I know of and so I guess I will wait to see if I ever hear from you again before I write much more of any thing because if you dont want to hear I cant afford to write.

Your aff son
Edward

April 28, 1862

Dear Mother   I have just been reading over part of your letter. You say March 1st "My last unanswered" & "but I must begin another the first of the month" and I guess the first of April you did not think of it. Or is it only once in two months that you write.   But if I could get as long & good a letter as that every month, I should be pretty well satisfied tho I would be pleased to hear oftener.   Why was not Father reappointed to Lancaster.   I saw in the paper that someone else had his place. Republicans <u>are</u> ungrateful.   <u>Good joke</u> on the letter to keep it unopened till the next day <u>wasn't</u> it.

Sept. 21, 1862

Dear Mother

How does it happen that I don't hear from you any more at all. What is the matter?   Even questions that I asked that had a bearing of the fate and prospects of others remain unanswered.   (I just this moment remember that a printed slip in relation to Mr. Hutchins that Geo. brot you wanted sent back.   I will hunt it up and send back in this letter.)   I suppose haying & mowing brush & cutting stalks are all done by this time and you are thinking of harvesting the corn and potatoes, perhaps Picking Apples.   By the way are you making cider this year?   Is the cider mill set up?   Or where do you get your own apples ground?   Are there many Winter Apples?   Did you have lots of Pears and Peaches?   We have Peaches here in abundance at 1.00 per bush.   Grapes, very fine ones, at 12 1/2 to 20 cts per lb.

As I am writing this Father sits at the table playing on my bass viol.   He is a good player on that or a violin, Flute, Clarionett and Melodeon.   Mr. Tritch, a man we have in the store, is a good singer so we have some good sings.

We are all pretty well now.   Charlie has been a little sick but has got over it now.

We are doing just a fair business at the store this summer, nothing wonderful at all.   We are thinking still of getting a Bindery to going but have not got it yet.   Shall probably do something about it soon.

I have been wondering how my face looked as I have not seen it for 7 years and over so I have had my wiskers shaved off to get a sight at it. I am expecting to get a picture taken tomorrow that I shall send to Appleton and ask him to send it to you after he sees it.   There have been three Books published by Ticknor & Fields of Boston this last summer: 2 "Recreations of a Country Parson",   "Leisure Hours in Town".   Have you seen and read them?   If not I guess I will send them to you or part of them.   Let me know please.

How is Aunt Mary Ann & where?   How does little George get along?   Does he go to school?   If so to whom?   How do the Schools get along?   Who has gone to the war that I know?   How are Mr. Websters folks now?   Give them my respects if you ever see them!   Are you at work for the soldiers now any.

I belong to a company that has been drilling three times a week all along but we are going to drill only once now.   All the State Militia has been called out in this county now and we may have to go if these theiving bands prowl around here much more.   The stores in town we all shut up for an hour and a half each day for two weeks but now they leave the stores open but a good many come out to drill.   Our Capt commanded one of the Lawrence Companies in the Battle of Wilsons Creek Aug 10 1861 and was wounded so that he had to leave the service.   He was shot thru the back while stooping over a man of his company who had just been shot down to get his last message to his wife.

I wish you would write and tell me the news from old Hopkinton. I would like to hear from there once in awhile.

Yours
Edward

Jan. 4, 1863

Dear Father

Enclosed you will find Draft for 70$ for the interest due on those Bonds.   Send us the Coupons that are due.   I told you you should have it by the first part of Jan.   We have a good many bills to pay about the first but we can manage to pay most of them.   We have had the past year a pretty prosperous year tho we are just now pressed for some money to use that we dont know just how to get.   We are talking of building a store on a lot immediately opposite where we now are.   I dont know yet for certain that we shall try it but we think of it and I am in hopes we shall make out.   How is it about this intst, do you pay Wood the whole 10 p ct? You had not ought to after giving a Mortgage on your farm for it to secure him.   And did you have to pay before you recd this?   How do the cattle etc get along this winter?   Is it pretty cold or an open winter?   We are having a very warm open winter here, very much like the first winter I was out here.   It was very warm Christmas so that we did not need any fire and we had what I'll warrant you did not and that was a thunderstorm with warm rain.

How much cider have you made?   Do you get the Agriculturalist yet?   I ordered it sent to you from the office.   Do you sell milk yet?   If so, how much?   And at what price?   I pay 8 cts per quart for milk and not much like the quarts I used to give others.

Where is Calvin and have you heard any thing from him since he went to N.C.?   Was he in those Battles under Gen Foster?   John I have not heard a word from since he left here for Fort Scott and the south.   I suppose he was in the Battle of Prairie Grove, Arkansas as I see the 13th Kan was there.   All I can learn however about them is that there were but two or three killed and comparatively few wounded in that Regiment. His name is not among these on either list.

I suppose he was with Blunt & Herron on that raid down to Van Buren, Ark.   They are doing considerable down there now.   Making the wool fly.

As to us here we are all well.   How is Little George?   Does he go to school?   Who keeps your school?   How does your stone digger do? etc. etc.

I should like to hear something about these things if nothing else about you could be got up to write upon.   How much are your taxes for the last year.   You spoke some time of their being high.   The taxes on my farm last year were 48$ which will be twice what I shall get off of the farm I expect, as my crop of corn was very small this year owing to the dry season.   We call that pretty high taxes and with the United States tax and all together we shall be nearly used up in this country.   If this war would only end sometime we might get along somewhere & somehow, but these prices are going up and the money going down so fast now that it is hard to pay taxes or any thing.   I wish you would write occasionally so that I may know if you are yet in existence and what is going on there at old Hopkinton.   How is Mr Webster & his folks now?   Or have you turned him off.   I have not heard anything about him for sometime.

I am very busy with the store so that I do not have much time to write letters.   I have to work late at night and early in the morning to do what writing I have to do and beside that Father does almost all of the regular bookkeeping.   If Father goes to Topeka during the Session of the Legislature I shall be driven worse than I am now.   If you hear any thing from Calvin I should like to hear from him.   I dont know how to write to him if I want to since he left Boston.

But my ideas are out, my paper is short.   It is almost daylight Mon. morning.   (Now I am writing by lamplight) so I guess I'll stop.
Yours,
Edward

256

Jan. 29, 1863

Dear Father

Your letter enclosing the Coupons came to hand last night all correct. You never have told me before to my knowledge that you paid Wood and borrowed of the Bank so I know nothing of it. Taxes are pretty high there I think.

You seem to intimate that you have a pretty hard time to keep your interest money up and I suppose you do. Now I enclose 20$ which I wish you to credit me on that Note of 400$ that I gave you in the fall of 59. That is, credit me on the interest. Also please give me the date of the Note so that I may see what interest is due up to this time. Or what is better still, do you calculate the interest on the note up to the date of it in 1862 (last year) and send me the statement and amt and I will pay it up to that time.

Then _we_ will send you by the first of March the 20$ that will be due at that time on the Note against Mr Wilmarth. We paid it up to Mar 1st 62.

Then we want you to let us know immediately if you would like to have that Note Paid at that time or if you would like 1/2 of it. If you would, we will pay 1/2 of it or the whole at that time. But if you get your money at six pct and we pay you _ten_, if you can get along without taking it up, I should think you was making something by the operation. But we can pay it on the 1st of Mar if you say so. Now let us know just what you would like to have us do in the matter. We are not particularly anxious to pay it, as we would like to keep the money to use very well; but we will make an effort to pay it-- so as to make our credit good in case we want any more, which is probable. We may sometime, so we leave it all to you to say whether we pay or not.

I suppose by your letter that you hold the Bonds that I left there. I dont know as they will be paid at Maturity but the Legislature are making some arrangement now to fix it up in some way, probably by giving State Bonds for them. If they do that we shall want to get those _Bonds_ and get them changed for the State Bonds. That will make them a little surer but will put off their payment somewhat. The reason of it making those surer is that those Bonds which were given to those who lost here during the troubles and which _Lane_ and others tried to get thrown up by Crying Bond Swindle etc. They were all put on the same footing with our Bonds and others that were given for things actually furnished to the Territory so if _they had succeeded_ or _should_ succeed in

Repudiating that part of the Debt -- which I think ought not to have been put in, we should have been put to much trouble to get ours separate from that, but if they are all put into State Bonds they can be sold now for a pretty good percent on this amount.   The Legislature has hold of the matter now. Just what they will do with it I dont know.   So much for money and such like things.   Now for you letter & the news, for which see next sheet.

Dear Mother,

Father says in his letter "You dont say a word about your wife & children, if they are all dead we dont know it."   Now I might return the compliment for he dont say a word about you.   So I dont know that you are dead, and not knowing, I will direct this part of the letter to you and see if I can find out.   I told Sarah she had better write but she says she had written you two letters and you have never even said that you recd them and she thot she should not write again until she found out whether you did or not.   Then she is kept pretty busy for our colored girl goes to school and so she has a great deal of work to do.   We have one boarder and expect to have another next week, a man that is coming into the store to stay.   He is a paper hanger and we are going to hang paper as well as furnish it.   I dont see that there is much news in your letter for me to say any thing about and I have not any to write, for there is nothing new that I know of that will be of interest to you.   We are all well -- wife, children and all as far as heard from.

We have heard nothing from John direct yet.   If that long letter from Calvin that you speak of was as good as one he wrote to us I should be glad to see it.   He wrote to us the best letter I ever saw from him.   If he gets home alive from the war I think his going into the Army will be the making of him.   Dont you think so?   I hope it will.   But I wish you would let me know the news from Hopkinton.   How all the folks get along that I know.   How is Mrs James [Long] and is Arthur in the clothing business yet?   That I want to know in particular.

Ys   Edward

Feb. 13, 1863

Dear Mother

You will perhaps think this a queer time to be writing letters -- and perhaps it is.   I have just got up after having lain down an hour or two while Sarah sat here with the children, for they are both quite sick. Julia is very sick indeed. She had another attack of that disease by which she came very near dying four years ago. Inflammation on the lungs. She was taken Monday night and for the last 24 hours has hardly spoken and she is not able to raise her head. Her breathing has been 80 times a minute which you can judge must be pretty fast & short and yet she does not complain. She is the most patient thing I ever saw so young. She takes all her medicine with no trouble.

Wed. Feb 18th. The children are better tho not so well but what we have to be up (Feb 19) with them much of the time nights. Julie is considerably better so as to be able to sit up considerable of the time, but Charlie was taken much worse this week Monday and from that time until now has been very sick. He is now lying in the rocking chair and looks terrible. He is a very sick child. We do not really know what is the matter with him. He has part of the time a great deal of fever and then he wont have so much. He has, we think, the Whooping Cough along with the rest, but of this we are not certain as neither Sarah nor I am enough acquainted with that cough to know really whether it is that or not and he has not coughed when the Doctor has been here. Charlie had not been very bad before, that is not so but what he was about part of the time until Monday and since that he has not stirred hardly except as he was obliged to, to drink or something of that sort. He is very sick; we are looking every moment now for the Doctor. He has not been here yet today.

Sunday Feb 22nd Charlie has been very sick indeed for the last three or four days but today he is evidently much better. He had no fever last night at all and would have slept pretty well if it had not been for his cough. This morning he has been cross enough to be better at any rate but he has now at noon just got to sleep and I think will feel better when he wakes up. Julia is gaining fast. She has walked around the floor considerable today without any help, which thing she has not done before since two weeks ago today. She has grown quite poor and Charley has even more than she, but I hope now that both of them are in a fair way to get better very fast. I have not been at the store, only a few minutes at a time, for two weeks now. I expect in a day or two the children will be well enough for Sarah to get along with them alone, tho I shall probably have writing enough that I can do for some days to keep me here if I want to stay. If I can only get a good sleep for a night or two I shall be all right again, for I am now, as well as Sarah, pretty well tired out. I am looking every day for that letter [from] Father telling me whether or not he wants us to pay that two hundred dollar note.   I hoped to have got it before this time but it has not yet come.   I am rather in hope that he will not want it for we had a little rather pay 10 pct on it than to pay it now but we will do as I said in regard to it.   I think I will finish this letter and send it today. I have been long enough about it.   Father is as well as usual.   Business is pretty dull tho we look for it to open bright in the spring.   I expect to go to Chicago & St Louis soon, say about the middle of March.   I may go as far East as Cincinnati, tho I hardly expect to now.

Your aff son
Edward

March 11, 1863

Dear Father

Your letter of Feb 17th was rec'd several days since and I have been waiting to find out something in regard to Quindaro before writing, but I have not been doing much for a month but take care of the children and write at home.   Their sickness will account in part for my not sending that money as I promised for the interest of the 200 Note.   I will send with this the 20.$ that is due on that acct and perhaps the other.   It may not be convenient for me to pay it just now.   We would like to have the note lay longer as the money is worth 10 pct to us now.   We are doing a pretty good business now if we dont fail of getting the cash for a large lot we have sold on time.

To show something [of] what we are doing I have just now tonight finished up a statement of acct to send to a man that we have sold considerable to.   We have <u>bought and paid for</u> and <u>sold to him alone</u> within the last two years over 8000$ worth of goods.   The statement which I am now sending him makes him owing us now pretty near 2000$ but we are expecting 800$ from him in a few days.   If we should happen to <u>slip up</u> on him we should be in a bad fix but I guess he will make it all right.   By this you can see that we do some business, whether we make much money or not.   I am expecting to go to St Louis & Chicago next week sometime on business.   <u>I may not</u> go however but think now I shall.

Four or five days ago I had a letter from John.   He is now at Springfield <u>Mo</u>, or was then.   The Reg he belongs to was in Blunt's fights at Cane Hill, Prairie Grove & Van Buren, but he was not in any of them being sick at the time.   He has had quite a hard time, has had Billious fever, then Small Pox or Variola, was sick so as not to be on Duty over two months.   I think likely you will hear from him but I dont know.   When he wrote to me Feb 26 he was on duty at the Court House [Prison] in Springfield Mo.   He is in the service for 3 years and thinks he may stay longer than that.   He says he will keep me posted in regard to his where abouts after this.   If he does I will post you.

A Letter Directed   John W Fitch,
Company E 13th Reg   Kan. Vols.
Care of   Col. Bowen Via, Springfield,   Missouri
would probably find him after a time at any rate.   I have not heard from Appleton for a long time.   I rather expect to see him within two weeks but I may miss it.

Today there came a letter directed to Sarah.   I got it but did not dare to open it for fear of the broomstick but finally it is now 12 Oclock at night and Sarah being very tired has gone to bed, so I have got hold of it and will answer a little of it so you may know that it is here.   When she opened it she saw Dear Brother & she said "I should like to know who wrote to me in that style".   The children are better -- in fact we call them about well, but they are not as strong as before and cant bear as much. Charlie is very fussy.   They were both very sick indeed, but I think soon they will be all right.   I suppose of course Sarah will answer <u>her</u> letter so I shall not say much about it, but content myself with what I have done in this line.

Yours,Edward

I shall write to John tonight.

March 12, 1863

Dear Father

Enclosed find Draft for Eighty four (84) Dollars.
Credit Mr Wilmarth for interest on the Note Due
Mar 1st $20.00
and E.P. Fitch interest on Note   <u>$64.00</u>

$84.00

Send statement of B N [Bank Note] so that we may see just how it is.

On acct of my going to St Louis it bothers me to pay this now but I thot if it would help you so much I would pay it.

Your af
E. P. Fitch

261

Spring 1863 (Est.)

This morning I got a Sewing Machine.   After it had been in the house 10 minutes I sewed this with seams.   Stitched two pieces together so as to show both sides of the seam on the same side of the cloth.   Also a hem so as I can show the same.   It is a Double Thread machine made by Williams & Orris of Boston.   It has a hemmer but I did not use it.   I sewed also a curved seam.   It can be used to embroider as well as every thing else.

Edward

The Machine cost 30$

The long piece of cloth is some that the lady did that we got the machine of.   One seam shows the different lengths of stitch that the machine will take.   I would not sell this machine for anything if I could not get another.

April 18, 1863

Dear Father

I returned home from the East on Sunday past Sunday, having been gone just 3 weeks.   I am pretty much tired out.   I expected to find a letter here for me from you acknowledging the recpt of that money that I sent you but I did not find any, but yesterday a letter came from you in which you say that you recd it.   Well!   I thot you would say that it was such an <u>unlooked</u> for <u>occurrence</u> as much as to say that "you never expected I <u>would</u> pay <u>you anything."</u>   Well, I did not know as I ever could.   I must say that if I had had to pay the same to some other person or not have any money I think I might have gone under before this time, but now I am in such a way that I hope to get along.   I have not paid Appleton any thing yet except to <u>pay him three</u> visits since I saw you.   If I charge him for them as professional (what puffery) perhaps that will pay my interest money.

I saw Mrs Garrett in St Louis (Lizzie Marshal), spent half an hour or so with her.   I was to spend an evening with them but did not have time.   She seems to be getting along well, not much to do I guess only. <u>'Eat Drink & Sleep</u>' instead of "Work" as Mother said in the family letter.

I also met John P. Wheeler on the street there and was in his office a few moments.   If he would return me the two hundred dollars that I consider he just about the same as stole from me I should have some patience to see him.   (For Conscience sake dont show this to any one) He looks as tho he would not live long. Sam'l Davenport told me he spit blood constantly. Sam told me of his Father's sickness and his sister's death. He told me what ailed his Father but I have forgotten and when you say the same as Grandfather Howe I dont know what that was, so am as much in the dark as ever. Sam is getting along well I guess. I bot 150$ worth of boots etc of him. Am to pay him as soon as I can. He thinks I'll do to trust. I spent the last Sunday in March and the Monday following with Appleton & Lizzie & the baby. The baby cried for me and thot I was her Dad, but Lizzie says I an't and she ought to know!!! They all seem to be doing well except that A. dont get that place as Principal that he wants yet. I wish he could.

I called at the office of the Adams Mills twice while I was in Chicago and saw all of the boys but none of them invited me to the house, so of course I did not return that call that Marilla made on Sarah at your house. But the last night that I was in Chicago about three hours before I left I met Ben. on the street and he told me Mrs Lee Claflin was at his house and wanted I should call and see her and I called and saw Mrs. C. She said she saw you at meeting the Sunday before. Mr Claflin had gone somewhere so I did not see him and I suppose it was just as well. I saw Willard Woodward, staid with him two nights. They have four children now, the youngest 5 weeks old. I had to work hard all the time I was gone and was tired out when I got home.

Now to answer your letter. About how Quindaro stands, I dont know for I have not had any charge to see about it yet, but if you can persuade Fitch to take it I think you had better, for the 500 that is, for I dont think it will be worth more than that for some time, tho the Pacific R.R. is going thru it. I will see and find out all I can about it and let you know. I am sorry we ever got into such a scrape with it, but it cant be helped now as I know of so we must make the best of it.

It seems funny to hear you tell of frost in the ground when at the same time we had peas up & flowers in the garden, tho we dont call it a very forward spring here. I hardly realise what you mean when you talk of Elijah taking the farm on shares but I hope he is going to make a farmer. If he is drafted, which I hope he will not be, you must get him clear under that claim--the <u>only son</u> having <u>two brothers</u> in the army or you being an <u>invalid</u>. I read a letter from John since I went away. He seems to be well now and feels pretty well. I have written to him several times and he has got them all I believe. I am sorry Mother is so unwell. Hope she will recover by warm weather. I am glad you bot no books for me at auction or any other way. The "Dear Brother" was from Elijah but the letter in which it was enclosed was directed to Sarah, that's all.   We here are in our usual health except that I have had the tooth ache for a week before I came home and <u>had it</u> (the ache) pulled the day after I came and I   got cold in it.   My jaw is very sore.   He broke two pieces out of the jaw, one came out with the tooth and the other had to be taken out afterward.   I kept in the house for fear of more cold in it.   No more that I can think of.

Your aff son
Edward P Fitch

I have not heard from Calvin for some time.   Have you any news.   It seems he was in a tight place there and I dont know as he's out yet.   I saw Mr Valentine Ed. H as I came home.   He is well but his wife is in poor health very.   He is keeping a hotel on the road from here to Leavenworth.

May 27, 1863

Dear Mother

<u>It is a Boy</u> and weighed 9 lbs

Julie says she is going to have the whole care of it for Mother is sick and beside she has so much to do that she has not time to take <u>care of it</u> . Sensible girl

He came by the 1/2 past nine train yesterday morning (Tues)

Sarah is very well considering.

Edward

Mid-1863 (Est.)

Dear Mother,

Father says in his letter "You dont say a word about your wife & children, if they are all dead we dont know it."   Now I might return the compliment for he dont say a word about you.   So I dont know that you are dead, and not knowing, I will direct this part of the letter to you and see if I can find out.   I told Sarah she had better write but she says she had written you two letters and you have never even said that you recd them and she thot she should not write again until she found out whether you did or not.   Then she is kept pretty busy for our colored girl goes to school and so she has a great deal of work to do.   We have one boarder and expect to have another next week, a man that is coming into the store to stay.   He is a paper hanger and we are going to hang paper as well as furnish it.   I dont see that there is much news in your letter for me to say any thing about and I have not any to write, for there is nothing new that I know of that will be of interest to you.   We are all well -- wife, children and all as far as heard from.

We have heard nothing from John direct yet.   If that long letter from Calvin that you speak of was as good as one he wrote to us I should be glad to see it.   He wrote to us the best letter I ever saw from him.   If he gets home alive from the war I think his going into the Army will be the making of him.   Dont you think so?   I hope it will.   But I wish you would let me know the news from Hopkinton.   How all the folks get along that I know.   How is Mrs James [Long] and is Arthur in the clothing business yet?   That I want to know in particular.

Ys   Edward

JUNE 29, 1863

Dear Mother

Three or four days since I recd a letter partly from you and partly from A. which I now return the whole of.   Also a few weeks ago I read a similar one.   In the first one there was nothing said by which I could judge of what you wanted me to do about it.   I only supposed it was sent to Appleton and from him to me to save writing two letters.   But Appleton copied a great part of yours in substance into his, the object of which I failed to see, but by this letter I see that you intended it to go around the family from me to John then to Calvin, but as I knew nothing of it before I of course had no idea of writing anything in the shape of a journal for it.   I think I will try and have some thing for the next one that comes on and will send it to John and I will let him know about it now, so that he may be prepared to act on the suggestion.   I have not heard from John for a long time.   His Regiment left Springfield and came to Fort Scott some time ago and as at that time a great many of the men had a furlough I expected to see him up here, but he did not come.   The Reg has now gone to the Indian Territory south of here where they will be likely enough to see some work.   There is no mail from here (or any where else) to where he is with any regularity to it so it would be of no use to send to him with any idea that a letter could go and come any way soon. So I shall not send him this letter, but I will write him the main points in yours to Appleton.   Then about sending it to Calvin, I see by the papers that his Regiment is to start home July 7th so it will be no use for me to send to him for it would not probably get to N.C. until he had left for Mass and there would be no knowing when it would get to him there.   So I shall send to you and you can keep it or send it to him as you choose. You will know better than I do whether it would get to him and where.

I am about as well as usual and so are the rest.   July [Julia] had a slight sickness yesterday but has got over it I guess.   The baby grows finely.   He is a great boy now, I expect will be a clerk in the store soon. The rest of us go on as usual in the even tenor of our way as you said. Work, eat, & sleep and so on day after day.   Some days a great deal to do, other days not so much.   The Fourth of July is at hand.   It makes us busy at this time tho we have no celebration here.   We are getting the toys and fireworks for others to celebrate with.   We have been bothered with poor help in the house for some time past and have just got a new girl, an American girl and from the few days she has been here we think we shall like her very much.   She appears to be a good steady girl.   O Dear here comes the baby and I must hold him and write because Sarah cant sew with him in her arms.   So he lies in my arms and I talk to him and write and he laughs.   Charlie is not up yet tho breakfast is nearly ready.   Julie is out helping the girl get breakfast, I suppose.

Yours
Edward

JULY 16, 1863

Dear Parents

I expect you will think this is quite a stretch of time from the date of the first part of my letter.   Well it is and this is the reason.   A day or two after I got the other sheet begun and when it was about ready to send I saw several men from John's Co. in the 13th and they told me that when they left the Reg all were to have a furlough that did not have one before and that they would be up thru here.   I talked considerable with one Mr Morton.   He said John was in the hospital sick with sore eyes and had been for some time but was better and that he (John) told him that if he could get a discharge from the hospital he was coming up and if he could get a furlough for 60 days he was going to Mass. but if he could only have the same furlough as the rest he should only come to Lawrence.   He said also that he (Morton) thot John would be out of the hospital in a few days, two or three, and then would come to Lawrence in the stage so then I looked for him every time the stage came in from Fort Scott and of course kept the letter here for him to see.

Then I did not know but he would go right to Leave from there East & not come here at all. I wrote to him, but last Sunday I found a Mr Brooks who was going down to Fort Scott and I concluded to send the letter by him and I directed them my self and put stamps on so that if he could not find John he would send them to you himself.   He left Tues. P.M. and that night I recd a letter from John.   He was enough better to have left the hospital.   His letter was dated Adjutant Office of 13th K.V. and he told me to leave off <u>Co E</u> in my direction of letters to him. Whether I am to infer from this that he is Adjutant of the Reg I dont know.   It may be that he is for Mr Morton told me that he thot "John would wear shoulder strips before long."   John never told me himself that he was a Sargeant so he might be Adj. and not say any thing about it. So I suppose you will rec the letter from him.

I see by the paper that Calvin's Reg has come home so I suppose he is at home now but will he not go in again to that new Corps that they are raising and get his 320$ Bounty.   I should think he would.   I think I stand a pretty good chance to be drafted here.   The Draft will take some 250 or 300 from this county, which will be a good many.   What an awful state of things in N.Y. City.   What a shame.

I was taken sick the 3 of July with vomiting.   (Father & McCoy, our clerk, had both gone to Topeka with the Band).   I was pretty sick so that I did not get up until 8 Oclock the next day.   Then I went and staid at the store a few moments and shut up, but I had to go up to the store again a little after noon to give out the Newspapers, tho I was not fit to sit up and ought to have been in bed.   I was sick three or four days, lost 6 lbs of flesh but I am better, in fact, well now tho I dont feel as smart as before. Yesterday the children were playing outdoors and Julia stuck the little garden hoe into Charles head cutting quite a little hole but Charles is around this morning nearly as usual.   He will get all over it today, I think, tho it may not all heal up.

E

Dear Father
The business with Wood is all settled.   I have paid Mr. Allen as his agent a draft of 150. on you and I have got a receipt in full so that if the draft is not paid I shall not lose it.

267

If I consider the interest on the three hundred dollar note then I in reality paid only ten dollars more for I get 10. taken off of the other note.   It is about as good a settlement as could be expected.

The Draft will probably be sent on soon.   How soon I do not know.

If my Claim was only fixed now I should be glad but we cannot tell how long it may be before the Land Office is open.

There is no news that I know of.

Emery sends his respects.   He says he will try and fill his appointment at Hopkinton when he gets East again and he starts pretty soon.   I tell him that if he fails to go to H. he will never do any business for me again.

Yours Edward P Fitch

The Draft is payable to Lyman Allen on order at Hopkinton Bank.   Three days after sight.

Sept. 2, 1863

The following letter was written by Sarah Fitch to her husband's parents less than two weeks after he had been killed in Quantrill's Raid. It was published in the Milford (Mass.) Journal for Saturday Nov. 7, 1863 but this transcription has been made from the original letter.

Lawrence "The City of Sorrow: Sept. 2 [18]63
Wednesday Eve.

My dear Father and Mother

I have been trying to summon strength to write to you all the particulars of the sad, sad day which has brought such gloom to this once happy place -- which has wrecked all my happiness -- which has bro't desolation to your hearts.   Oh! My dear mother how I longed to help you bear this burden!   Never before did I feel the meaning of that word -- crushed -- oh I feel as tho' I was crushed into the dust with the weight of sorrow which has rolled upon me! -- oh the utter desolation -- the heart breaking despair I have endured.   My brain reels! -- my reason totters -- had it not been for our children -- Edward's darlings -- that I had to live for, I do not think I could have endured -- How have those poor hearts endured that could not feel "thou didst it."   -- where shall I commence?

268

What shall I say -- there is so much I want to tell you -- and my mind is so confused -- I have yet hardly strength to perform the task --

Two short weeks ago -- on Thursday eve -- this place was so happy -- so prosperous -- on that evening I went up town and was at the store some time. E. [Edward] & I walked home together -- going down the whole length of our principal business street speaking of all the new building & all the projected improvements -- How bright -- how glowing with happiness & prosperity seemed the future -- How little we dreamed of the horror which even then was hovering over us -- Oh! that evening -- can it be -- oh can it truly be, it was <u>the last!</u> I cannot -- <u>cannot</u> endure it -- oh how little I tho't as Lulie & Charlie kissed "Dear Papa" -- and bade him "goodnight" -- that it was <u>the last</u> -- Oh Mother - Mother - those sad words the last time. I know now what they mean -- such a quiet, happy evening as we spent - <u>together</u> - in our sweet, happy home - oh as I look back to that evening - it seems as tho' my heart would break -- why cannot it break -- how can I bear this burden on thro' dreary month & years -- I will try to tell as well as I can the events of that next terrible morning that fatal Friday morning -- when horror & despair fell upon us -- at sunrise I was up -- it had been a warm, still night & was a lovely morning -- as calm and quiet as any of these mornings to you -- but few were out nearly all were just rising -- I went to call Miranda the girl who lived with us - (she had been out to meeting late & was very tired) I then went to the baby who was nestling as tho' about to wake -- Edward was in Lulie's room -- as it was cooler than in ours -- In about five minutes I heard the report of a pistol -- then another & another -- twenty or thirty shots -- "Edward" said I -- what's all that about. There was a camp of recruits -- just back of our house & the shots were in that direction "Oh" answered E - "it's the boys having some fun" but the shots came thicker & faster -- Edward sprang to the window - "It's more than fun" - said he - "<u>the rebels are upon us</u>" -- you must know that two weeks before there had been a great fright here about Quantrell's coming - & troops were sent here, guards were out constantly & all was excitement -- but it had passed away - the soldiers removed the guards discharged, the Independent Company of which E. was a member disbanded -- the arms taken from them & every one was entirely defenceless - they had plenty of <u>spies</u> in town to inform them of the condition of things - & they had chosen that time of all others when we should be off our guard - oh why was it permitted - a half hours notice would have saved all! but altho they avowed their intention to burn L. all the way up no one was friend enough to try to put us on our guard - oh such a strange fatality that such a body of 250 or 300 mounted men were

269

sweeping on & we, not to dream of danger! - But they were <u>here</u> - stealthy - silently they came on till they reached the heart of town - then they commenced firing - quicker than I can write it - they broke their ranks & scattered in every direction - firing constantly - shooting down every unfortunate one who was out & as they were <u>every where</u> -no one who did not live on the outskirts of the town could escape. In five or ten minutes fires were springing up in every direction - first the "Republican" office was in flames - then barns & houses all around - <u>What are they intending to do</u> - was our anxious question - They very soon came to the house opposite us - where G.W.E. Griffith, a public man in the State lived, took his watch, what money he had - the key to his safe - & then ordered him to go up town with them   His wife with her little child, came immediately over to us almost crazy   with fright & apprehension - Edward was perfectly calm - He said we had better get all the clothing we could take, tied up - & if they came to our house try to save it & ourselves - of course we could not venture out before they came, for they were firing all about us constantly & I forgot to add they were screaming & yelling like so many demons from the infernal pit - oh how can I go on - so as I try to think it over & place in order those terrible details my brain reels - I can scarcely think - we had got the most of necessary clothing tied up - & carried down stairs to take out - when all at once twenty or thirty of them swept up to the house, surrounded it, and in an instant, a ruffian, a demon burst open the door - oh that face!   it haunts me day & night, a coarse, brutal, blood thirsty face - inflamed with hellish passions & strong drink for he was evidently intoxicated - with horrid oaths he said not one of us should leave (he had not seen E. then) another one was behind with perhaps one spark more of humanity in his bosom & he said "let the women & children go" - I was almost beside myself with terror for Edward - I <u>knew</u> his doom was sealed - that <u>demon</u> - who was there swearing - shouting - screaming - in <u>our</u> dear little parlor, with his revolver cocked in one hand - the matches lighted to fire our home in the other - I felt there was no mercy there - oh my friends - do you wonder that in that instant - (for all passed much more quickly than I can write it) - that my heart almost stopped its beating - and in utter despair, I almost doubted if there was a God who loved us - He - that <u>wretch</u> - turned & saw my Edward - oh Mother - so calm so self possessed - and without a word the deadly aim was taken - shot after shot in rapid succession - emptying his own revolver, then taking the weapon from the hand of his companion, and using all its load to make sure work of death - oh can you picture that moment - I begged, I implored - I looked around on that circle of hard cruel faces - and I know there was not help - no help - oh had God forgotten us - the match was applied to our home - I pleaded, I begged thrice to take him out - not to burn that precious body - But with an oath, a terrible oath - he pointed his pistol to my breast & said he would shoot me too if I didn't leave - & I took my screaming children - & went across the road & three ourselves on the grass - how did I live - I know not - In the meantime Mr. Griffiths house (opposite ours) had been fired & soon the flames made it too hot for us to remain there &   we went further away & threw ourselves upon the ground - & watched the work of death & desolation go on - no one who did not see it can form any conception of it - no words can convey an idea - By this time houses in every direction were burning - the crash of falling walls - the constant firing - the unearthly yells of the mounted invaders, rushing in every direction - the shrieks of the bereaved, the groans of the wounded - could anything more be added to the horrid picture - Before ten o'clock all were gone - and in that short space of four or five hours - what a change - 150 killed & most of them our best men - 25 wounded (their aim was sure & in most cases they shot again & again, as in E's case) and of these last, several have since died - 86 widows over 200 children fatherless - was not their work complete?   "The city of sorrow" we are justly called - scarcely a house but was in mourning - scarcely a family but had lost husband - father or friends - Many were burned in the building - others were lying here & there, scattered all over town - People say they know at once who belong to this place & who not by the saddened look - all are mourning &   great many houses were burned & the people barely escaped with the clothing they had on, some even had not time to dress - we only had the clothing we had on,   every thing was burned - house - store - all, all gone - Father was at Topeka - or he too would have fallen - I thank God he was spared - thee were many different bands - all seemed to have their work laid out in order - they knew just who they were after & where they lived.   They had marked their victims & especially the members of the "Independent Company" of which E. was one of the first members - they had a list of that company I could tell you of heart-harrowing incidents without end.   Such cold blooded butchery was never before seen - such deliberate, hellish cruelty - not one of the newspaper reports that I have seen exaggerated - the half is not told - after they had left we got up & went to a friend's whose house was not burned tho' they took from her everything of value - even to the rings from her fingers - It was Mrs. Martin F. Conway - & fortunately he was East.   Here I staid a week - Father came down as soon as he heard the news - He at once found another small building & opened business again

& the next week - a friend of ours, Mrs. Lowe, whose husband was killed
went East to Fitchburg, Mass., with her husband's body - Father's hired
the house she was living in. took enough of her furniture for two rooms -
the rest of the house our minister, Rev. Mr. Cordley, (whose house & all
they had was burnt) has taken & we are <u>comfortable</u> - I have had plenty of
clothing for present use sent me by friends from Leavenworth & Topeka &
I am trying to sew & get once more enough for the children to be
comfortable - but - oh it is so hard to put my mind on things that pertain
to <u>living</u> to <u>live without</u> the one who was <u>all</u> I lived for - for I believe he
was <u>my idol</u>. And now I must tell you of <u>today</u> - and did you but know
how my heart has today been racked you would not wonder at my
unsatisfactory, desultory letter. E. having been burnt in the house, it was
many days before it was possible to work there, on account of the heat -
We intended to have had the funeral exercises on last Sabbath but there
were so many other services that our pastor Mr Cordley was completely
exhausted - and it was deferred until today - and here this afternoon we
consigned his precious remains to their last resting place - I had him
buried in our garden, where I can have it close to me & keep constant
watch of the dearest spot. I had our dear baby baptized over his coffin by
the name of <u>Edward Payson</u>. You will love the dear baby, won't you! for
his name? - Oh it seems as tho' my heart would break - two short weeks
ago - such a happy home - such a happy family - such bright prospects
now all that is left is a heap of blackened ruins & <u>my husband's grave</u>.
On, my God, why layest thou thine hand so heavily upon me? - But I
know <u>he</u> is happy - I know he was prepared - that it is well with <u>him - and
I</u> believe - my torn & tortured heart still clings to this one faith - <u>God rules
-</u> For some good end this was permitted - "What I do now, ye know not -
but ye shall know hereafter" - for some wise purpose my darling was
made a martyr to freedom - and mother, with all my grief is one <u>proud
thought</u> - <u>Edward never faltered - nor hid nor showed any fear</u> - he <u>knew</u>
the danger but with calm trust in God's will - he was as calm & self
possessed - as ever you saw him in the world & I look now almost with
reverence, upon that last memory of him - If it was God's will he should go
- how much more noble, facing death with manly firmness than to be
found & murdered when in some hiding place as many were - and mother
so many friends as he had - all loved him - they have come & mingled
their tears with mine & said so many times "how we all loved him." He
will be so much missed - in the church - in the S. school particularly; his
place cannot be filled - and my rebellious heart will murmur, why <u>was</u> it
so - when life was so bright - every prospect so flattering - I feel as tho'

God could not have meant <u>him</u> to be taken - Perhaps you will think it so strange for me to talk so - but it seems as tho' I have drunk the cup of misery to the full - as I told one of my friends today - "I am <u>completely crushed</u> in the dust."   I wish I could see you.   I have written so much & so wandering - & still I could fill sheets more with what I wish to tell - I thank you all for the sympathy you expressed for me - for this evening your letters were handed me - Oh I have tho't so many times "what will his mother say?   how can she bear it" - and I wished I could fly to you & tell you myself & help you bear it - but God who has taken him will be with you - May his strength uphold you!   Perhaps I have been selfish in torturing your hearts with all my moans - but it seems as tho' I could not restrain myself - I try to control myself before father for his grief is very deep - he loved Edward as his own son - he had placed all his hopes upon him - all his business was soon to be left entirely in E.'s hands - & he is old - & it is so hard for him to see all his plans so crushed - and for the children's sake I try to keep a cheerful face - for Lulie says - "Mamma why do you cry!   Isn't dear papa in Heaven with God?   and don't he love us now just the same as he used to?   - and dear little Charlie says "Don't cry Mamma - papa's with God."   Dear little comforters!   They little know what they have lost - I wish you could see Charlie.   He is Edward's image in looks & disposition - so loving - so affectionate to all - I see Edward's eyes every time he looks up - I must not write more tonight - Probably you have received father's letter before this time - May God sustain you - as I believe He has sustained me - For had He not I should have sunk under it. I must tell you of one thing more - As we were watching those invaders & with intense anxiety trying to determine their intentions, I put my arms around his neck & said - "God will take care of us - He will protect us" - and it gave E. & myself such strength - Edward's trust was there - & he is safe - God took him - and he did not suffer.   He must have been almost instantly killed.   The one who murdered him was close beside him & aimed at the heart & Edward made no sound.   He did not have to suffer as many have such agony & then die.   One good noble man died yesterday after so many days of terrible suffering - was it not a mercy that he did not suffer!   But oh! he is gone - there is such desolation - I miss him so every moment & it was so sudden - oh was there ever such wickedness done! - Is there not a righteous Judge who will bring them into judgement!   Will not the wails of anguish which rise from this city of mourning reach the ear of a pitying Father & call down terrible retribution.   I feel that God has mingled mercies even with this bitter cup - for I have one of the kindest fathers in the world & a great many friends

& everything that love & kindness could do, has been done to sustain me under this burden - but there are many who have none to look to - many poor women whose only friend was taken & they left to struggle alone - a great amount of provisions & clothing is being sent here from Leavenworth & Kansas City & other places - but - as is usually the case those who need it most are the last to apply.

By mistake this half-sheet was left & I cannot let blank paper go. A letter came from John last night to Edward.   He is near Fort Blunt Cherokee Nation & expects soon to be ordered to Texas.   I am going to write him immediately.   I will tell you of a few who fell that day.   You remember Mrs. Collamore whom you went to see in Boston with Edward? Her husband Gen. Collamore   was our Mayor.   He was killed, his oldest son severely wounded, his house burned, everything of value taken - his second son made sick with brain fever in consequence of excitement, and last week she returned to Boston with her dead husband & two sick sons - without a dollar & scarcely a change of clothing - tho she has abundant means in Boston.   Have we not mentioned in our letters a young man by the name of Tritch who was clerk in the store & boarded with us.   For nearly a year he was an inmate of our family & loved by us all as a brother. Edward loved him so much.   He was found dead in the street - pierced by six bullets - & on us devolved the sad task of sending the news to his friends, among them a sweet young girl he was soon to be married to. God help all the desolate hearts.   I must tell you of one sad house.   Dr. Griswold, a warm friend of E's had on <u>Thursday</u> returned from a visit East with his wife & two children.   When I was up at the store on Thursday Eve. he came in & he was <u>so happy</u> to be home.   At his house boarded Trask, editor of State Journal, son of Rev. Mr. Trask of Mass. - L.M. Thorp a splendid man, member of the Legislature - & Mr Baker one of our first merchants.   A detachment of the ruffians went to the house, called out these four men by shouting as they rode up.   "The rebels are in town. Rally & help us drive them out" & the four victims rushed to the door to learn more & were deliberately shot down with their wives shrieking & pleading by their sides.   Dr. G. and Mr. Trask were instantly killed.   Mr. Thorp died next day.   Mr. Baker is still lingering on suffering & may possibly recover - all young - noble men - Trask & Baker married last winter, the other two but a few years.   From the windows of my room, I see in one direction - the blackened ruins of two homes - from the back window - six ruined houses & in   full view a large brick house lately built by one of our most promising young lawyers Judge Carpenter - married last winter to Miss Barbour from Sherburne, Mass.   He was fired upon, he ran thro the house, thro the cellar his life blood gushing at every step. The ruffians followed; still firing till C. fell to the ground - his wife threw herself upon him & tried to protect him but the wretch cooly lifted her arm placed his pistol under it & fired again to finish the deed - But its too harrowing to both of us to relate such details.   I will send this to you - & I judge Appleton and his wife are still with you - as he does not mention his return to Peoria.   If he is not there would you not send this letter to him - as I would like him to know all - & it seems almost more than I can do to go over all again now; I love you all.   I feel for you all - All that Edward loved, and all who loved him will ever be sacred to me - & I wish we were nearer you that E's children might learn to know & love their father's friends. Pray for me.   I need strength more than human hands can give. Sometimes I can rise above & seem to see beyond the cloud - & can say - "Do all Thy will - for it is good."   but tis only for a short time & poor nature sinks & the clouds seem impenetrable & God seems afar off - must I live so for years, perhaps without my Edward - my stay - my support - my almost idol - I am thankful that I have his children to live for - to do for - to train them to fill his place - may God help me to do my duty to them for his dear sake.   Will you not write to me as you used to him for I need your letters & I will try to write for him for I cannot bear that <u>his children</u> should grow up without a knowledge & love for his friends.

Yours in love & sympathy,
Sarah

Thursday Morn

   Perhaps I have already written too much for once - but I thought you would like to know of the funeral.   Mr. Cordley first baptized dear baby - after a very few appropriate remarks - Dear little <u>Edward</u>! sweet unconscious baby!   smiling while tears fell like rain from all eyes - little does he know what loss is his - God bless my baby - "<u>papa's dear baby</u>" - as Edward so often called him - then after the prayer a few friends with whom E's voice had often mingled in songs of praise - sang these words - "Forever with the Lord!

   Amen! So let it be!
Life from the dead is in that word!
   <u>Tis immortality!</u>
My Father's house on high
   Home of my soul!   how near
At times, to faith's fore seeing eye
   Thy <u>golden gates appear</u>!

275

"Forever with the Lord!"
  Father if 'tis thy will,
The promise of thy gracious word
  Ever here to me fulfill!
Be thou at my right hand!
  So shall I never fail -
Uphold Thou me and I shall stand
  Help, and I shall prevail

Mr. C. spoke so feelingly of E. for he loved him much - and feels his love deeply.   Our friends again sung --

When we hear the music ringing
  Thro' the bright celestial dome
When sweet angel voices ringing
  Gladly bid us welcome home
To the land of ancient story
  Where the spirit knows no care -
In the Land of light and glory,
  Shall we know each other there?

When the holy angels meet us
  As we go to join their band,
Shall we know the friends that greet us -
  In the glorious spirit - land?
Shall we see the same eyes shining
  On us, as in days of yore?
Shall we feel their dear arms twining
  Fondly round us, as before?

Yes! My earth worn soul rejoices,
  And my weary heart grows light -
For the thrilling angel voices,
  And the angel faces bright -
That shall welcome us in heaven
  Are the loved of long ago,
And to theirs tis kindly given
  Thus their mortal friends to know.

O! Ye weary, -- sad & tossed ones

Drop not, faint not by the way,
Ye shall join the loved & just ones
   In the land of perfect day!
Harp strings touched by angel fingers
   Murmured in my raptured ear,
Evermore their sweet song lingers,
"We shall know each other there!"

   Then we laid his dear remains away to rest till the last summons shall call him to rise, & we went back to what we now call "home" - I try to feel that - God does all things <u>well</u> & to feel that I am willing He should do as seemeth to Him good with his own.   But tho' the spirit be <u>willing</u>, the flesh is very weak, and the moan <u>will</u> come - when I miss him every moment.   I am copying to send to you Mr. Cordley's sermon of last Sabbath.   It was thought excellent by all who heard it and I thought you might be interested in it, as you so often heard E. speak of Mr. C. I will send it soon.
   I will write no more now - God be with you all and sustain you by unwavering faith in His love, "He will not return to us, but we <u>may</u> go to <u>him</u>"   Let us do the duty which God sets before us & patiently wait till called to go & meet our loved ones <u>there</u> –
                         Yours ever in love
                              Sarah

[The letter continues after this with the following:]

   There was one significant fact connected with the atrocities committed at our home, which, if a full account is prepared, as I hope it will be, I should like to have mentioned - as it fully shows the <u>spirit</u> which moved these fiends.   In some respects they did worse with us than many others - murdering E. at first sight - not allowing his body to be removed - not permitting a <u>single article</u> to be taken from the house - it seemed as tho' they could not do worse.   And two or three days ago I found out the reason, which I had often thought must be something mysterious.   A colored woman who lived back of our house (whose son was killed,) came to see me - and, said she "Did you know there was a <u>Union flag</u> on your house?"   On our <u>woodshed</u> she explained   and it all came over me where it was & when put there.   Our children had a flag about 2 x 3 feet, which they played "soldier" with - a day or two before a little boy playing with them had climbed up on the shed & firmly placed the flag staff there.

277

Altho' we knew it was there before this morning it was out of sight from the house & we never tho't of it - but in full view from the street-back, as there was a vacant lot back of ours - So, as a large body of them swept down the street, a breeze blew out those "starts & stripes" in full view, and they seemed perfectly infuriated, cursing & swearing horrid vengeance on <u>that house</u> - yes, our dear flag - the glorious "stripes & stars" - for that Edward fell, murdered in cold blood, that beautiful emblem exasperated them to the utmost - & they meant to glut their vengeance - to show their deadly hatred & <u>they did it</u> -may God bless that flag & soon may it wave over our whole country.

AFTERMATH

Poet Robert Frost hadn't yet uttered his famous three words about life, but residents of 1863 Lawrence already had learned them firsthand: It goes on.

Even young Julia "Lulu" Fitch had figured that out. Lulu was the oldest of Edward and Sarah's children, just a little more than five years old when her father was killed in Quantrill's raid. In 1928, she wrote a letter to one of her nephews describing some of the family's early history, including the days after the raid. She reported that her grandfather – Sarah's father, Otis – was spared from the raid because he was attending to business in Topeka. When he returned, he secured a couple of upstairs rooms in a house that hadn't been burned by the raiders.

"Furniture and clothing was sent by friends from near and far and life went on!" Lulu wrote.

But not without scars. Lulu remembers the day that her father was buried.

"Because Papa's body was burned in the house, it was some days before his bones could be gotten together to be buried –at the funeral the baby was baptized 'Edward Payson,'" Lulu wrote in the letter. "I remember that scene perfectly – the casket – the minister holding the baby – it was a sad, sad day."

By 1868, Sarah Fitch had traveled back East and a year later was married to Henry M. Stevens. The family set up a home in Kansas City, then Topeka and then in Council Bluffs, Iowa where the family would settle for a good long time.

For Sarah, life would continue to go on, but it would include more pain. She would have three more children, but two of them would die before they turned three years old. But the "tragedy of her life" would forever be that August 1863 day when her morning began with the crack of gunfire outside her tidy home.

"Mamma's happy married life with her dear husband Edward was a short one – only six years and five months," Lulu wrote. "Then came the tragedy of her life – the Raid Aug. 21, 1863 – when she saw her husband shot down before her eyes and the murderers would not allow her to even

279

remove his body from the doorway where he had met his death and his body was consumed with the house and all its contents! And Mamma was left with her three little children. I was 5 ½ years old, Charlie 2 years and 2 ½ months and the baby 2 ½ months. Those were indeed tragic days!"

Tragic, but not fruitless. Edward Fitch didn't live to see it, but Lawrence, Kansas went on to rebuild itself. The front lawn of Lawrence City Hall continues to feature a sculpture called The Flame, which evokes the image of a phoenix rising from the ashes. The community is now home to the University of Kansas, a thriving arts and culture scene and regularly receives national attention during the community's beloved Kansas Jayhawk's basketball season. Try as they might, Missouri raiders didn't destroy Lawrence. Residents of Lawrence on a daily basis enjoy a vibrancy that reminds them of a simple fact: William Quantrill was a failure.

Slavery, of course, was a failure too. That would have pleased Edward to no end. It surely didn't happen fast enough to suit Edward, but he could have taken some comfort in knowing his hand played a role in its demise. While it has never been documented that Edward even as much as fired a shot for the Union army, he was a warrior nonetheless. While the country spent much time talking about slavery and its future, Edward and his fellow settlers of Lawrence Kansas set about shaping the future. They moved to the spot where it was decided the line would be drawn in the sand. They moved to the spot where beliefs turned to blood. From that blood, a war was born.

Edward Fitch and his fellow settlers may have just been ordinary men and women. But they took an extraordinary stand. They held the line. In the end, it matters not so much whether the history books ever list Lawrence or Douglas County or eastern Kansas as the spot where the Civil War began. But it is important that Edward Fitch and his kind not be forgotten.

To defeat an evil as great as slavery, it would take more than men who wore a soldier's uniform. It would take men and women who lived the cause. They lived it in Bleeding Kansas.

A Note to the Reader

I hope you found the letters of Edward and Sarah Fitch an interesting look into the important role that early settlers of Kansas had in shaping the Civil War. If you would like this history to be shared on a broader stage, please consider posting a review of Postmarked: Bleeding Kansas on the book's Amazon.com Web page.

Made in the USA
San Bernardino, CA
28 March 2017